Rethinking Christendom
Europe's Struggle for Christianity

Rethinking Christendom

Europe's Struggle for Christianity

Jonathan Luxmoore and Jolanta Babiuch

GRACEWING

First published in 2005

Gracewing
2 Southern Avenue
Leominster
Herefordshire HR6 0QF

ISBN 0 85244 647 0

Typesetting by
Action Publishing Technology Ltd, Gloucester, GL1 5SR

Contents

Introduction

When French and Dutch voters rejected the European Union's Constitutional Treaty in national referenda in the early summer of 2005, the future of Europe seemed to be in question. If ratified by parliaments and electorates, the lengthy document was intended to establish the EU's institutional direction for the next half-century, drawing its disparate laws and treaties together into a single statement of procedures and objectives. Yet the Constitution drew strident criticism. Many Europeans were convinced it transferred authority and power from Europe's nation-states to EU bureaucrats, while failing to express the Continent's social and cultural richness, its unity in diversity.

The place of Christianity featured prominently in debates at the European Convention which drew up the Constitution in Brussels. Why has it caused such division? What do the arguments around it say about the new Europe now being created – a secular, pragmatic, technocratic Europe, or a Europe united at a deeper level by shared ethical values and spiritual intuitions? Would the rediscovery of Europe's Christian roots help or hinder the search for workable unity? This book sets out to explain the background to the latest controversy, drawing on views and perspectives from East and West. It shows how positions have been influenced by contrasting attitudes to the spiritual and secular. It looks at how Christianity has contributed to Europe's historical development and at how it can be expected to contribute in future.

* * *

The European Union has been only the latest expression of this Europe. In ancient times, it was said that Europe was populated by descendants of Japheth, the son of Noah, and bordered to the east by the River Don and Sea of Azov, and to the west by the Pillars of Hercules at Gibraltar and Ceuta. In the late eighteenth century, the philosopher Jean-Jacques Rousseau insisted there were 'no longer French, Germans or Spaniards, or even English, but only Europeans'.[1] Yet it was debatable where Europe's cultural boundaries lay, and whether its inhabitants really thought of themselves as having anything in common. Did 'Europe' include Russia and the territories it controlled, backing out on to the vast wastes of Siberia and the Asian steppe? Did it include Britain, which had been linked to Europe since 1066 but also looked further afield to an empire 'where the sun never set'. Even on the Continent proper, there were competing outlooks and attitudes at play. What did it mean to be European? Was there a European identity?

If there was, it was largely Christian in origin. Christianity would take many forms, from the Orthodoxy of the Russian empire to the Anglicanism of the British dominions, from the Lutheranism of Germans and Scandinavians to the Catholicism of Poles and Austrians. As a source of ideas and images, however, Christianity was the essential badge of Europeanness. Even among those who criticised or rejected it, it was the only universal reference point for peoples and societies drawn together by external threats and internal aspirations. Europeans no longer called themselves 'Christendom'. But they were conscious of their inherited Christian culture.

Today, buffeted by competing secular and spiritual winds, most are no longer Christians by religious faith. Yet at least three-quarters still describe themselves as Christians, and signs of the faith are visible in every town and village.[2] If European history is a verdant plain, then Christianity is the river which flows through it. It is a river with various sources: Judaic tradition, oriental faiths, Greek philosophy, Roman law. But it has also been broadened by incoming streams over two millennia – Celtic, Germanic, Slav and Finno-Ugric culture; Islam, humanism and Romanticism – embracing and re-directing them, but also being enriched and deepened by them. If the Christian God created the world, he left mankind to name its contents and devise its laws and customs, without the detailed directives found in the Koran and other holy texts. This capacity for dialogue has been Christianity's strength. It has fuelled dilemmas and conflicts. But it has also helped other faiths, philosophies and ideologies contribute to European civilisation, a civilisation full of contrasts and contradictions, but flowing from the same inclusive river of Christian norms and values.

Pope Benedict XVI has made the Continent's future a theme of his pontificate. His predecessor, John Paul II, talked about the 'multiple spiritual roots' underlying Europe's commitment to human dignity and freedom of thought and speech. 'These roots have helped lead to the submission of political power to the rule of law and to respect for the rights of individuals and peoples,' the Polish Pope argued.

> Yet it must be acknowledged that these inspiring principles have historically found in the Judaeo-Christian tradition a force capable of harmonising, consolidating and promoting them . . . In the process of building a united Europe there is a need to acknowledge that this edifice must also be founded on values most fully manifested in the Christian tradition. Such an acknowledgement is to everyone's advantage.[3]

Not everyone will agree. But they can concur that Christianity has been the foremost influence on Europe's formation. It is, quite simply, the only religion to have played a direct, consistent part in the emergence of its institutions of law and government, and the only faith to have placed a coherent, permanent stamp on its cultural and social traditions. How has Christianity played such a role?

One of its strengths has been a constant dialectical struggle between self-confidence and self-criticism, which has spurred a permanent dissatisfaction with the current state of the world and a constant yearning to improve it. Christianity borrowed heavily from other religious and philosophical traditions, accepting those which reflected its values and embodied the same creative restlessness. It preserved the heritage of Greece and Rome by incorporating them into its teaching. It raised the myths and symbols of ancient cults to a higher universal plane. Meanwhile, it recognised its debt to other religious faiths, including Judaism, which searched, like Christianity, 'among shadows and images for the God who is unknown yet near'.[4]

Another strength has been Christianity's liability to internal disputes. The divisions which beset it from the beginning culminated in the 1054 Great Schism between eastern and western Christianity, and led on to the Protestant Reformation of the sixteenth century. Even then, however, the disputes continued, generating hundreds of separate denominations, all with their own interpretations of the faith. This proneness to discord, especially in western society, marked Christianity off from other faiths – including Islam, which suffered only a single great division between Sunnis and Shias since the death of Muhammed in AD 632. It fuelled pluralism, typefied by the proliferation of literary and artistic styles: Byzantine, Romanesque, Gothic, Renaissance, Baroque. In so doing, even if unintentionally, it became a motor for intellectual, cultural, social and political development.

Another strength has been Christianity's rootedness in the world, thanks to its doctrine of Christ's Incarnation. 'The spirit of God really dwells in you,' St Paul explained. 'You are no longer strangers and sojourners, but you are fellow citizens with the saints and members of the household of God, built upon the foundation of the apostles and prophets, Christ Jesus himself being the cornerstone' (Ephesians 2:19–22). Christianity became a creative force because it rejected the doctrine that the ruler was also divine, which had been upheld by imperial regimes from the Epyptian pharoahs to the Roman emperors.

In this way, Christianity contributed four golden rules to human society. The first was that the individual had dignity since all were equal in the sight of God. The second was that secular and spiritual powers are separate and must compete for human loyalties. The third was that human society necessitates a balance between the individualism of self-interest and the universalism of the common good. The fourth was that faith and reason, tradition and innovation, convention and conviction could be linked in a creative tension.

Christianity taught that the human person was responsible,

with the imagination to look beyond everyday realities. Christians had a duty of loyalty to state and nation. But they could also appeal to higher principles. If the ethics of a later secular liberal society would be based on contract and reciprocity, Christianity's ethics were founded on the unconditional love of neighbour. Even if Christians failed to match this requirement, it nevertheless remained dynamic and binding.

Instead of despairing of the world, Christians have gone on trying to make it better by interpreting and searching the Gospel for its meanings. The secular and spiritual powers who struggled for dominance in Christian Europe both ultimately realised there could be no absolute earthly authority. Each had to be responsive to external judgement, whether from God or from society. In this way, they created the mechanism of checks and balances which lies at the heart of democracy. Though frequently in conflict, they shared the same sense of unfulfilment, and a readiness to explore ideas in a constant dialectical search for answers and solutions.

If Christianity has developed with the passing of time, it has been thanks to a creative sense of its own incompleteness. Christianity has moved a long way from the era of rival popes, crusades and religious wars. Its churches and denominations remain places of contrast, of saints and sinners, combining the best and the worst of human nature, without any simple typology. Yet the wicked acts committed in its name cannot compare with the positive spiritual energy Christianity has brought to bear. Alternative philosophies and ideologies have come and gone, some modified and humanised by interaction with Christianity, others driven to extremes by rejecting it. But all have made reference to it.

The anti-Christian movement which began in the eighteenth century had roots in a pluralisation of values, and a certainty that reason could flourish without faith in a world of cultural advance and social emancipation. It believed the Christian churches of the day were hostile to progress, and that their conservative, other-worldly values would be displaced by scientific, utilitarian solutions. The result was a rift between Europe's traditional Christian establishments and the new forces of secular radicalism, which fuelled polarisation and helped spark the explosions of the twentieth century.

It took a century of totalitarianism and war to rid secular forces of their utopian revolutionary illusions, and to purge the Church of its association with a reactionary order of power and privilege, as well as its fear of change. When Europe was reunited, there was, at last, an opportunity to bring both into harmony, helped by an awareness of contrasting historical experiences in a Europe of multiple local, regional and national loyalties. The debate on the future of Europe suggests this has not happened. While some Europeans see Christianity as a means of liberation, others still view it as a barrier to freedom. Yet if today's divisive discussions have highlighted something, it is that Christianity is still important. Most Europeans see a need to clarify its status – past, present and future.

This, then, is the purpose of this book.

Jonathan Luxmoore and Jolanta Babiuch
Oxford and Warsaw, 2005

CHAPTER 1

The Quest for Europa

Europa lost her fear. With her innocent hands she stroked his breast when he offered it for her caress, and hung fresh garlands on his horns; and finally she ventured to mount the bull, little knowing on whose back she was resting. Then the god drew away from the shore by easy stages, first planting the hooves that were part of his disguise in the surf at the water's edge, and then proceeding further out to sea, till he bore his booty away over the wide stretches of ocean. The girl was sorely frightened, and looked back at the sands behind her. Her right hand grasped the bull's horn, the other rested on his back, and her fluttering garments floated in the breeze. Ovid, *Metamorphoses*, Book II, pp. 833–875

By the time this Roman writer was completing his epic poem some time around AD 8 – about how chaos was transformed into an ordered universe – the event which would herald a new era had taken place in Palestine. The abduction of Princess Europa by the lustful Zeus, disguised as a bull, from Tyre to Crete may well have been a metaphor, in Ovid's hands, for how the ancient civilisation of the East came to be transferred to a new society growing up across the Mediterranean. Europa would give her name to a continent, whose cultural and ethnic boundaries would shift, concertina-like, over centuries of invasion and conquest. Christianity, also born outside Europe, would give that Continent its fundamental identity.

Religion had been present in Europe from the earliest times. It had flourished in the three centuries since the death of

Alexander the Great in 323 BC, as oriental and Hellenistic cults competed with the deities of the Roman Empire. Yet Christianity would be something different.

Its creator, Jesus of Nazareth, was a Galilean nurtured on Jewish scriptures, whose prophets talked of a single God commanding love, humility and charity. Unlike other religions, Christianity's New Testament offered no detailed guidelines for human society. It had its Ten Commandments. But it had to turn to other traditions for practical insights.

St Paul, the Greek-speaking son of a Pharisee and Roman, popularised Christian teaching in thirteen epistles during his travels through the eastern Mediterranean. Instead of seeing Christianity as a reversal of human history, he saw it as its fulfilment. This meant drawing together existing forms of wisdom, and transforming them through the Christian message of an all-embracing creator. 'There is neither Jew nor Greek, there is neither bond nor free, there is neither male nor female,' Paul told the Galatians. 'For you are all one in Jesus Christ' (Galatians 3:28).

There were numerous elements of that message which could be traced to parallel systems of thought. Christian ethics contained echoes of Judaism, as well as of Socrates and the Greek philosophers, whom St Paul described as 'Christians before Christ'. Its notions of responsibility and final judgement could be linked to the Stoicism of the apostle's native Tarsus, whose Roman exponent, Seneca, often spoke 'like a Christian', according to the theologian Tertullian.[1] So could the idea of a universe governed by the Word, or Logos, the seed of truth in every human being – 'In the beginning was the Word, and the Word was with God, and the Word was God' (John 1:1).

Christianity also inherited ideas and emblems from other religious traditions. Purgatory, the incarnation of deities, acts of mediation between God and Man had featured in the Greek legends of Orpheus and Theseus. The laying on of hands and ordination of ministers had been used among Jews. The concepts of a sacramental union with the divine, of a God dying and reborn, had occurred in the oriental cults of Isis and Mithras, as had Christian symbols of wood and water, sun and moon, light and darkness.

By the time of St Paul's execution in AD 64 during the emperor Nero's persecutions, Christianity was seen as something distinctive. The Roman historian Suetonius, writing after the dispersal of Jews following the destruction of the Second Temple in AD 70, spoke of 'a set of men adhering to a novel and mischievous superstition', who shunned all pleasure, practised pacifism and refused to sacrifice to the emperor. A better characterisation of St Peter's *koinonia*, or catacomb church, was provided by the Christian apologist, Justin Martyr:

> We who formerly rejoiced in uncleanliness of life and now love only chastity; who used magic arts and have now dedicated ourselves to the good, unbegotten God; we who loved money and possessions more than anything, and who now actually share what we have and give to everyone in need; we who hated and killed one another, and would not eat with those of another race, now since the manifestation of Christ have a common life, and pray for our enemies and try to win over those who hate us without just cause.[2]

The description captured the way Christianity, though developing in the Greco-Roman context, had begun to transform moral values and breathe a new spiritual awareness into culture. Though thinly spread across the Roman Empire, it had already assumed a coherent pattern. Christianity represented a new civilisation born through persecution – a velvet revolution from below which showed no interest in political power. The Greek word *katholikos* (related to the whole) had not appeared in the New Testament. By the time it was used in AD 110 by Bishop Ignatius of Antioch, the Church had become in Latin the *ecclesia catholica* with its own established order of deacons, priests and bishops.

Why had it taken root? One reason was its solid missionary organisation, based on charity and solidarity towards the poor and suffering. Another was its monotheism, which seemed attractive and progressive compared to the fluid, ecclectic cults of Roman society. Christianity's talk of liberating captives and dignifying the poor presented a more advanced ethical system than pagan morality. It offered clearer, more accessible answers to life's great questions; and it could assimilate itself into diverse social and cultural contexts by showing that faith and wisdom were open to everyone, not just to the elders and the elect. Although Church Fathers like Bishop Ignatius insisted salvation was only possible through the Church, this meant those with the opportunity of following Christ. 'The gifts and the call of God are irrevocable,' St Paul had told the Romans (Romans 11:29). There were elements of truth in other faiths too, whose followers could be saved if they truly sought God.

Christianity was destined to lose its other-worldly innocence.

When the emperor Constantine embraced Christianity after seeing a vision of the Cross before the Battle of Milvian Bridge near Rome in 312, it brought persecution to an end. Yet Constantine's conversion to a more powerful God of victory had its costs. For one thing, it laid the faith open to hybrid influences – as head of the Church, the emperor kept the pagan title *pontifex maximus* and combined faith in Christ with worship of the Sun God, *Sol Invictus*. For another, it linked the Church with the Roman state and made it an instrument of secular rule. 'By his divine will, God has entrusted rule over the whole world to me,' Constantine told a Roman governor in 313, the year 'immoral sacrifices' were banned and toleration decreed for Christianity under the Edict of Milan. 'I shall not be really or fully secure, and able to trust in God's almighty goodness, which freely dispenses happiness and salvation, until all men offer worship in harmony and brotherhood to the all-holy God in the prescribed forms of the Christian religion.'[3]

The first ecumenical council, convened at Nicaea in 325, based orthodox beliefs on the divinity of Christ – 'God of God, light of light, true God from true God, begotten not created, of one substance with the Father.' By the end of the fourth century, heresy was a crime and pagan cults were banned. The emperor's new capital, Constantinople, founded at the eastern Greek city of Byzantium in 330, had become the centre of an imperial creed. Of the Church's five patriarchates, four – Alexandria, Antioch, Jerusalem and Constantinople – were based in the East. Only Rome was situated in the West. Its Latin Christianity seemed a poor substitute for the glories of the 'New Rome' a thousand miles away.

* * *

All of this was about to change. As the *Volkerwanderung*, or barbarian invasions, made inroads into imperial territory far to the West, the Church of Rome was drawn into the resulting power vacuum, and assumed greater control over western Christianity. Rome gained prestige as the place of martyrdom of St Peter and St Paul. As its authority developed, it began to claim primacy over other patriarchates. The title of Pope, or father, was first used by Bishop Siricus in the late fourth century.

Meanwhile, Latin became the language of western worship and ecclesiastical government, in place of the Greek of Constantinople. Whereas Byzantine theology was speculative and metaphysical, Rome's was empirical and practical. The Roman Church was beginning to assert its rights against the secular power, through the work of men like St Ambrose and St Jerome, whose Vulgate Bible was the first Latin translation.

It was in its first great theologian that western Christianity's depth and richness became apparent. St Augustine (354–430) was the son of a pagan father and Christian mother. He had an unmarried relationship before his conversion, which produced a son; and he came to Christianity via Manichaeism (believing all matter to be fundamentally evil) after studying Platonic philosophy at Carthage and Latin rhetoric in Rome. As Bishop of Hippo Regius in North Africa for thirty-five years, Augustine believed it was essential to uphold the unity of a single universal Catholic Church. It was a time of heresies, when Donatists were preaching that salvation came only for a few, and Pelagians were rejecting the doctrine of original sin and defending Man's free will. Against this turbulent background, Augustine showed the need for a combination of divine grace and human faith. He gave the Church a clear sense of direction by tackling its dilemmas for the first time in a comprehensive, systematic way.

Augustine's greatest work, *The City of God*, was written in the wake of Alaric the Visigoth's capture of Rome in 410, an event which shockingly highlighted the Church's vulnerability. Hippo itself would be sacked by the Vandals a year after Augustine's death, while Rome would be seized again in 455, three years after Attila the Hun, the 'Scourge of God', had been narrowly bought off by Pope Leo I. Yet the eternal Kingdom of God would endure, Augustine reassured Christians, whatever destruction was wreaked on the world.

> The earthly city, which does not live by faith, seeks an earthly peace, and the end it proposes, in the well-ordered concord of civic obedience and rule, is the combination of men's wills to attain the things which are helpful to this life. The heavenly city, or rather the part of it which sojourns on earth and lives by faith, makes use of this peace only because it must, until this mortal condition which necessitates it shall pass away.[4]

Augustine's notion of the visible, transient world as merely symbolising a more perfect everlasting world drew on Platonist philosophy. It gave Christianity its first great theology of history and humanity, and was to dominate the Church for centuries.

It also had profound political implications. If worldly powers were merely a reflection of a higher spiritual order, kings and emperors must ultimately yield to the authority of bishops and popes. Such thinking provided a cue for gradual consolidation by the Roman papacy. It would be helped by alleged documentary evidence like the forged Donation of Constantine, in which the first Christian emperor had supposedly given the popes permanent possession of 'all provinces, palaces and districts of the city of Rome and Italy, and of the regions of the West'.[5] It was also justified, however, by the steady separation between East and West after the Council of Chalcedon in 451, and Rome's gradual assertion of independence from the emperor in Constantinople.

The conversion of the Germanic tribes gave the Western Church a vital new source of support, whose innovative, creative power could be harnessed for building up a united Europe. Since kings like Theoderic the Ostrogoth, who ruled from Ravenna at the turn of the fifth and sixth centuries, were unable to read and write, the Roman clergy held a monopoly on education. They preserved and handed on the ancient texts of Judaic, Greek and Latin civilisation, and became responsible for creating a new European culture around art and literature, law and administration.

Pope Gregory I (*c.* 540–604), an ascetic and polyglot, has been called the 'Father of Europe'. His Pastoral Rule was the first document to standardise the work of priests. His depiction of the Pope as *servus servorum Dei* (servant of the servants of God) survives to the present day. Gregory saw the Church as the 'Body of Christ', made up of nations and kingdoms which formed a *societas republicae christianae* (society of the Christian state). It was a society which already combined the splendour of great cathedrals with the austere simplicity of distant missions – from the ornate Hagia Sofia in Constantinople, consecrated in 537, to the Irish St Columba's bare stone cell on the windswept isle of Iona.

Not surprisingly, the Church had gained some powerful backers.

Its first great patron, the Frankish king Clovis (481–511), founder of the Merovingian dynasty, had realised the value of establishing Christianity as an integrating force throughout his dominions. Although the Merovingians were overthrown in the mid-eighth century by the Carolingian Pepin the Short, the Franks' alliance with Rome continued. Anointed king on the Pope's authority by the English St Boniface, Pepin was given the title 'Patrician of the Romans'. When his son, Charlemagne, was crowned in St Peter's basilica in AD 800, the title was raised to 'Emperor of the Romans'. If Gregory the Great had been the father of Europe, Charlemagne was *Europae veneranda apex* – Europe's revered chieftan.[6]

Charlemagne believed he had a mission to unite all European tribes under a single Christian empire, using the clergy as his civilising instrument. He founded the first school for nobility at his court, and encouraged cathedrals and monasteries to set up others. Meanwhile, he decreed the death penalty for refusing baptism and appointed bishops to supervise the 300 counties under his rule. It was a fusion of cross and sword. In return, the Church gave a religious sanction to Charlemagne's conquests.

The Carolingian Empire broke up at the Treaty of Verdun in 843 into the separate states of France, Germany and Italy. It was the Christian faith, however, which kept European civilisation intact. Tribal bonds were superceded by spiritual loyalty to the Church. To be Christian was to be admitted into the fellowship of civilised nations.

This was a great age of Christian missions, when intrepid priests and monks spread the Word far and wide to the fearsome Vikings of Scandinavia and to the Slavs of the Danube plain. The kingdoms of England opted for the Roman Christianity brought in 597 by St Augustine of Canterbury and thirty-nine monks, in preference to the austere faith offered by Celtic missionaries from Ireland. Saints Cyril and Methodius evangelised central Europe with joint backing from Rome and Constantinople, translating the Bible into Old Slavonic and inventing the first Cyrillic alphabet. Poland's first Christian king, Mieszko I, founder of the Piast dynasty, was baptised in 966, making his country a bastion of Christianity via its first bishopric at Gniezno. Hungary's Prince Geza was baptised in 975, a century after the Magyars – named, according to legend, after the satanic giants of the Apocalypse, Gog and Magog – had invaded Pannonia from the Asian steppe. His son, Istvan (Stephen) was crowned on Christmas Day 1000, exactly two centuries after Charlemagne, and established a Christian kingdom. The ruler of Kievan Rus, Prince Volodymyr, embraced the faith in 988, acquiring the title *Ravnoapostolny* (equal to the apostles). Baptising his whole nation *en masse*, he too set up a Christian kingdom stretching from Ukraine to the Baltic, and laid the foundations for a massive empire running all the way to the Pacific.

These gains to civilisation were often achieved at ferocious cost. St Wojciech, the first Bishop of Prague, was martyred by the Prussians in 997, and the Lithuanians were not converted until 1386. Step by step, however, Christianisation brought the northern peoples into the European family. When the Estonians finally adopted the faith, their territory was dubbed 'Maarjamaa', Land of Mary, by a grateful pope, who authorised pilgrims to travel to Talinn as an alternative to Jerusalem.

* * *

Long before that, another factor had made a major impact on the emerging Christendom. When Islam had begun its meteoric expansion in the seventh century, Christians had given the Muslims a biblical name, Ishmaelites. Their armies spread like a tidal wave out of Arabia – to Syria and Egypt, Persia and the Punjab – with the sword in one hand and the Koran in the other. Like the later onslaughts of Genghis Khan and Tamerlaine, the challenge forced Christian Europe together.

That took time, however. The eastern empire of Constantinople had already faced down attacks by Goths, Slavs, Avars, Bulgars and Persians. It now bore the brunt of the latest offensive. As Christianity was all but wiped out in Byzantine-ruled North Africa and Asia Minor, the historic patriarchates of Jerusalem, Alexandria and Antioch were left stranded *in partibus infidelium* (in the lands of the infidel).

The key to Islam's successful expansion (besides its fruitful taxation system) was said to be its tolerance. The Koran spoke well of Christians as 'people of the Book', and recognised 'Jesus son of Mary' as a prophet and teacher. Muhammed himself was said to have advised his followers to take refuge after fleeing Mecca with the Christian King of Ausum in Ethiopia, 'under whom no man is persecuted'.[7] Christian architects later helped build the mosques of Egypt.

It was a selective tolerance. Muslim Persians massacred Jerusalem's inhabitants after sacking the city in 614, and the Christian faith was tightly restricted in conquered territory. Yet the Five Pillars of Islam were simpler to understand than the often confusing Christian faith. They offered one God, one Arabic language and one sacred book, written by a single author in a single period. Whereas Christianity had faced multiple divisions from the outset, there would be only one serious schism in Islam over the succession to Muhammed. With millions of Christians given incentives to convert, some welcomed the arrival of the Muslims as a means of reasserting their local beliefs and practices.

The effect was to remove Christianity finally from its original Middle East heartland and make it a European force, with Rome as its focal point. With Muslim armies invading Visigothic Spain in 711, and attacking Constantinople at the other end of the Mediterranean just a few years later, Islam began to give Christendom its first frontiers.

They were contracting ones. Having overrun Toledo, Valencia and other cities, the Moors pushed on across the Pyrenees into France under their commander, Abd ar-Rahman, capturing Bordeaux. 'The unbelieving Saracen people burned the churches and slew the inhabitants,' a contemporary chronicler recorded. The Muslim force was finally turned back at the battle of Tours in 731 by the Frankish ruler, Charles Martel. 'The Europeans noticed the tents set up in the distance by the Arabs,' the chronicler continued. 'In the power of Christ, Charles utterly destroyed them.'[8]

The writer's wording suggested Europe's identity had come to be linked with Christianity. Yet the truth was a lot more complex. At the time of the Muslim invasions, the Continent's Christianisation was still underway. It had barely touched northern Europe and the word 'European' was a rarity at best. Meanwhile, if Islam saw elements of a common heritage in Christianity, Christianity also took much from the cultural life of Islam, as it flowered over four centuries. Its stress on monotheism influenced the Christian monophysites, who rejected the Council of Chalcedon's dogma that Christ possessed two natures, human and divine. Its prohibition of sacred images helped inspire the Iconoclasm movement which swept the Eastern Church in the 720s.

Unlike the barbarian tribes, Muslims could not easily be converted to Christianity. But Christianity was an egalitarian faith, which had continually assimilated non-Christian elements into its teaching and infrastructure. Christmas festivities, popular from the fourth century, drew heavily on Roman religious imagery, while ancient symbols, from fountains to dragon-slayers, acquired Christian patrons. In Rome, the temples of Aesclepius and Mithras ('the light-bearer') were turned into Christian churches, and the Pantheon re-dedicated to the Virgin Mary and Christian martyrs. In England, where the feast of the Resurrection acquired the name of the Anglo-Saxon goddess Eostre, the Christian missionaries were instructed not to destroy pagan temples: 'For if these temples are well built, it is requisite that they be converted from the worship of devils to the service of the true God; that the nations, seeing their temples are not destroyed, may remove error from their heart.'[9]

*   *   *

The new Christian peoples, whether Goths or Vikings, were admitted to the faith on equal terms and encouraged to rise to high office in the Church. Meanwhile, the idea of a Christian commonwealth, founded on a shared faith, was helped by wider cultural and social developments. One was the growing popularity of pilgrimages. The main destinations were Rome and the Holy Land, whose Muslim occupiers found the practice profitable. But the shrine of St James at the Campus Stellae, or Field of the Star, at Santiago – a site once used by Druids, Celts and Romans – also attracted pilgrims from all over Europe after the northern Spanish town was liberated from the Moors in 834.

Another was the rise of monasticism, which spread rapidly from the eastern Mediterranean. The hermit-founder of the monastic ideal, St Antony, was said to have been inspired by Christ's words – 'If you will be perfect, go, sell all you have and give to the poor.' Its greatest champion, St Benedict (*c.* 480–547), gave his name to a movement after retreating to Subiaco and Monte Cassino to escape contemporary decadence. Benedict's Rule offered an ordered and stable way of life – 'nothing harsh, nothing burdensome' – for those who wished to enter 'a school for the Lord's service', in which 'the strong have something to yearn for, and the weak have nothing to run from'.[10]

The monastic network quickly expanded, gaining over 500 centres in France alone. Versions were brought by Irish monks to Britain and Anglo-Saxon missionaries to Germany. When its observances became lax, a reform was launched in 910 under the same Benedictine Rule by a new house at Cluny in eastern France.

The role of the monasteries in conserving culture and learning would be gradually supplemented by new universities at Paris, Oxford and elsewhere, which strengthened the Church's intellectual and moral resources. The Church needed this. In the ninth and tenth centuries, something had gone drastically wrong in Rome. Of the forty-one competing popes elected after the violent murder of John VIII in 872, one-third died unnatural deaths amid infighting and intrigue by rival families.

They were, as one cardinal put it, 'not apostles, but apostates – vainglorious Messalinas filled with fleshly lusts and cunning in all forms of wickedness'.[11]

By the eleventh century, however, the papacy had made a recovery. The Church had gained a tighter structure of parishes and dioceses, while its authority had been strengthened by its participation in the coronations of the German Otto I as Holy Roman Emperor in 962, and of King Edgar of Wessex as overlord of Britain in 973. The consequence was a growing struggle over where supreme power rightfully lay, with secular or with ecclesiastical rulers. Its focal point would be the right to invest, or appoint, bishops in return for pledges of loyalty.

Papal polemicists argued that a *plenitudo potestatis* (fullness of power) had been bestowed on St Peter, the first Bishop of Rome. 'You are Peter, and on this rock I will build my church,' Christ had told the Apostle. 'I will give you the keys of the kingdom of heaven, and whatever you bind on earth shall be bound in heaven, and whatever you loose on earth shall be loosed in heaven' (Matthew 16:19). When Gregory VII became Pope in 1073, a man dubbed the 'holy satan' by an associate, the feuding reached a spectacular head. Gregory's *Dictatus Papae* contained twenty-seven postulates which amounted to the most explicit assertion of papal supremacy ever made. 'The Roman Church was founded by God alone', the document began, before going on to claim the right of the Pope to 'use the imperial insignia', 'depose emperors', 'absolve subjects of unjust men from their fealty' and 'be judged by no one', as sole head of a Church 'which has never erred, nor ever, by the witness of scripture, shall err to all eternity'.[12]

Defenders of the Pope would say he had a vision of a Christian society, uncorrupted by secular interference, which had to remain firmly under Church authority to fulfil the will of God. Critics argued that papal pretensions had no basis in scripture, history or tradition. Unluckily for them, they lacked the intellectual tools to compete effectively. Biblical texts were appealed to, including St Luke's account of how Christ had approved the existence of 'two swords' (Luke 22:38). But Gregory VII stuck to his claim. Two years later, when the

German emperor Henry IV insisted on his right to appoint bishops, he was declared deposed and excommunicated for 'rebelling against the Church with unheard-of audacity'. The young emperor hit back. He in turn deposed the 'so-called Pope', who 'presides in the Apostolic See not with the care of a pastor but with the violence of a usurper'.[13] When his bishops and nobles threatened to rise against him, however, Henry capitulated, standing barefoot in the Alpine snow outside the Pope's castle at Canossa until Gregory VII deigned to receive him. Reinstated, he was later dethroned by the German princes and excommunicated a second time, this time taking revenge by marching into Rome in 1084 and setting up a rival pope.

Gregory VII died after fleeing to Salerno under protection from the Normans in Sicily. But papal power remained intact, reaching its highpoint a century later under Innocent III. At the Fourth Lateran Council in 1215, attended by over 2,000 bishops and priests, an elaborate system of laws and procedures was codified for all areas of Church life. It reaffirmed the Church's independence under a celibate clergy. 'The Creator of the Universe set up two great luminaries in the firmament of heaven: the greater light to rule the day, the lesser light to rule the night,' Pope Innocent explained:

> In the same way for the firmament of the universal Church, which is spoken of as heaven, he appointed two great dignitaries: the greater to bear rule over souls (these being, as it were, days), and the lesser to rule over our bodies (these being, as it were, nights). These dignities are the pontifical authority and the royal power.[14]

* * *

By then, a deep split had occurred in Christianity, with mutual excommunications in 1054 by the Pope and Patriarch of Constantinople. The Great Schism had followed centuries of alienation, as the Western and Eastern Churches drifted apart in liturgy and theology, language and culture. The music, architecture and scholarship of Constantinople were unsurpassed, as were the devotion and contemplation symbolised by the 'Republic of Monks' founded at Mount Athos in 885. But the

East had avoided the struggles over temporal and spiritual power which marked the Investiture Contest. The eastern emperor still saw himself as Melchisadech, the 'king-priest' of the Old Testament, with the right to supervise the Church and appoint its leaders. Though much reduced in power, he had not abandoned his claim to overlordship of Rome and the West. 'We beseech you in the Lord to turn aside from these childish follies,' Pope Gregory II had accosted the emperor Leo.

> You ought rather to know and to hold for certain that the pontiffs who have ruled at Rome preside there in order to maintain peace, like a wall joining East and West, occupying the middle ground between them, and that they are arbiters and promoters of peace ... One thing we take badly is this, that while the savage and barbarous people have become peaceful, your peacefulness turns to savagery and cruelty. The whole of the West faithfully offers its fruits to the holy prince of the apostles.[15]

By the late eleventh century, something else had happened to cement the East–West division. The Crusades were formally intended by Pope Urban II as a common effort by western Christians to recapture the Holy Sepulchre of Jerusalem from Islam – an end enthusiastically endorsed by otherwise peaceful luminaries such as St Bernard of Clairvaux, founder of the Cistercian order. But they also served the purpose of extending papal supremacy. They were to have the opposite effect. When Constantinople was sacked and temporarily occupied during the Fourth Crusade in 1202–4, the East–West schism was sealed.

Officially at least, the popes disapproved of the brutal crusader methods. They continued to view Islam as a threat to Christendom and went on defending attempts to push it back. Yet they also allowed some cross-fertilisation of cultures. St Francis of Assisi undertook a peace mission to Egypt, while King Ferdinand of Castille showed tolerance after reducing the Moorish rulers of Toledo, Saragossa and Seville to tributaries. Islam was accepted, along with Christianity and Judaism, in the five kingdoms of medieval Spain, where six main languages were spoken. Two Cordoba-born thinkers, the Muslim Averroes (1126–1198) and Jewish Maimonides

(1135–1204), had a far-reaching influence among Christian philosophers and theologians.

Muslims and Jews were the two principal non-Christian minorities living within the confines of Europe. The Jews were barred from public office by the 1215 Lateran Council, which also ordered them to wear special dress and pay a tax to the Church. In reality, however, Jews remained influential, thanks to their skills in finance, medicine, trade and administration. The Catholic King of Poland, Kazimierz the Great (1333–1370), whose territory was largely spared plague and famine, later offered a homeland to Jews fleeing pogroms in the rest of Europe, and allowed them to develop under his protection into a thriving autonomous minority.

The Lateran Council also turned with a vengeance against the Church's internal enemies. A bloody crusade against the Cathars in southern France, who taught that the world was irredeemably evil, was launched in 1208, while the Church persecuted groups such as the Waldensians, who rejected established doctrines. Heretical movements proclaimed a return to the purity of Christianity over the power and wealth of the contemporary Church. They had social and political implications. But Rome succeeded in incorporating the new movement towards apostolic poverty which grew up around the Franciscans and Dominicans in the early thirteenth century, suggesting it was not hostile to reform as such, provided it remained loyal. When St Francis of Assisi met Pope Innocent III in 1209, it brought together two starkly contrasting images of Christianity. Yet it also expressed the Church's capacity to institutionalise radical ideas. The new orders were to maintain tense relations with the Church's leaders. But they also gave it a new generation of theologians, teachers, chroniclers, illuminators and doctors.

The surge of energy was expressed in works of art and culture, as well as in charity and care of the sick. In the single century after 1170, over 80 cathedrals and 500 large Gothic churches were built in England alone. With its popular cults and devotions, the Church helped ward off dangerous lingering attachments to magic and superstition. It brought order and peace to social life, as well as ideas of just governance, contracts and fair prices, chivalry and honour. It also promoted the advancement of women through education, and offered equal opportunities in its own ranks to peasants and nobles alike. It did so, furthermore, on a continental scale, providing a powerful motor for Europe's development. The simplicity of St Francis and splendour of Pope Innocent both played a creative and instructive part.

Certainly, the absolute power of the Pope looked like the downside of these achievements. But this too was open to interpretation. In the struggle to define the right relationship between spiritual and secular forms of power, critics accused the popes of theocratic megalomania, while apologists insisted they had always accepted the necessary autonomy of secular rulers, even if some popes were guilty of political abuses. Whatever the truth, the Investiture Contest forced a distinction between the 'two swords' which had been merged in most systems of government from the Egyptian pharoahs to the Roman caesars. Neither was able to dominate the other, despite a formidable array of instruments and arguments. The result was a dualism, in which two power structures were obliged to compete for loyalties. Thanks to its well-defended independence from the state, the Church was able to erect a barrier against total state control. Once applied, Christ's exhortation from St Luke – 'Render unto Caesar the things that are Caesar's, and unto God the things that are God's' (Luke 20:25) – meant limited power and greater freedom. It would become built into European politics and society.

*   *   *

Of course, it was in the interests of *sacerdotium* and *regnum* to co-operate as far as possible. Finding the right kind of coexistence would be largely the achievement of the Church's great political philosopher, St Thomas Aquinas (1225–1274). His thought marked a symbolic shift away from the all-embracing Augustinian system, grounded in the Church Fathers and historic councils, towards a new type of theology which delineated forms and levels of knowledge.

Aquinas's *Summa Theologica* (1266–73) presented a comprehensive system of research and argmentation, based on questions and answers, which distinguished between reason and faith, natural and revealed truth. St Thomas defended the papal system, whereby 'the secular power is subject to the spiritual as the body is to the soul'; but he also spoke up for the state. Both forms of power were 'derived from the divine power', he pointed out. The secular power was under the spiritual only in matters that 'pertain to the salvation of souls'. In issues that 'pertain to civil good', the secular power was to be obeyed.[16]

Aquinas argued for a strong authority; but he also set out conditions for the legitimate overthrow of unjust rulers. He called for a vigorous moral order; but he also stressed the need to tolerate certain evils – 'If you do away with harlots,' Augustine had written, 'the world will be convulsed with lust.'[17] Meanwhile, he also approved of the Crusades to prevent the infidel 'from hindering the faith of Christ'; but he differed from Augustine in doubting that Jews and infidels should be converted.

In the course of his writing, St Thomas drew on authorities from St Paul to Seneca, and ranged over conscience and moral duty, forms of law and justice, statesmanship and property. But his greatest debt was to Aristotle, whom he referred to as 'the Philosopher'. The works of the ancient Greek had been the subject of Jewish and Arab commentaries, but had only recently been rediscovered by Christian writers. His distinction between different spheres of knowledge and virtue challenged the single compact metaphysics embodied in St Augustine's neo-Platonism. It offered a new outlook – a 'theologically founded worldliness' – which was rooted in faith but also accepted the reality of the visible world.[18]

Although his conclusions reflected thirteenth-century preoccupations, Aquinas set a new standard for Christian discourse which still applies. His theories of natural law, the pursuit of virtue and Just War – and of the relationship between religion and politics, human intelligence and freedom – were all of permanent relevance. So too was his stress on the need for faith to be informed by reason, not divorced from reality but challenged to change it.

The Bishop of Paris, where St Thomas taught, condemned many of his propositions, fearing the revival of Greek philosophy would endanger faith and order. In 1323, however,

Aquinas was declared a saint, another sign of the Church's capacity to absorb novel, refractory elements. In the 1870s, his philosophy became official teaching.

Aquinas was decidedly orthodox on one point – that obedience to the Pope remained 'utterly necessary to the salvation of every human creature'. By his death, however, a new crisis was shaping up, as a rising intellectual stratum in Europe's universities, spearheaded by Marsilius of Padua and William of Ockham, questioned the papacy's *plentitudo potestatis*. Pope Boniface VIII defended the medieval status quo. 'Both are in the power of the Church, the material sword and the spiritual,' he reiterated in a 1302 bull, *Unam Sanctam*. 'Therefore, if the earthly power errs, it shall be judged by the spiritual power; if a lesser spiritual power errs, it shall be judged by its superior; but if the supreme spiritual power errs, it can be judged only by God, not by man.'[19]

Boniface came to grief trying to excommunicate King Philip IV of France and died imprisoned at Anagni. The next popes were all French, and the seat of the papacy was moved for seven decades from Rome to Avignon in what became known as the 'Babylonian Captivity'. Rival pontiffs came and went (there were at least seventeen anti-popes before 1500), culminating in three contesting claimants in the early fifteenth century. The schism ended with the Council of Constance in 1414–18, which decreed that a general council, rather than the papacy, should henceforth wield 'immediate power from Christ' over the Church. The Council, best known for its savage condemnation of the reformers John Wycliffe and Jan Hus, was summoned by the Holy Roman Emperor, Sigismund of Luxembourg, and was followed by others. But Europe's secular rulers feared the disruptive potential of 'Conciliarism', and the Papacy recouped its power. In 1460, Pius II declared the Constance decree 'condemned, reproved, quashed, annulled', and warned against the 'pestilent venom' of general councils.[20] The way was open for a new autocratic papacy, ruled intermittently as a personal fiefdom by the Borgia and Medici families.

* * *

In the new climate of political intrigue and social unrest, many Christians turned for reassurance to the *Devotio Moderna*, represented by mystics such as the German Thomas à Kempis, whose emphasis on scriptural teaching and personal holiness offered a refuge from the oppressive formalities of scholastic theology. The philosophy of Greece and Rome came back into vogue, with Antiquity providing a new refreshing counterpoint to accumulated tradition.

Despite this, the Renaissance developed firmly within the cultural and intellectual framework of Christianity. The talents of the day – Dante, Leonardo da Vinci, Raphael, Dürer – combined a new respect for human dignity and feeling with a reverence for nature and the material world. They placed Christianity, however, at the centre and remained loyal to the Church. 'In earlier times, the Rhine divided the French from the Germans, but it does not separate one Christian from another,' reaffirmed Erasmus of Rotterdam. 'The Pyrenees separate Spaniards and Frenchmen, but they do not undo the commonality of the Church. The sea flows between the English and the French, but it can in no way split the unity of faith.'[21]

The rediscovery of ancient learning was considered compatible with Christian tradition. More eccentric figures such as Pico della Mirandola (1463–1494), with his precocious talent for Hermetic and Kabbalist thought, were concerned to prove, rather than undermine, the truth of Christianity. The wisdom of the Orient had provided steps in man's ascent to a more perfect union with God – just as the story of the Three Kings, or magi, from the East, who had identified the New King by the star over Bethlehem, had symbolised the induction of ancient wisdom to the new Christian faith. Where conflict with the Church occurred, it was largely over issues of influence and power.

For all its good intentions, the Renaissance nevertheless chipped away at the Church's authority. At a time when there was more talk of a personal link to God, independently of ecclesiastical institutions, that authority was no longer taken on trust. With theorists such as Niccolo Machiavelli (1469–1527) advocating a secularised, opportunist model of political science, it would take sharper evidence and argumentation to justify the Church's divine claims. Yet the traditional view that the subsequent Reformation was necessitated solely or primarily by church decay and corruption is questionable. There were indeed negative features: intolerance, bureaucracy and politicisation. But there were many more positive aspects of church life. Blocked attempts at reform told part of the story, as did popular agitation against clerical privilege. But few sought a revolution which would overthrow traditional beliefs. Nor did the Reformation's figurehead, Martin Luther (1483–1546), see himself as breaking with Catholicism. Instead, he insisted on his loyalty to the Church and the universal faith according to the Bible.

Luther's doctrine of Justification and Grace was rooted in Augustinian theology. What made his teaching subversive was his appeal to the primacy of Christ, and to the original Christian message elaborated by St Paul over the accretions and distortions of history. The three theological treatises he published in 1520 alone – *To the Christian Nobility of the German Nation*; *The Babylonian Captivity of the Church* and *Of the Liberty of a Christian Man* – mixed intense spirituality with obscene polemic. They attacked the 'walls of the Romanists': the primacy of spiritual over secular power and the papacy's claim to be sole interpreter of Scripture. But they recognised the same God, Gospel and Eucharist, and took their stance on the same Christian faith.

It has been argued that the Reformation brought a paradigm change – 'a move away from the all too human ecclesiocentricity of the powerful Church to the christocentricity of the Gospel' – which renewed the emphasis on freedom which had been part of Christianity's message.[22] It would, indeed, be associated with new ideas of governance and social organisation, as well a novel notions of political protest and solidarity. Initially at least, though, Luther's revolution was self-limiting. Fearing anarchy, Luther denounced the German peasants when they rose, citing biblical verses, against their landowners in 1524–5 under the Anabaptist Thomas Muntzer. 'Brandish your swords!' he told the German princes. 'Free, save, help and pity the poor who are forced to join the peasants – hit the wicked, stab, smite and slay all you can.'[23]

The reaction to the Anabaptists indicated a preference for

more peaceful groups like the Hutterites, Mennonites and Socinians, who favoured a less politicised return to the simplicity of early Christian communities. Yet it was not seen that way at the time. Concern for the stability of Christendom impelled the English humanist and martyr, Thomas More, into a epic struggle against the Bible translator, William Tyndale (1494–1536), penning 750,000 words against him, the largest polemic ever published in English. Reformers might rail against the arrogance which denied people the right to read the Word of God. But thinkers like More also realised intuitively and immediately the threat posed by men like Tyndale – who 'would in this worlde liue in lewd libertie, and have all runne to ryot'.[24] They accurately forecast that Protestantism would fuel unprecedented conflict.

Sure enough, the Reformation soon moved in various directions. The first split occurred in Luther's lifetime as followers of Ulrich Zwingli in Zurich rejected his theology of the Eucharist. Zwingli was killed in a battle between Switzerland's Protestant and Catholic cantons. But his radicalism was taken up by the Frenchman John Calvin, who demanded reform not just in the Church, but in Christian life and doctrine too. Calvin's *Institutio Religionis Christianae* (1536) called for abolition of the Mass, singing, images and crucifixes. Far from advocating an other-worldly existence, however, it envisaged an active Christian involvement with the world.

The German sociologist Max Weber (1864–1920) would see a link between Calvin's teaching and the rise of capitalism and a modern work ethic. The city of Geneva, where he established himself, became a Taliban-style mini-state, in which church elders collaborated with city councillors and the boundaries between religious and civil authority were blurred. But it was also a state which protected the poor and weak, imposed a strict moral code on business and encouraged profitable but just commerce. Protestant refugees flocked to Geneva and the city became a reformist beacon, as well as a source of inspiration for the traders and financiers of London, Amsterdam and Hamburg.

Capitalism would never be a Protestant monopoly. But Calvin's alternative church structure of synods and offices

●

also had a wide influence, particularly on the Free Churches which emerged from the more radical wing of the Reformation. Luther's movement had been predominantly a young people's affair. It concided with the development of printing, the spread of biblical scholarship, the growing use of vernacular languages over Latin, and the rise of an educated and assertive middle class. Its activists formed only a small minority. But they were socially motivated and tapped into a much wider popular mood.

They also attracted interest from secular rulers hoping to restrict the powers, privileges and properties of the Catholic Church. As the power of nation-states grew, the creation of state-churches, exemplified by Henry VIII in England, became a Reformation side effect. England's new Anglican establishment was not typical. After being pulled in opposing directions by rival Catholic and Protestant factions, it would settle on a *via media*, or middle way, under Elizabeth I, which combined a Reformed liturgy with a Catholic structure of priesthood and sacraments. The Church of England was lucky to have a clear set of beliefs and procedures in its Thirty-Nine Articles and 1611 Authorised Version of the Bible. The possibilities of compromise and accomodation were more restricted elsewhere.

The 'religious wars' which wracked Europe in the sixteenth century may have had more to do with political and economic competition than with issues of faith. The famous formula of the 1555 Treaty of Augsburg, *cuius regio eius religio* (whoever rules decides the faith) recognised the new power of secular rulers in Church life, whether in Catholic Portugal, Protestant Germany or Orthodox Russia. Yet Europe, now divided North and South, as well as East and West, was still governed everywhere according to Christian precepts and beliefs.

The bloody conflicts did, however, leave Europe fatally weakened at a time when Christendom's eastern frontiers were being pushed inwards by new Islamic invasions. Constantinople had been captured by Ottoman armies in 1453, and Greece seven years later. There had been constant fighting along the Danube in Bulgaria, Transylvania, Wallachia and Romania, as the Hungarians Janos Hunyadi and Matthias

Corvinus attempted to halt further Turkish advances, periodically assisted by intrigue-ridden local rulers such as the Romanian Vlad Țepeș and the Serb George Brankovic. In years to come, various nations would claim to have saved Europe's *Respublica Christiana* from the Turks. By the early sixteeth century, however, the eastern borderlands were in mortal danger. Serbia and Croatia fell in the 1520s to Sultan Suleiman the Magnificent, while the rout of a Hungarian and Bohemian army at Mohács in 1526 laid Central Europe open. In 1529, the Ottomans laid seige to Vienna, raising alarm throughout the Continent. Although they withdrew, leaving a trail of destruction, the presence of Islam was now established from the Balkans as far north as the Tatar settlements of Lithuania. The threat to Central Europe would last until 1683, when the Catholic Polish king, Jan Sobieski, finally defeated Turkish armies at the gates of Vienna.

* * *

More penitential Church leaders had recognised the need for change if Christendom was to hold together. 'We are well aware that for some years now abominable things have taken place at this Holy See,' Pope Hadrian VI told Germany's nobility in 1522; 'abuses in matters spiritual, transgressions of the commandments; indeed, that all has turned for the worse. So it is not surprising that the sickness has spread from the head to the members, from the Pope to the prelates. All of us, prelates and clergy, have departed from the right way.'[25]

Putting words into action was more difficult. In the 1530s, Pope Paul III tried for reconciliation with Protestants through secret negotiations, but failed over the issue of papal authority. Although other attempts followed, the differences had become irreconcilable. Roman apologists maintained that salvation was only possible inside the Catholic Church, while Calvin dismissed Catholicism totally, claiming he could find only 'traces of Christianity' in it.[26]

Yet a more dynamic Catholic response was not long in coming. In the single momentous year of 1492, Izabella of Castile had completed the reconquest of Spain from the Moors and presided over the discovery of America. On a darker side, she had also expelled Spain's Jews and founded the Inquisition, under which 125,000 heretics and infidels would be put on trial and in some cases killed. Catholic Spain had become a land of both reaction and reform, defending Church and faith, but also in the vanguard of revival and discovery.

Similar contrasts would be evident as the Church of Rome began its own Counter-Reformation. The Council of Trent opened in 1545, three years after the papacy had founded its own Inquisition, and ran for the next eighteen years. Its 400 participating bishops re-established papal authority and the orthodox Church position on scripture and sacraments, rejecting Protestant reforms such as clerical marriage and the vernacular liturgy. They also shook off the Church's remaining medieval shackles, however, and made it more efficient and effective. Priestly training and catechetical teaching were all streamlined and improved. In 1588, the year Philip II's Spanish Armada was routed off the coasts of England, Rome introduced a modern system of curial departments. It also founded a network of colleges for the different nations of Europe.

The Counter-Reformation was, in short, not just a Catholic response to the Protestant Reformation, but a parallel movement of reform and adaptation. It took shape under pressure from Protestantism and had much in common with it. But its essential purpose was to restore Europe's Christian unity. Catholic rulers like Philip II resisted the Council of Trent, which appeared to give the papacy renewed power and prestige. In the resulting surge of activity, however, new religious orders – Jesuits, Capuchins, Oratorians – brought new standards of education and pastoral care to the Continent, while a new wave of mystics – St John of the Cross, St Teresa of Avila, St Francis de Sales – introduced a purer, more evangelical form of devotion. Countless churches were built in the new ornate Baroque, Europe's last unitary architectural style. Meanwhile, 123 Catholic priests paid with their lives attempting to re-establish Catholic worship in the England of Elizabeth I and James I, while others, such as the Czech St Jan Sarkander, were martyred in other parts of Europe.

Spanish, Portuguese and Italian missions to America, Africa, China and Japan, associated with such great names as

Bartolomé de las Casas and Mateo Ricci, would debate how far the Christian culture of Europe could be imprinted on native traditions. 'Do not regard it as your task, and do not bring any pressure to bear on the peoples, to change their manners, customs and uses, unless they are evidently contrary to religion and sound morals,' the secretary of Rome's new De Propaganda Fide congregation offered a warning.

> What could be more absurd that to transport France, Spain, Italy or some other European country to China? Do not introduce all of that to them, but only the faith that does not despise or destroy the manners and customs of any people ... Do not draw invidious contrasts between the customs of the peoples and those of Europe; do your utmost to adapt yourselves to them.[27]

There were significant instances of acculturation closer to home. Polish Catholic rulers showed tolerance towards the Orthodox inhabitants of their conquered territories. Under the 1596 Union of Brest, Orthodox Ukrainian communities incorporated into the Catholic Habsburg empire were permitted to keep their eastern liturgy and ecclesial order, serving as a prototype for other 'Uniate' churches in Ruthenia and Transylvania. The Protestant Reformation and Catholic Counter-Reformation turned out to be complementary movements. Both in their own ways breathed life back into Christianity through a new wave of spiritual endeavour and new impulses of social and cultural development.

Unfortunately for Europe, national politics intervened. In France, up to 10,000 Protestant Huguenots were massacred on the eve of St Bartholomew's Day in 1572 against a background of dynastic feuding. Catholic-Protestant coexistence was not achieved till the Edict of Nantes twenty-six years later. In the Low Countries, a Dutch revolt against Spanish rule triggered an eighty-year war which resulted in a Catholic Flanders and Protestant United Provinces. In Bohemia, another Protestant revolt was crushed by Catholic Habsburg armies at the Battle of the White Mountain in 1620, touching off the Thirty Years War.

* * *

Under the Peace of Westphalia which ended that war in 1648, the rulers of Germany, France and Sweden agreed to allow 'exact and mutual equality' in religion to Europe's newly demarcated Catholic and Protestant territories, decreeing that 'all violence and physical force in these as in other matters shall be perpetually forbidden for either side'.[28] The Peace was heavily expedient, taking Europe a big step closer to a political order divorced from religious considerations. It was also bitterly condemned by Pope Innocent X, who was alarmed at the implications of placing Protestants on the same social and political level as Catholics. A 'very great prejudice' had been done, he was sure, to the Catholic Church's 'jurisdiction, authority, immunities, franchises, liberties, exemptions, privileges, affairs, possessions and rights'.[29]

Yet the political influence of churches was decreasing, and the Peace merely confirmed this. The previous century's wars had shown the destructiveness of an alliance between religion and politics. If peace was to last, Europeans needed to agree certain principles of coexistence, and ensure religious rivalries did not intrude too far on the business of governance. Religious tolerance was a political, social and economic necessity. It was beginning to look like a spiritual necessity too.

This tolerance needed careful definition. The new age was bringing a shift of power away from Germany and Italy to the new maritime powers of France, Britain and the Netherlands. It was also becoming a time of absolutism, in which traumatised societies looked for an all-powerful sovereign – the Leviathan conceived by the English Thomas Hobbes – to keep a lid on fanaticism and anarchy.

France itself was ruled by a Catholic monarchy which believed firmly in its divine right. But it was also a centralised nation-state, guided by *raison d'état*, in which nobility, peasantry and parliament were kept firmly in their place. That it had taken a Catholic cardinal, Armand de Richelieu (1585–1642), to steer France to this position, as chief minister under Louis XIII, was a sign of the Church's capacity to modernise. Yet religion would remain a political instrument. In 1685, when Louis XIV revoked the Edict of Nantes and gave Reformed ministers fifteen days to leave his country, he made clear the toleration established a century earlier had been little more than a tactical retreat under pressure. It was now time, the Sun King decreed, to restore true *Chretienté* – 'to efface entirely the memory of the disorders, confusion and evils which this false religion has caused in our kingdom'.[30]

The French king's move damaged the French economy and set back the Catholic cause in Europe by strengthening Protestantism's identification with personal liberty. Even the Pope viewed it with deep reserve. But it also showed how secular rulers continued to use Christianity for their own ends.

Austria's Habsburg emperor, Joseph II, also championed the idea of religious toleration – 'being convinced, on the one hand, that all coercion of consciences is detrimental and, on the other, that great profit arises to religion and the state from a truly Christian tolerance'.[31] But this was limited in practice to private worship by Lutherans, Calvinists and Orthodox Christians. It was also accompanied by high-handed reforms of the Catholic Church, made without Rome's consent, which caused widespread popular resentment.

In Russia, the Orthodox Church had assumed leadership of eastern Christianity after the fall of Constantinople to the Turks. It remained deeply subservient, however, to the secular power. The Russian Tsar had become, in the words of one Orthodox apologist, 'on earth the sole emperor of the Christians, the leader of the Apostolic Church which stands no longer in Rome or Constantinople, but in the blessed city of Moscow. Two Romes have fallen, but the third stands and a fourth there will not be'.[32] A Moscow patriarchate was founded in 1589. But pro-Greek reforms by Patriarch Nikon in the early seventeeth century provoked a schism with Old Believers. It paved the way for Peter the Great (1672–1725) to impose total control over the Church, replacing the patriarchate with a dependent synod as part of a programme of Westernisation.

* * *

Yet the real challenge to Christianity was coming as much from new types of secular culture. By the mid-seventeenth century, the development of disciplines such as geometry and optics were having knock-on effects, as reformers tried to rationalise the structures of the state and society, and find natural explanations for human activity. Much of the new thought emanated from within the Church. It was Catholic religious orders like the Jesuits and Piarists who did most to promote education and cultural awareness in Central Europe. The Polish astronomer, Nicolaus Copernicus (1473–1543), whose heliocentric theory of the solar system appeared to undermine the Christian concept of the universe, was a Catholic cathedral canon in Torun. The Italian physicist, Galileo Galilei (1564–1642), who was forced by the Inquisition to recant his views, was said to have worked out a theory of motion from watching a swinging chandelier in Pisa cathedral.

Yet there were many who sought to play down confessional differences in favour of a shared faith, and to highlight the common humanity of a world divided between Catholic and Protestant rulers. The slogan, 'dare to think', expressed the new mood. The English father of scientific experimentation, Francis Bacon (1561–1626), had rejected the Aristotelian system of thought codified by Aquinas, and set out to demonstrate how consciousness was acquired through standard forms of knowledge and perception. His philosophical successor, John Locke (1632–1704) argued that it was experience which provided the key to ideas. The mind of each human being was, at birth, a *tabula rasa*, a bare table, which was furnished in the course of life through contact with the natural world of mind and body.

Locke remained a believing Christian, rejecting atheism as much as the rhetorical aspects of contemporary religion. But his notion of Christianity was grounded on reason, rather than revelation. His book, *The Reasonableness of Christianity*, published anonymously in 1695, set out to restore the Gospel to the pristine shape intended by Christ, before 'vice and superstition held the world' and 'priests everywhere, to secure their empire, excluded reason from having anything to do with religion'.

> I do not remember that he anywhere assumes to himself the title of priest, or mentions anything relating to his priesthood ... But the Gospel, or the good news of the kingdom of the

Messiah, is what he preaches everywhere and makes it his great business to publish in the world.[33]

Locke's view that nothing was innate contradicted the Christian view that Man was marked by Original Sin. It spread quickly in the form of a profound scepticism, which scorned the magical, incantatory aspects of Christian worship summed up in the 'hocus pocus' (*hoc est corpus*) uttered by the priest during the Catholic Mass. The 'God in the Gaps' spoken of by Deists was a God who occupied the realm beyond attested human knowledge. As such, the space available to him was continually shrinking. The formula of the French philosopher René Descartes (1596–1650), *Cogito ergo sum* (I think, therefore I am), placed the foundation of awareness in Man's existence rather than God's. This apparently reversed the core of certainty inherited from earlier times. The faith of the Enlightenment had no need of miracles and dogmas. The 'true light' spoken of by St John – 'which lighteth every man that cometh into the world' – was God-given reason. It had enabled society to advance through historical stages. As such, it deserved to be viewed as Man's supreme authority, over and above the Grace of Catholics or the Faith of Protestants.

The developing study of politics and economics strengthened the idea of progress, as did the new disciplines of sociology and anthropology. Both contributed to the emergence of critical democratic attitudes in reaction to the divinely ordained order of monarchs and hierarchs. Education and secularisation went hand in hand with emancipation and self-determination. Yet they also fuelled instability and confusion in a world which had not yet learned to absorb them. It was left to the German Immanuel Kant (1724–1804) to restore the 'categorical imperative' of an absolute moral law, by finding the right balance between the empirical experience of John Locke and David Hume, and the mediating reason of Descartes, Gottfried Leibnitz and Benedict Spinoza. Reason made experience possible by imposing understanding on the raw material supplied by the senses. Practical reason could be present, Kant concluded in his famous critiques, in the moral action of human beings, who could have certainty in morality as much as in mathematics.

The precondition was, however, a transcendental idealism. On this point at least, Enlightenment thought was rooted in Christianity. Descartes had remained a Catholic all his life, arguing for the existence of God, while the French theorist of mathematical probability, Blaise Pascal (1623–1662), had pledged trust for 'the God of Abraham, the God of Isaac, the God of Jacob, and not of the philosophers and men of science'. The English Francis Bacon had written prayers and translated the Psalms, insisting 'depth in Philosophy bringeth Menn's Minds about to Religion'. The English physicist and mathematician Isaac Newton (1642–1727), discoverer of gravity and inventor of calculus, wrote extensive theological commentaries and saw no threat from God, whose creation of the world he dated from biblical evidence to around 3500 BC.[34]

'No age, since the founding and forming of the Christian Church,' the English Daniel Defoe lamented in 1720, 'was ever like, in open avowed atheism, blasphemies and heresies, to the age we live in now.'[35] That was plainly an exaggeration, even by the later eighteenth century. For all its doubt and scepticism, this was also a great age of Christian renewal. New impulses were given to Protestantism by Baptists, Quakers and Methodists, whose founder, John Wesley, travelled 250,000 miles over half a century, preaching 40,000 sermons. If Protestantism was associated with a forward-looking ethic of individual responsibility, which had fostered political reform and economic advance in northern Europe, it had no monopoly over them. In the Catholic Church too, groups as diverse as the Jansenists and Redemptorists offered more rigorous forms of spiritual and moral discipline. In many cases, they also posed a cultural and social barrier to absolutist power, a stance which contributed to the suppression of the Jesuits in 1773.

By the late eighteenth century, the best minds would have agreed with Kant that Locke's *tabula rasa* was wrong. Human experiences were always shaped and interpreted by ideas, while some ideas (as the Irish Bishop George Berkeley argued) did not originate with experiences at all. They would also have concurred deeply on the need for Christianity. Even the agnostic Hume (1711–1776), with his theory of cause and effect, called history the 'march of the providence of God' and recognised that the 'enthusiasm' of Puritans and other religious reformers had fostered human freedom. 'The proper office of religion,' Hume conceded, 'is to regulate the heart of men, humanise their conduct, infuse the spirit of temperance, order and obedience.'[36]

* * *

Luckily for Hume and others, Europe remained profoundly Christian anyway. The term *respublica christiana*, or Christian commonwealth, had been used again in the treaties of Utrecht in 1713–14 which brought an end to Louis XIV's expansionism. Later in the century, the French Enlightenment prophet, Voltaire (1694–1778), advanced the case for a 'Christian Europe' defined by 'reason, arts and sciences'. Yet Voltaire conceded that all European countries still had 'the same religious foundation, even though divided into several confessions'.[37]

Ironically, it was in the Catholic culture of Voltaire's France, rather than in Protestant England, that Enlightenment philosophy had advanced most, thanks to thinkers from Montesquieu to Diderot. The *Philosophes* attacked the French establishment, with its cloak of religious mystification, and provided, in their 35-volume *Encyclopaedie* (1751–80), a compendium of rational knowledge, freed from religious obscurities, which influenced the liberal elites of Europe.

Their followers applauded the freedom of conscience embodied in the American constitution of 1787 and Polish constitution of 1791, and looked with fascination at the discovery of religions in Asia and Latin America which appeared older that Christianity itself. Although coining the slogan, *Écrazez l'infame!* against the Church, however, Voltaire himself was far from being an atheist. He believed in the immortality of the soul and never doubted the usefulness of religion in a world of fear and uncertainty. 'If God did not exist, it would be necessary to invent Him,' the French writer and philosopher acknowledged famously.[38]

In decades to come, the French Revolution would be viewed as a savage warning of what was to follow when the order provided by customary rights and duties broke down. Initially at least, however, the Revolution was not directly hostile to the Church. The notion of *Laicité*, or secularity, implied a distinction between Church and State offices, rather than an anti-Christian or irreligious mindset. Anti-clericalism had been a marginal phenomenon in France, mainly aimed against Church wealth. Although most Catholic bishops were aristocrats, who sided with king and nobility against the abolition of traditional privileges, many of the lower clergy joined the Third Estate in supporting the new Declaration of Human and Civil Rights after the fall of the Bastille in 1789.

The National Assembly which adopted the Civil Constitution of the Clergy after heated debates a year later appeared to believe Pope Pius VI might accept it as a practical rearrangement, largely dictated by economic considerations, which placed the Church under secular control but fell short of interfering in spiritual affairs. Section I pledged to uphold 'the unity of the faith and the communion which should be reserved with the visible head of the universal Church'. But it also undermined the French Church's links with Rome, by forbidding citizens to recognise 'under any pretext whatever the authority of an ordinary or metropolitan bishop whose see should be established under domination by a foreign power'.[39] This was what brought papal condemnation. With only a minority of priests and bishops consenting to take the new civil oath, most of the Church was forced into opposition, as civil war erupted in the Vendée, accompanied by terror, persecution and massacre.

With its ideological slogan, *Liberté, Egalité, Fraternité*, the French Revolution established a model for two centuries of struggle against the established social order. It set a precedent for confrontation with the Church, characterised by the seizure of its schools and hospitals, the nationalisation of its lands and properties, and the dissolution of its religious orders. It also pioneered an alternative culture, capped by the abolition of the Christian year in October 1793 and the crowning of the 'Goddess of Reason' in Notre Dame Cathedral a month later. 'It is time, since we have arrived at the summit of the principles of a great revolution, to reveal the truth about all types of religion,' the de-Christianiser, Jacques Thuriot de la Rozière, declared. 'All religions are but conventions –

legislators make them to suit the people they govern ... It is the moral order of the Republic, of the Revolution, that we must preach now'.[40]

Yet the *culte de la raison et de la loi* failed to take hold. Although further anti-clerical laws were issued by the Directory in the late 1790s and copied in Belgium, Italy and Switzerland, the secularist mood dissipated and Christianity recovered. The Jacobin leader, Maximilien Robespierre, who presided over 16,000 executions in ten months, had been a practising Catholic until 1789. He equated atheism with aristocratic arrogance and considered the festivals of Reason to be 'ridiculous farces' by 'men without honour or religion'. Popular writers extolled the virtues of Christian Europe against the anarchy and despotism brought by the Revolution. 'Of all the religions that have ever existed, the Christian religion is the most poetical,' the writer Chateaubriand insisted in his *Génie du Christianisme* (1802). 'It is the most favourable to freedom, art and letters, and the modern world owes everything to it, from agriculture to the abstract sciences.'[41]

The terror-struck idealism of 1789 gave way to a new era of nationalism and imperialism. Rising to power on the back of the Revolution, Napoleon concurred that Christianity provided a useful instrument for social cohesion. With diplomatic ties now broken with the papacy, a Roman republic was proclaimed by occupying French troops in 1798. The Pope was hauled off, a prisoner, to Valence, where he died a year later, described in a registrar's report as 'Jean Ange Braschi, exercising the profession of pontiff'. His successor, Pius VII, was made to sign a Concordat in 1801. This restored religious freedom 'in conformity with police regulations which the government shall judge necessary for public tranquility'. It also recognised Catholicism as 'the religion of the vast majority of French citizens', which had 'received and is receiving at the present time the greatest benefit and prestige' from its establishment in the country.[42] Three years later, Pius VII personally crowned Napoleon emperor. A suitably pacified Church, Napoleon had concluded, could be harnessed for state purposes in a French-administered *Association Européene*.

Some would argue that Christianity had been forced to

change under relentless pressure – others that justice, democracy, freedom of conscience and the rule of law had been Christian ideals all along. Whichever views were held, Christianity had adapted over its long history through a constant interaction with the forces of change. As a universal civilisation, it still incorporated the contrasting vices and virtues of the age – ostentatious wealth and saintly simplicity, pluralism and authoritarianism, tolerance and prejudice. In that sense at least, it reflected the character of society, the open house of Europe which remained Christian in its foundations and structures.

Belonging to that Europe did not have to mean becoming Christian. When troops of the new French republic had entered Rome, they had been welcomed as liberators by the Jews of Catholic Italy, still smarting from the mistreatment meted out to them in southern Europe over the previous century. In the Catholic Polish-Lithuanian Commonwealth, by contrast, Jews were protected by the wealthy and powerful, and appeared to have found favourable conditions. In Warsaw, Krakow and other towns, synagogues and churches stood side by side, Jewish and Christian streets interlinked. Having proliferated fourfold to 800,000 by the time of the first partition in 1791, Poland's Jewish population made up four-fifths of Europe's total and played a key role in Poland's national anti-Russian uprisings of 1831 and 1863.

The Christian river, with its sources in Judaic tradition, oriental cults, Greek philosophy and Roman law, had gained many streams and tributaries over its long history. All had found value and originality as part of the common heritage of Christian Europe, which had been able to incorporate cultures and ideologies which reflected its basic values. The fellowship and intimacy of the first Christian communities, the theological disputes of early centuries, the separation of loyalties of medieval Christendom, the radical reforms of the Reformation, the self-purifying urges unleashed by the French Revolution – these had all played vital roles in the creation of a modern Europe.

There was, however, trouble in store. The forces of change would not be dormant for long. Under its constitution of 1831, adopted a year after independence from the Kingdom of the

Netherlands, Belgium had become the first predominantly Catholic state to come to terms with liberal democracy, promising 'freedom of expressing opinions on any matter', and declaring that 'no one can be compelled to join in any manner whatever in the rites and ceremonies of any religion'.[43] Putting such noble-sounding principles into practice would not be easy. The stage was set for Christian Europe's greatest test.

CHAPTER 2

The Great Divide

*Death, near and seemingly inescapable, threatened the
Catholic Church, but God took pity ... He opened the
treasury of His mercy and sent the Revolution. People
saw only its horrible side; they still had to see its salutary consequences. Without it where would it be?
Nothing less than this storm could have swept away the
deadly fog which covered a stagnant and polluted
society.*

The words of a Roman Catholic priest, Hugues-Robert de
Lamennais (1782–1854), expressed the polarisation which had
swept over Europe by the early nineteenth century.[1]
Disillusioned writers like Edmund Burke and Alexis de
Tocqueville argued that the Revolution had betrayed its ideals
by clearing the way for demagogues and dictators. 'The
nations of Europe have had the very same Christian religion,'
Burke observed. 'The whole of the polity and economy of
every country in Europe derived from the same source.' It was
essential to defend Europe's 'ancient civil, moral and political
order,' he added, against 'a sect of fanatical and ambitious
atheists'.[2]

Yet the Revolution was still an inspiration for the generation of poets, artists and dreamers raised in its wake. The
'archangel of the terror', Antoine de Saint-Just, who in his
twenties had sent thousands to their deaths, personified the
purifying, erotic combination of youth and power which had
seemed to promise a better world. 'Great men do not die in
their beds,' Saint-Just wrote before accompanying Robespierre
to the guillotine on 10 Thermidor. 'I wish to go my way
without arms, without defence – followed by love, not fear.'[3]

As the origin of the terms, 'Left' and 'Right,' the Revolution had become a test of political attitudes and philosophical worldviews. The rift between them would help make the century a breeding ground for ideological conflict, in which the yearning to understand and improve the world competed with the urge to maintain order and wholeness. The river of Christianity had flowed on. But it would come close to bursting its banks under the pressure of rival streams and currents. A great divide was opening up between the Church and the new radical forces of secular democracy.

Industrialisation was its fundamental impulse. New methods of production and organisation were being ushered in, as the advance of science allied to capitalism brought economic and social change. Urban slums were growing up in the heart of Christian Europe, fuelling the appalling conditions described by the German socialist, Friedrich Engels, at his factory in Manchester, a city whose population would expand tenfold during the century. British reformers spoke of a new slavery to replace the one officially abolished by William Wilberforce in 1807. There were Christians among them, from Lord Shaftesbury to Charles Kingsley, who agreed that the Bible was being used as 'an opium-dose for keeping beasts of burden patient while they are being overloaded'.[4] People like this founded co-operatives and education circles in a bid to keep the workers Christian, as well as the Sunday School movement, Salvation Army and Young Men's Christian Association.

More radical figures liked Engels looked contemptuously at Christian philanthropy, believing it merely diverted pent-up resentments and defused legitimate protest. For them, the Church still embodied the *ancien régime*: it was not the solution, but part of the problem. The Revolution's anti-Christian impulses had run into the ground. But secularism and anti-clericalism remained strong, especially among a new stratum of Europeans born and bred outside the Church's embrace, for whom the revolutionary notions of national sovereignty and inalienable rights had only grown in attractiveness.

The conservative powers, led by Austria-Hungary, were determined to preserve the Christian order of Europe. At the Congress of Vienna in 1814–15, which followed Napoleon's defeat at Waterloo, 'Legitimism' had triumphed, with monarchies restored in half a dozen states, including France and Spain. Meanwhile, a Holy Alliance had been invoked to ensure government and society stuck to 'the sublime truths which the Holy Religion of our Saviour teaches ... namely, the precepts of Justice, Christian Charity and Peace'. The Austrian foreign minister, Furst von Metternich, whose policies dominated the Congress, conceded that the Holy Alliance was, in practice, a 'high-sounding nothing'. But the tone of the Congress disappointed those looking for a new vision to end the Napoleonic era. It was intended to quell revolutionary fervour. Instead, it merely provided a new source of grievances, intensifying social and national frustrations. 'I have simplified my politics into a detestation of all existing governments,' declared the English poet Lord Byron.[5]

The papacy had signed the Final Act of the Congress, along with the 'pentarchy' of Austria, Russia, Britain, France and Prussia. Back in 1800, Pope Pius VI had urged Europe's rulers to keep out the 'ravening wolves' of revolution, by taking steps to suppress 'the great licence of thinking, speaking, writing and reading'.[6] Church leaders everywhere concurred on the necessity of preventing any reversion to the savagery of the late eighteenth century, to what the French Jesuit Joseph de Maistre branded the 'satanic character' of a Revolution which had presaged the downfall of Christianity. Yet they had no real answer to the pent-up tensions of a fast-changing society. The exiled Russian writer, Alexander Herzen, called de Maistre the 'bloodthirsty terrorist of Catholicism', who 'stretched out one hand to the Pope, and the other to the hangman'.[7] However exaggerated, this explained the polarisation.

Although the Church's structure and influence had been battered by two decades of war and instability, the nineteenth century was to be a new time of Christian enthusiasm, symbolised by the Anglican Oxford Movement and a resurgence of vocations and pilgrimages in France. A total of forty-four new Catholic bishoprics were established by Pope Gregory XVI alone in the 1830s and 1840s. Meanwhile, the Anglican Church Missionary Society, founded in 1799, was matched by Lutheran and Presbyterian initiatives in Asia and

Africa. In 1888, when representatives of 140 missionary societies gathered in London, Britain and Germany between them
had over 5,000 missionaries in the field, making Christianity
a worldwide faith.[8]

Yet none of this would be enough to hold back the secularising tide in culture and education, and the steady breakdown
in communication between the Church and Europe's intellectual elites. In Britain, where the overall population doubled in
the first half of the century, Catholics gained civil rights under
an 1829 Emancipation Act, while smaller Protestant denominations were almost as numerous as the official Church of
England in an 1851 census. Christian influences would,
however, weaken throughout the century, as industrialisation
and social change took their toll on traditional allegiances and
life patterns.

There were politicians on the international stage who
managed to adapt to every environment, such as Charles
Maurice de Talleyrand (1754–1838), the Catholic priest
excommunicated for helping emasculate the French Church
during the Revolution, who survived as foreign minister from
the Directory to the restored Louis XVIII. There were also
moderates like Talleyrand's Protestant compatriot, François
Guizot, who believed Europe's Christian order could survive
only if all power was kept within bounds. 'European civilisation has entered into the eternal truth, the plan of Providence,'
the French historian noted in his *Histoire de la Civilisation en
Europe* (1828–30). 'It progresses according of the intentions
of God.'[9]

For most, however, the growing fault line between
Christian teaching and demands for reform and emancipation
posed deeper dilemmas of loyalty. The choice was becoming
increasingly stark: to accept republican experiments, or to
help preserve the reassuring power of established institutions,
which might still, via small-step reforms, keep the lid on
social discontent. The Church would opt for the second. But
the lines of division ran through Christian communities – and
sometimes through Christians themselves.

For all the challenges of previous decades, the Church was
ill-prepared, intellectually and psychologically, for the flood
of new ideas. Its reservations were understandable. What the

Church feared most was a comprehensive breakdown in order, brought about by reckless, irresponsible social engineering. Pope Pius VI had warned before the Revolution against 'accursed philosophers', who 'keep proclaiming that man is born free and subject to no one'. They saw society as no more than 'a crowd of foolish men', he added, 'who stupidly yield to priests who deceive them and kings who oppress them, so that the harmony of priest and ruler is only a monstrous conspiracy against the innate liberty of man'.[10] Though aimed at Rousseau and the *Philosophes*, it was a fair description of the mood among radical Europeans half a century later.

Initially at least, people like this were not hostile to Christianity. The 'Charcoal-burners', or Carbonari, who plotted the overthrow of Italy's Papal States, were fiercely anti-clerical. But their slogan, 'Faith, Hope and Charity', appealed to Christian virtues and they had priests among their members. The Carbonari were soon upstaged by Guiseppe Mazzini's Young Italy movement, which plotted the Risorgimento, or reunification of Italy, in the 1830s. This too took 'God and People' as its motto, and even called on the Pope to lead a united Italy in a fraternity of liberated nations. Mazzini spoke of 'a moral unity, a Catholicism of humanity'. His opposition to the Church was 'not in name of philosophic rationalism', he insisted, 'but in that of a new mysticism, which claims to be more in conformity with the humaner spirit of the Gospels'. 'Religion and politics are inseparable,' the Italian revolutionary wrote. 'Without religion, political science can create only despotism or anarchy.'[11]

What turned the radicals against Christianity was the lack of any responsive dialogue. The Church saw it all differently. 'Eradicate those secret societies of factious men,' Pope Pius VIII urged Europe's leaders in 1829, 'who, completely opposed to God and to princes, are wholly dedicated to bringing about the fall of the Church, the destruction of kingdoms, and disorder in the whole world.' Three years later, Gregory XVI went further, deploring the 'fraud of the wicked' who advocated 'restoration and regeneration' in the Church as well. 'Depravity exults; science is impudent; liberty, dissolute,' the pontiff added despairingly. 'All that is sacrilegious, infamous and blasphemous has gathered as bilge water in a ship's hold, a congealed mass of all filth.'[12]

Not all Catholics saw the new radicalism in such a drastic light. Gregory's denunciations came two years after the 1830 July Revolution in France, which had directed popular anger at the Church as much as the Bourbon monarchy, evoking the atmosphere of 1789. There were important figures who believed the ideological gap could still be healed – not by building bridges between Christianity and secular ideals (that would only come a century later), but by enlisting the Church's participation in radical change.

The Breton priest, Félicité de Lamennais, was one. A convert from Legitimism, Lamennais believed the Church could calm Europe's revolutionary chaos by embracing positive aspects of the Revolution: the rights of man, liberty of conscience, freedom of thought and speech. He called his proposals, outlined in 1830, a 'great Magna Carta for the century'.

Lamennais's vision was of an alliance between the forces of Catholic spirituality and popular emancipation against the corrupt, reactionary monarchies of Europe, whom he was sure would merely exploit the Church's support before dragging it down with them. This made it essential to separate Church and State. If the Revolution had been sent by God to purify and reclaim Christianity from its *ancien régime* accretions, then the people were God's chosen instrument – *vox populi, vox Dei*. The Church could harness their creative energies to establish a fraternal order for the children of God, free of state interference.

Lamennais's newspaper, *l'Avenir*, proclaimed *Dieu et liberté* on its masthead, and was Europe's first daily paper to champion the interests of Christianity. It attracted leading lights of French culture and became a focus for other liberal Catholics, including the priest Jean Baptiste Lacordaire and Charles de Montalembert. 'The question of the poor is a question of life and death for society,' the paper declared in 1831, 'since it is a question of life and death for five-sixths of the human race.'[13] Yet its talk of a new era, of a Christianity that saved the people from despotism, quickly drew hostility. Powerful figures as far afield as Metternich in Austria prevailed on the Pope to intervene.

In 1834, Gregory XVI duly obliged with an encyclical letter, *Singulari Nos*. Its immediate target was Lamennais's *Paroles d'un Croyant*, a book 'small in size but enormous in wickedness', whose 'false, calumnious and rash propositions' could be compared to the heresies of Wycliffe and Hus.[14] The Pope's fear that Lamennais would stoke anarchy by 'igniting the torch of revolution' became something of a self-fulfilling prophecy. Lamennais left the Church, proclaiming that Christ would overthrow the social order, liberate the oppressed and win victory over the corrupt rulers of both Church and State.

It also forced a division among the liberal Catholics. Lacordaire stuck to his ideals. 'There are two victorious forces – the nation and religion, the people and Jesus Christ,' he declared in a new paper, *Ère Nouvelle*, founded in 1848. 'If they part company, we are lost. If they understand each other, we are saved.'[15] Montalembert, by contrast, concluded that radical reform was incompatible with Christianity. It had left the hearts of workers 'profoundly polluted by unbelief and immorality,' he warned.

As his ultimate volte-face, Montalembert declared support for Louis Napoleon's 1851 coup and called on fellow-Catholics to do the same. With the Church's bishops also welcoming Napoleon III as an 'instrument of providence', the division was sealed. Lamennais himself conceded that liberal Catholicism was an illusion. It had yielded to a regime based on 'the priest, the soldier and the spy', he wrote – 'a damp, cold cave where in the silence and darkness venomous reptiles crawl and make your skin creep'.[16]

* * *

In reality, the efforts of liberal Catholics had shown it was possible to combine radical thinking with Christian devotion, and to envisage a Church which stood for freedom and dignity amid the squalor and repression of the nineteenth century. What prevented the new ideal from gaining followers had a lot to do with lack of mutual understanding. Unresolved social problems threatened to spark uncontrolled popular violence. Not surprisingly, the Church shrank away from proposing real solutions of its own.

When a new pope had been elected in 1846, aged just fifty-five, he had aroused hope among liberal groups – reforming government in the Papal States, amnestying political prisoners and lifting restrictions on Roman Jews. All that had changed in 1848, the year of revolutions, when a Roman republic was proclaimed by Mazzini and Garibaldi, and Pius IX was forced to flee Rome's Quirinal Palace from a besieging mob, disguised as a servant. Churches were ransacked and priests murdered. Across Europe, the Archbishop of Paris was killed by a stray bullet while attempting to mediate on the barricades.

Not surprisingly, the Church took the side of order in the bloodshed which ensued. French troops occupied Rome a year later and ended mob rule, calculating that a reinstated papacy would keep Italy disunited. In France itself, the crushing of disorder was lauded by right-wing Catholics as a victory for 'La France honnête' over 'La France anarchique et corrompue'. During the same year, Pius IX warned against the incitement of disorder among 'those of the lower class', who had been 'deceived by lies and deluded by the promise of a happier condition'. The agitators' aim, he added, was to 'profane all law, human and divine'.[17]

He had some powerful voices to back him up – men like the editor Louis Veuillot, who assured his readers Catholic Europe would 'reject parliamentary government just as it rejected Protestantism, or perish in its efforts to vomit it up'. People like this failed to understand that social consciousness was irreversible. The genie of emancipation, once released, could not be forced back into its bottle. 'An abyss is opening up,' lamented the Catholic reformer, Frédéric Ozanam (1813–1853). Like Lamennais, Ozanam believed the Church's strength lay with the new worker communities, the 'barbarians of the modern age', who could be drawn into the Church's civilising embrace just as their Dark Age forerunners had been. Charity was not enough – social justice was needed too. The task of Christians was to 'rekindle the vital fire' of a 'world grown cold'. 'We do not have enough faith: we always want to restore religion by political means,' Ozanam continued. 'We dream of a Constantine who will, at one stroke and with a single effort, bring the nations back into their stall.'[18]

The atmosphere was similar elsewhere. In Britain, the

established Anglican Church was rooted in a rural, gentry-dominated society and held a privileged position in national life. The Oxford Movement fostered a religious revival by reminding the Church of its Catholic structure and sacraments, and reasserting its independence from the state. But Anglicanism reflected the class system. Its clergy were predominantly upper-class, at a time when the Roman Catholic Church was peopled with Irish labourers and slum-dwellers, and Nonconformist Churches like the Methodists and Quakers recruited chiefly from the lower levels of society.

In Germany too, the churches were poorly equipped. Berlin had places of worship for only 25,000 people, a small proportion of its inhabitants. In the new worker districts, pastors from the Evangelical Church were dubbed the 'Black Police' and distrusted.

This failure to adapt had fuelled recalcitrant attitudes among Europe's discontented youth, culminating in the rise of Romanticism and nationalism. The two were inextricably linked. Romanticism spread from England to France, Spain and Italy, and then East to Poland, Hungary and Russia. It could be seen as a reaction to the dry rationality and elitism of the Enlightenment – an appeal to emotion and passion over restraint and convention, to the untamed spirit against civilised society. It was critical of all forms of imperial rule, whether by the Tsar or Emperor, the Sultan or the Pope. It also cut across religious divisions, drawing in the Orthodox Aleksandr Pushkin and Protestant Johann von Goethe, as much as the Anglican John Keats and Catholic Alphonse de Lamartine.

Though hostile to the established order, most Romantic poets and artists were religious by temperament, championing the spiritual imagination against the godlessness of the late eighteenth century. Yet they scorned the imposed authority of established churches and demanded fresh answers from a faith which seemed to have lost hope. 'Réponds-moi, Dieu cruel!' was the cry of the anti-clerical Victor Hugo, who returned to Christianity in the 1820s after rejecting it in a rush of disaffection. Like other writers, from Dickens and Balzac to Tolstoy and Lermontov, Hugo felt a responsibility for highlighting Europe's mounting social problems. But he also used religious metaphors to sanctify national feeling. It was in that fusion of images that the link between Romanticism and nationalism had been born. It was an age of 'nation-building', when the small nations of Eastern and Central Europe were rediscovering their collective memory and identity, and rebuilding the strength to conspire for independence. In the 1830 November Uprising, young Polish officers made enthusiastic use of Catholic symbols. From his exile in Paris, the poet Adam Mickiewicz denounced the 'Satanic Trinity' of Russia, Prussia and Austria which had 'crucified' his country in the 1790s partitions, and prophesied that Poland would rise again, the 'Christ of Nations'.[19]

A similar blend of messianic nationalism surfaced among Czechs and Slovaks, as well as in the work of Hungarian poets such as Imre Madách and Mihaly Vörösmarty after the defeat of Hungary's insurgent army in 1848-9. All the peoples of Eastern Europe claimed to have preserved the true frontier spirit of Christianity. Ukraine's greatest poet, Taras Shevchenko, argued that the Slavic peoples had received Christianity as a holy destiny. His Serb counterpart, Vuk Karadzic, claimed to have retraced the national culture over 5000 years, revealing in the process that Jesus and His Apostles had actually been Serbs. Russia's Decembrist revolutionaries of 1825 accused the Tsar of acting against God's will and claimed a Christian sanction for conspiring to remodel their country's governance on European lines.

Some revolutionaries had set about reshaping the Christian faith to suit their causes. Mazzini, disillusioned by clergy reticence, proclaimed 'a new Revelation to supersede effete Christianity', while Garibaldi villified Pope Pius IX as the 'vampire of Italy', allowing his followers – the *mangiapreti*, or priest-eaters – to popularise a travesty of the Lord's Prayer which included the line 'Give us today our daily cartridges'. In France, the historian Jules Michelet called for service to the *patrie* to 'fill within us the immeasurable abyss which extinct Christianity has left there'. He saw the Revolution as a Second Coming, the birth of a new God, and compared the Versailles tennis court, where the Third Estate had taken its revolutionary oath in 1789, to the stable of Bethlehem.[20]

*　*　*

The urge to reject the Church in favour of a 'new Christianity' also typified the early socialists: men like Charles Fourier, who sought the abolition of marriage and other 'constrictions', and Pierre Joseph Proudhon, whose famous slogans – 'God is evil', 'Property is theft' – equated anarchy with atheism. Socialism's premise was opposition to discrimination and exploitation, and a conviction that individual rights had to be subordinated to the common good under a state which intervened to help the weakest. It leant on ideas formed around trade unions and worker co-operatives. But it also drew inspiration from Christian ideals, from the solidarity of early Christian communities and medieval monasticism, to the utopian writings of Thomas More and the communal living of Russian peasants.

French socialism's idealistic founder, Claude Henri de Saint-Simon, envisaged a fraternal industrial state in which poverty was eradicated and science replaced traditional religion as a spiritual authority – an idea outlined in his *Nouveau Christianisme* (1825). His younger disciple, Auguste Comte, constructed a calendar of scientists to replace that of the saints. 'Humanity has passed through three stages,' Comte wrote: 'a theological stage, in which free play is given to spontaneous fictions admitting of no proof; a metaphysical stage, characterised by the prevalence of personified abstractions or entities; and lastly, a positive stage, based upon an exact view of the real facts of the case.'[21]

New approaches to moral philosophy were widespread, too. The work of Kant, with its emphasis on duty and responsibility, had been seen by contemporaries as a reference point for philosophical attempts to defend transcendent values. By the early nineteenth century, however, Kant's sense of universal morality was being comprehensively challenged, not least in his native Germany.

In the work of Georg Wilhelm Hegel (1770–1831), both religion and science yielded to philosophy, the highest form of knowledge. Hegel was pessimistic about Christian Europe, believing it would be reduced to a heap of ashes by the coming 'middle-class society', a society 'driven over its own boundaries in order to look for consumers and essential raw materials'.[22] Instead of God, he imagined a Spirit of the Age, or *Zeitgeist*, who revealed his purpose through the dialectic of ideas, the constant rise of humanity through history. The Kingdom of the Father had lasted from the Roman Empire to Charlemagne; the Kingdom of the Son until the Reformation; and the Kingdom of the Holy Ghost was the modern Protestant world, in which heaven and earth, faith and science, Church and State, individual and community were reconciled. In this way, the *Zeitgeist* had moved through every political state, embodying the onward march of progress and freedom.

In *The Philosophy of Right* (1821), Hegel offered a new language in which state, society and citizen replaced the traditional Christian concepts of nation, community and person. When the harmony between them broke down, he argued, the result was alienation and conflict.

While some interpreters of Hegel's thought believed it was compatible with Christianity, the Young Hegelians thought otherwise. One of the most influential, Ludwig Feuerbach (1804–1872), rejected Hegel's idealism and gave his dialectical view of history a materialistic application. Far from being a higher synthesis of Jewish and Greek religion, as Hegel had argued, Christianity was a mere illusion, the 'dominance of subjectivity'. Divine revelation was no more than a fable. God had not created man, Feuerbach insisted: it was man who had created God, as a means of explaining and attenuating human suffering.

Feuerbach's book, *The Essence of Christianity* (1841), had a profound influence on the man who was to take socialism from the realm of ideals to practical politics. Karl Marx (1818–1883) was the son of a Jewish rabbi, who had been baptised but rejected Christianity in favour of atheism. Besides Feuerbach's historical materialism, he drew on Hegel's notion of dialectical progress, Saint-Simon's theory of class struggle, François-Noel Babeuf's egalitarianism and Adam Smith's labour theory and doctrine of self-interest. What Marx came up with was a historical analysis of human society, a society driven by the laws of production and acquisition, which was far more precise than the musings of earlier theorists. He also offered a practical programme which could be taken up and applied by political organisations.

Hegel's idea that a positive outcome, or synthesis, could be produced by the creative clash of opposites (thesis and antithesis) was applied by Marx to show how ends could justify means, good be obtained from evil. There were those who saw messianic, quasi-religious elements in Marx's programme. In his scheme, however, all religion was an illusion, a barrier to be destroyed – the 'sigh of the oppressed creature, the soul of a world without soul, the mind of a world without mind ... the opium of the people'. It would disintegrate with the advance of science. But Communism's enemies should be identified too. They included the Pope, who had formed a 'holy alliance' – in the words of the *Communist Manifesto* (1848) – with the powers of old Europe: 'the Tsar, Metternich and Guizot, French radicals and German police spies'.[23]

Marx befriended numerous fellow-refugees, from Mazzini to Proudhon, in his squalid London apartment. He sent approaches to Lamennais, who found his doctrine of class war unpalatable. But he was contemptuous of other Christian reformers like the German 'Social Catholic', Wilhelm von Ketteler. Ketteler's book, *The Labour Problem and Christianity* (1868), had merely 'flirted with workers' problems' while professing a sympathy for socialist aims.[24]

Marx had good reason for his doubts. Pope Pius IX condemned the 'unspeakable doctrine of Communism' in 1846, warning that it was 'most opposed to the very natural order' and would 'completely destroy men's rights, property and fortune, even human society itself'.[25] At that stage, he saw Communism as little more than a conspiracy, the extreme wing of the revolutionary republican movements making a bid for power in Rome and Paris. He was a lot more concerned about the new post-Enlightenment doctrines of liberalism articulated by men like Jeremy Bentham and the utilitarian John Stuart Mill, with their stress on limited government and individual liberty, and their opposition to the prerogatives of Crown and Altar.

As an ideology of the new middle class, liberalism had produced benefits in less developed countries like Hungary, where statesmen-reformers such as István Széchenyi, József Eötvös and Ferenc Deák calmed the frenetic idealism fuelled by the independence leader, Lajos Kossuth, or by the poet Sándor Petöfi, who disappeared, aged twenty-six, battling

Austrian and Russian lancers at Segesvár. In others, Germany included, it was quickly equated with the abandonment of stable values. This was what the Church had trouble with.

In his famous *Syllabus Errorum* (1864), the Pope tried to set the record straight on new anti-Christian notions of law and philosophy. The most widely quoted 'error' was the last, No. 80, that 'the Roman Pontiff can and should reconcile himself and reach agreement with "progress", liberalism and recent departures in civil society'. But there were other much-cited items too, grouped under ten headings. One was that 'authority is nothing other than a number and total of material forces'; another that 'all moral discipline and goodness ought to aim at the enlargement and increase of wealth'.[26] The Syllabus was widely viewed as a response to Montalembert's call in 1863 for a rapprochement between Catholicism and liberalism, a 'free Church in a free State'. It was also a reaction to anti-clerical legislation in Piedmont, whose King Victor Emmanuel had incorporated part of the Papal States, slaughtering an international brigade when it tried to retake them with the Pope's blessing.

Yet it was a clumsy document – a highly condensed, badly drafted index of propositions which damaged the Church's image. The Pope's real aim, as the English John Henry Newman and French Bishop Félix Dupanloup pointed out, was not to condemn modern civilisation as such, only its materialistic and irreligious aspects. Yet there were Catholics like Lord Acton who blamed Church reactionaries for forcing the Pope's hand. He meant polemicists such as de Maistre, whose lies and slanders had 'justified those grave accusations of falsehood, insincerity, indifference to civil rights and contempt for civil authorities which are uttered with such profound injustice against the Church'.

> The present difficulties of the Church – her internal dissensions and apparent weakness, the alienation of so much intellect, the strong prejudice which keeps many away from her altogether, and makes many who had approached her shrink back – all draw nourishment from this rank soil. The world can never know and recognise her divine perfection while the pleas of her defenders are scarcely nearer to the truth than the crimes which her enemies impute to her.[27]

In reality, the Syllabus had to be read along with the encyclical it formed part of, *Quanta Cura*. In this, the Pope made clear what he feared most: the 'impious and absurd principle' that human society could be governed without religion.

> Where religion has been removed from civil society, and the doctrine of divine revelation repudiated, the genuine notion itself of justice and human rights is darkened and lost and the place of true justice and legitimate right is supplied by material force ... Who does not see and clearly perceive that human society, when set loose from the bonds of religion and true justice, can have, in truth, no other end than the purpose of obtaining and amassing wealth.[28]

In the course of his thirty-two-year reign, Pius IX presided over a revival of Christian devotions, pilgrimages and missions, as well as a substantial internationalisation of the Church's upper ranks. Tensions remained between liberal and Ultramontane groups in the Church, as well as with minorities such as Eastern Europe's hard-pressed Greek Catholics, who were pressured to adopt the Latin liturgy. But the Pope rejected accusations of intransigence. All he had tried to do, he asserted, was to maintain 'that mutual fellowship and concord of counsels between Church and State which has proved itself propitious and salutary for both religious and civil interests'.[29]

The year of the Syllabus, 1864, saw the First International meeting in London to debate the rival programmes of Marx and the anarchist Mikhail Bakunin, and to reach out to the budding unions. The agitators were organising among Europe's expanding worker population. Yet the Church's counter-initiatives gained little response. The divide between the Church and secular radicalism was as wide as ever.

In 1870, a *postulatum* at the First Vatican Council urged the Church to clarify its teaching on employer-worker relations. The Council became better known, however, for something else – its declaration of papal infallibility, which made the Pope infallible when defining a doctrine *ex cathedra*. 'With this decree, the claims of Innocent III over mankind have been resurrected in the nineteenth century,' wrote the English statesman William Gladstone (1809–1898), 'like some mummy picked out of its dusty sarcophagus'.[30] In reality, the declaration was nothing new – popes had always reserved the right to make binding proclamations on faith and morals. It was intended to further the Council's aim of safeguarding 'the integrity of the faith, the gravity of divine worship, the eternal salvation of men ... .' It did not imply any extension of the Pope's temporal power, as Gladstone feared.

Yet it did come at a time of high international tension.

The Franco-Prussian war broke out a day after the Infallibility declaration, forcing Napoleon III to withdraw his troops from Rome. Piedmontese troops duly seized the Papal States two weeks later, proclaiming Rome capital of a united Italy and ending 1500 years of papal rule. A Law of Guarantees in May 1871 reduced the Church's temporal power to the Vatican. But it recognised the Pope's 'sovereign honours and pre-eminence in dignity'. It also gave him wide-ranging rights – from free movement and communication, to tax exemptions and control of city churches.[31]

Arguments abounded over this momentous change in the papacy's fortunes. Some commentators viewed it as an all-time humiliation which fatally compromised the Pope's independence. Others believed his release from secular entanglements would actually enhance the Pope's authority.

However interpreted, the end of the Papal States failed to appease anti-Church feeling, which reached a highpoint in the Paris Commune after France's defeat by Prussia in 1871. Another archbishop was killed, along with at least fifty priests, before the Commune was bloodily suppressed, leaving 36,000 dead on the city's streets. A succession of pro-Church monarchist governments followed. But these did little for the Church's social prestige. By 1875, when the Church was allowed to set up its own universities, France was home to 51,000 parishes, five times as many as modern-day Poland, and its religious orders had doubled. But anti-clerical sentiment was rife among workers and intellectuals. 'The clergy of France has finally convinced everyone who believes in things popular and democratic,' wrote the Abbé Georges Frémont, 'that between the Church on the one hand, and progress, the Republic and the future on the other, there is no relationship possible but the most deadly hatred.'[32]

The Church was in trouble in Germany too, where a new chancellor, Otto von Bismarck (1815–1898), had set out to curb its influence on behalf of a Protestant Prussian state. Bismarck was said to be fearful that German Catholics might provide a fifth column if France and Austria launched a new war. Whatever the motives, his May Laws of 1873 cut state support for the Church, brought its seminaries and appointments under state control, and required clergy to take exams at state universities. Diplomatic ties were severed with the Vatican and over 1,000 priests and bishops jailed. The measures required a change in the constitution and were followed by others, banning religious orders and threatening Church property. By 1876, all Catholic bishoprics were empty. 'We shall not go to Canossa!' the Iron Chancellor boasted, in a throwback to Henry IV's humiliation eight centuries earlier.

Pius IX seemed unperturbed by Bismarck's repression. 'Sometimes, God sends a scourge to awaken men from their sloth,' the Pope told German pilgrims. 'And this modern Attila, who prides himself that he is destroying, does not know that he is really creating. He thinks he is eliminating the religion of Jesus Christ in Germany – in reality he is reinforcing it.'[33] Sure enough, with Germany's Social Democrats gaining ground, Bismarck realised he needed support from the Catholic Centre Party, which became the largest in the Reichstag in 1881 elections. The Iron Chancellor's *Kulturkampf* petered out, and the May Laws were gradually rescinded. 'The German Empire, defended by a million bayonets and with a legion of public and secret policemen at its disposal, celebrated, sung and idolised by an unnumerable court of panegyrists as the first power in the world,' boasted the English Cardinal Henry Manning, 'was forced to bow before 200 defenceless priests.'[34]

The anti-Church legislation did, however, find emulators elsewhere. In Italy, Church property was seized and religious education banned from state schools, while a secret society, the Alfieri, demanded 'abolition of the papacy, the expulsion of priests and the burning of all churches, beginning with the Vatican'. In Spain, an anti-clerical government deposed Queen Izabella II, while secularising reforms were imposed in Austria-Hungary, Switzerland, Portugal and Belgium.

* * *

This was the picture in Europe when a new pope was elected in 1878. Leo XIII was not a soft touch. His first encyclical, *Quod apostolici muneris*, denounced the 'wicked confederacy' of 'socialists, communists and nihilists', who were waging a 'deadly war' against Christianity. Successive popes since the Enlightenment had warned of the consequences, the Pope recalled. But 'no adequate precaution' had been taken, and the whole of Europe now stood in 'extreme peril'.

Yet liberalism and unrestrained capitalism were as much to blame. Leo added. God had intended there to be various orders in civil society, differing in 'dignity, rights and power'. But He also required that rulers use their power 'to save and not to destroy'. He held 'over the heads of the rich the divine sentence that, unless they succour the needy, they will be repaid by eternal torments'.[35]

In 1885, *Immortale Dei* switched the emphasis to liberalism entirely, pointing out how its advocacy of a secular state endangered social stability. The Church was not opposed to 'real and lawful liberty', the encyclical made clear, nor to any form of government if it contained nothing 'contrary to Catholic doctrine'. It was not against democracy – 'for at certain times, and under certain laws, the participation of the people may not only benefit citizens, but may even be an obligation'. But it believed all public power must proceed from God, the 'true and supreme Lord of the world'. Government functioned best when Church and State were 'at one, in complete accord'.

> There was a time when states were governed by the principles of Gospel teaching. Then it was that the power and divine virtue of Christian wisdom had diffused itself throughout the laws, institutions and morals of the people, permeating all ranks and relations of civil society ... Christian Europe has subdued barbarous nations, and changed them from a savage to a civilised condition, from superstition to true worship. It victoriously rolled back the tide of Mohammedan conquest; retained the headship of civilisation; stood forth in the front rank as the leader and teacher of all, in every branch of national culture; bestowed on the world the gift of true and

many-sided liberty; and most wisely founded very numerous institutions for the solace of human suffering. And if we enquire how it was able to bring about so altered a condition of things, the answer is: beyond all question, in large measure, through religion.[36]

Leo XIII knew his predecessor had been too unbending in a range of areas. What was needed now was some fresh thinking about the Church's relationship with society – 'the Christianisation of modern life, and the modernisation of Christian life'.[37] In 1891, a new encyclical reaffirmed the link between economics and ethics, which had become increasingly blurred, and attempted to show, through copious use of Thomist precepts, how Christian teaching could offer an alternative to both liberalism and socialism.

Rerum novarum accepted the Church's political subordination to the State. But the Church had a right to make moral demands, the encyclical added, and the State could not claim omnipotence. Inequalities were inevitable – it was impossible to 'reduce civil society to one dead level'. But the condition of the working classes had now become 'the pressing question of the hour'.

> Public institutions and the laws have set aside the ancient religion. By degrees it has come to pass that working-men have been surrendered, isolated and helpless, to the hard-heartedness of employers and the greed of unchecked competition . . . The hiring of labour and the conduct of trade are concentrated in the hands of comparatively few; so that a small number of very rich men have been able to lay upon the teeming masses of labouring poor a yoke little better than slavery.[38]

Yet if abusive capitalism was the root cause of modern poverty and misery, socialist proposals – a community of goods, abolition of private property – also violated Christian teaching and natural law. In fact, Leo XIII insisted, they would make the working classes poorer still. 'Capital cannot do without Labour, nor Labour without Capital,' the encyclical stressed. 'The great mistake is to take up the notion that class is naturally hostile to class, and that the wealthy and the working men are intended by nature to live in mutual conflict.' Workers were by nature 'members of the state equally with the rich'. They should therefore have equal rights, even if they were unequal in property and possessions, as well as a living wage and associations or unions to protect their interests. These principles all belonged to Christianity, Leo XIII insisted. Without a return to Christianity, 'all the plans and devices of the wisest will prove of little avail'.[39]

Rerum Novarum appeared a year before the Pope, encouraged by moderate republicans, urged France's discontented Legitimists and Bonapartists to cut their losses and make peace with the Third Republic. Republics were 'as legitimate a form of government as any other', Leo noted. In the United States, the Church was developing and flourishing, despite 'unbridled liberty'. It had no quarrel with the state, and this could apply in France too. What the Church did condemn were unjust laws, which Christians would continue to fight against.[40]

Thanks to its detailed treatment of worker issues, *Rerum Novarum* would be widely seen as heralding a new era in Catholic social teaching. Yet the encyclical appeared late in the day – twenty-four years after Marx's *Das Kapital* had set a new baseline for socialist and communist agitation. It was said to have inspired the creation of an International Labour Organisation at Geneva, as well as early legislation on social security and worker protection. Yet if Christians were exhorted to improve the social order, they were not expected to change it. The encyclical accepted that the Church's concerns extended to 'temporal and earthly interests', as well as spiritual ones. It showed a deep awareness of the nineteenth century's social and economic disorders, and accepted much of the argumentation of the Social Catholics. But Leo XIII failed, even so, to recognise the full anthropological dimensions of the crisis, the growing impatience of humiliated masses pressing for a better, more dignified life. The task of Christians was, in the end, philanthropic rather than political.

* * *

In 1901, the Pope fired a warning shot at self-styled 'Christian Democrats', who had attempted to give Catholic social

reformism a more political direction since *Rerum novarum.*
The very term contained a 'perilous ambiguity', he said.
Those who used it must steer clear of politics and stay loyal
to the Church's hierarchy. They must also avoid any confusion with 'Social Democracy' – the difference between them
was 'nothing less than between the sectarianism of socialism
and the profession of the Christian law'.[41]

Despite everything, many believed the Pope had moved the
Church in a conciliatory direction. 'Where Pius IX opened an
abyss, Leo XIII traversed it with a bridge,' was the verdict of
France's *Le Monde.* Yet the Church's defence of the Christian
order continued to set Catholics at odds with socialists – those
prophets of utopia who threatened, in Leo's words, to 'spew
the paths they travel with blood'. Meanwhile, the confrontation with anti-clerical liberals was unabated, too. Far from
bringing the sides closer, the passage of time was widening
the divisions. 'We are either wolves or lambs,' the German
Friedrich Naumann, proponent of the concept of *Mitteleuropa*,
wrote in *Letters on Religion* (1900). 'We either side with
Bismarck or with Tolstoy, either with the Gospel of the mailed
fist, or with the Gospel of the brethren of communal life.'[42]

In 1892, the Pope's policy of *Ralliement,* urging French
monarchists to accept the Republic, had reflected the Church's
weakening relationship with Europe's ruling regimes in the
wake of the Germany's reunification and the Risorgimento in
Italy. Clearly, the Church had to begin building up its social
influence, rather than relying on the wielders of power. Yet
the conciliatory gesture had failed to prevent further anti-clerical measures, summed up by Léon Gambetta's slogan,
'Cléricalisme – violà l'ennemi!' In 1879, France's Minister of
Public Instruction, Jules Ferry, had taken steps to secularise
education, proclaiming his ambition 'to organise humanity
without God and without kings'.[43] The ultimate republican
aim, Church leaders suspected, was full separation of Church
and State.

Although the new governments presented problems, there
were new opportunities as well. For centuries, the popes had
dealt with kings and princes who ruled autocratically but
respected the Christian order. They were now having to
coexist with socialists and liberals who stood for democracy

but often rejected the faith. Yet the new rulers needed Christian votes, as Bismarck had discovered. In the 1870s alone, Italy went through nine governments, as public disillusionment was fuelled by rising taxation, corruption and crime. Coping with the challenges of democracy required new adroit forms of statesmanship.

The Church was still fatally weak, however, where it mattered most – in Europe's industrial heartlands. There were plenty of Catholic reformers who still regarded all socialists as conspirators and extremists, and resented their evident success in mobilising the working class. But their own organisations were marginal by comparison, and inhibited by their Church alignment. In France, the Catholic reformer Albert de Mun had sought the middle ground, by promoting social change 'without the overthrow of kings, the unchaining of popular passions and bloody riots'. His working men's clubs, or *Cercles*, had amassed tens of thousands; but they were hidebound by what their own founder called their 'counter-revolutionary pathos'.[44] Another Catholic movement seeking to educate young French workers in the spirit of democracy, Marc Sangnier's *Sillon*, was branded extremist by the Vatican.

By 1906, Catholic labour organisations in Italy could claim just 70,000 members, compared to 570,000 enrolled in the socialist-dominated General Confederation of Labour and Chambers of Labour. They accounted for no more than 12.5% of the country's organised labour-force.

A new pope, Pius X, continued to resist any attempt to give Christianity a harder-edged political application. In the course of his eleven-year reign, Pius reformed Canon Law and the liturgy, reorganised seminaries, rationalised the Church's structures and defended its independence. But it was his campaign to re-establish the Church's 'disciplinary, dogmatic and liturgical authority' which most defined his pontificate. Catholic 'Modernists' who had responded to Leo XIII's perceived reformism by attempting to bring Christian teaching up to date were brought to book by a new condemnation of this 'synthesis of all heresies' in *Pascendi* (1907). 'It is in conformity with the order established by God in human society,' the Pope reiterated, 'that there should be princes and subjects, employers and proletariat, rich and poor, instructed and ignorant.'[45]

He had reason to feel anxious. Biblical scholarship had developed in leaps and bounds throughout the nineteenth century, with writers like David Friedrich Strauss and Ernest Renan questioning the divine origin of the Gospels. The Vatican had responded with its own Biblical Commission in 1902. But while applauding Christianity's moral teachings, many voices had accused the Church of betraying Christ's summons to brotherhood and purity of heart. 'The Roman Church is the most inclusive and the mightiest structure, the most complicated and yet the most homogeneous, that history as so far known to us has brought forth – all the forces of human intellect and soul, all the elemental powers of which man is possessed, have laboured at this structure,' the Protestant Adolf von Harnack, enthused in his end-of-century Berlin lectures, *What is Christianity?* 'Yet Roman Catholicism, as a secular Church, as a regime of privilege and power, has nothing to do with the Gospel and indeed contradicts it fundamentally.'[46]

Already in the eighteenth century, the Jesuit-trained naturalist, George-Louis Buffon, had computed the Earth's age as 75,000 years, far beyond biblical claims, while the mathematician, Pierre Laplace, had attributed the universe's origins, not to the hand of God in Genesis, but to an expanding gas cloud. Charles Darwin's *Origin of Species*, appearing in 1859, claimed that mankind had evolved, not from Adam, but from 'a hairy quadruped, furnished with a tail and pointed ears'. This caused a sensation. Aspects of Darwin's natural selection theory were soon overtaken and improved upon. But scientific claims of this magnitude naturally challenged traditional religious explanations. As contemporaries observed, science itself had a huge potential for good. It was science's anti-religious subtext – the power of discovery without responsibility – which caused concern.

Scientists, for their part, saw the Church's authority as incompatible with freedom of thought – and with the kind of progressive understanding which could liberate the rational mind from irrational beliefs. Science was 'true knowledge', since it was observable and measurable. The laws of Nature elaborated by Darwin and other scientists – such as the Austrian monk-botanist, Gregor Johann Mendel – must be applicable to human beings too.

The advancement of scholarship and science also made this an interesting time for religious enquiry, along with expanding literacy and the arrival in Europe of exotic faiths such as Buddhism and Hinduism. Strange things were happening in art and literature, where the dark rebellious reflections of Romantics like Byron and Shelley had given way to the even darker preoccupations with evil and death of Gustave Flaubert, Charles Baudelaire and others. Writers like this had gained an international, inter-denominational appeal. So had many theologians, from the Prussian Protestant Friedrich Schleiermacher to the dissident Catholic Ignaz Dollinger, who helped lead resistance to papal infallibility at Vatican I. Cardinal Newman, an Anglican convert to Catholicism, was another. So was the Dane Søren Kierkegaard (1813–1855), whose quest to 'reintroduce Christianity to Christendom' led him to reject both science and traditional religiosity in favour of a personal approach to truth which would influence twentieth-century existentialism.

Christianity had become, in short, the object of a passionate, critical discussion. It reached deep inside the Church itself, questioning its doctrine and authority; and it was the aggressive deployment of scientific knowledge in this debate which Pius X was nervous about. He responded with a clampdown. Another 1907 decree, *Lamentabili*, listed sixty-five Modernist errors which 'rejected the legacy of the human race', and were 'to be held by all as condemned and proscribed'.[47] A secretive organisation, the Sodalitium Pianum, was set up in Rome to co-ordinate the counter-revolution, with 'diocesan vigilance committees' ensuring censorship of Catholic publications and gatherings.

It was questionable whether 'Modernism' actually existed. Pius X had in mind figures such as the French Alfred Loisy, the Italian Romolo Murri and the English-Austrian Friedrich von Hugel, who all concurred, in their different ways, on the inadequacy of Christian thought and practice to meet contemporary needs. Yet the Pope's critics disclaimed any conspiracy. The likeliest answer was that Modernism was deemed to threaten the Church's integrity as an attitude of independent criticism, rather than any coherent set of ideas. The French writer, Maurice Blondel, accused Catholic apologists of 'taking refuge in an ostrich-like policy', as 'mystical ideologists claiming to impose their systems upon the concrete truth of history'. The English George Tyrrell defined Modernism more simply, as 'a synthesis of Catholicism and science'. 'The cry of the spiritually starving multitudes, robbed of the bread of life,' Tyrrell prophesied, 'will at last drown the chatter of idle theologians and wake the great heart of the Church to the weightier realities of the Gospel.'[48]

Those were not the kind of sentiments the Pope wanted to hear. In 1905, a new law in France, drafted by the socialist Aristide Briand, formally abrogated Napoleon's 1801 Concordat, ending clergy stipends and nationalising church buildings. All religious communities – Christian, Jewish and Muslim – were to be run by 'associations cultuelles' and require permits to worship. The guiding French principle, *Laicit*é, now meant total Church-State separation. It could be interpreted positively, as ensuring freedom of conscience and finally relieving Church and faith of state interference.

It was not, however, seen that way. Although Christian life went on, a large proportion of France's Catholic parishes found themselves priestless within two years of the law. Pius X deplored the new measures as violating 'the constitution on which the Church was founded by Jesus Christ'. The new French premier, Émile Combes, a former Catholic seminarian, took little notice. 'Citizens, we have to undo in a very short time the clerical reaction of a century,' he told the Chambre de Députés. 'Once again, the Catholic Church has organised itself into a despotic hierarchy, leading the people to an ideal totally opposed to modern society, plotting the destruction of the political and social edifice erected by the glorious French Revolution.'[49]

The Separation Law was said to have been copied as far afield as Mexico, where anti-clerical measures under Plutarcho Calles sparked a civil war in 1926. The Church had vigorously supported Mexican independence in the early nineteenth century, in contrast to its cautious attitude to the small nations of Eastern and Central Europe. Here too, socialist agitation had intensified, especially among the workers of

Hungary and Bohemia, chiming in with the anti-clericalism of Czechoslovakia's founder-president, Tomáš Garrigue Masaryk (1850–1937).

Masaryk's dream was of a 'creative synthesis' between modern philosophies, based on 'scepticism, criticism, positivism, historicism and humanism'. His key influences included Augustin Smetana, a former Catholic priest. But there was little space for 'ecclesiastical religion', or even a 'reformed Catholicism', in Masaryk's vision of Slavic nations freed from Russian, German and Austro-Hungarian control. The democratic order he had in mind would be one which rejected the Church's 'medieval theocratism'. Its citizens would be 'morally re-educated' by enlightened leaders such as himself to create a new 'Homo Europeus'. 'Religion will not lose thereby its weight of authority; on the contrary, it will gain if it is freed from the state and the arbitrary will of deified dynasties,' Masaryk wrote. 'What was right in medieval theocracy – the idea of catholicity, universality, mankind as an organised whole – will not be lost by democracy. Democracy also hopes and works to the end that there may be one sheepfold and one shepherd.'[50]

* * *

Masaryk's paternalistic agnosticism was a far cry from the extreme sentiments coming out of Russia, where anarchists such as Prince Peter Kropotkin had long since rejected all forms of organised authority. The anarchist creed had been close to socialism, but had concluded that the Revolution merely strengthened state control, leading to bureaucratic government by the bourgeoisie which destroyed the rights of the common people. 'The social revolution is a path to be travelled – to stop on the way would be the same as turning back,' Kropotkin wrote. 'It cannot end until it has run its course and achieved its object of conquest: the free individual in a free humanity.'[51]

Kropotkin's influence, with its will to destruction and re-creation, would be felt by early twentieth-century architects of 'stateless socialism', such as the Pole Edward Abramowski. His fellow-Russian, Mikhail Bakunin, had also rejected

Marx's revolutionary programme at the First International as authoritarian and deterministic, insisting it would merely install a new state tyranny. At the Congress of Anarchist Revolutionaries six years later, Bakunin announced the end of another barrier to freedom – Christianity. The world would only be won, he proclaimed, 'when the last king is strangled with the guts of the last priest'. The time had come to abandon dreams of immortality in favour of faith in man. 'I seek God in men, in their love, in their freedom; and now I seek God in revolution,' Bakunin proclaimed. 'There is nothing I more earnestly desire than to serve intact to the end the sacred spirit of revolt.'[52]

What was it that had spurred such profound disillusionment with Christianity?

The Orthodoxy of Bakunin's native Russia told part of the story. Self-governing Orthodox Churches had been formed during the century in Greece, Romania, Bulgaria and Serbia, with reluctant agreement from the Ecumenical Patriarchate in Constantinople (now Ottoman-ruled Istanbul). As a social and cultural force, these had helped rally local Christians to throw off Turkish rule. Despite Islam's historic victories, most of Ottoman-ruled Europe had remained Christian. Only in Albania, Bosnia and parts of Bulgaria had significant numbers converted.

Though tolerant in religion, the Turks reacted savagely to political opposition. When a Greek uprising was proclaimed in the 1820s by an Orthodox bishop, Germanos, Patriarch Gregorios of Constantinople was hanged in retaliation and 30,000 Greeks slaughtered on the island of Chios. Greek independence was finally settled in 1830, when the Ottomans were defeated by a British-French force. The struggle had been viewed universally as a defence of Christian civilisation against barbarism. It had revived interest in Hellenic culture and philosophy, whose ideals of truth and beauty seized the imagination of the Romantic poets as a superior, older alternative to Christianity. 'Our laws, our literature, our religion, our arts have their roots in Greece,' mused Shelley, with studied exaggeration. 'But for Greece, we might still have been savages and idolators.'[53]

In reality, it was Christianity which provided the source of identity for Greeks, just as it did for Romanians, Bulgarians, Serbs and Macedonians. It gave the rest of Europe a moral impulse for intervening, such as in 1876, when 20,000 Christian peasants were killed in Bulgaria after the murder of 136 Turkish officials, or when Armenians, whose adoption of Christianity as a state religion predated the Emperor Constantine, were subjected to genocide in the early twentieth century. By 1914, the Ottoman presence had been pushed back to Constantinople. Christianity's ancient north African heartlands had been reoccupied by the British, French, Spanish and Italians. Further east, Russian rulers had brought Christianity to Central Asia, occupying the old Mongol capital of Samarkand in 1868, and the Pamirs in 1895, allowing Orthodox missions to reach China, Japan, Kamchatka and Alaska.

There were those like the Slavophile philosopher, Vladimir Soloviev, who believed Orthodoxy could act as a mediator between Catholicism and Protestantism, as a prelude to being liberated from autocracy and reunited within a single universal Church. Yet the Orthodox Churches were deeply conservative. There had been no Reformation to force through modernising changes, and no Enlightenment to separate religion from politics. Church leaders remained subordinate to ruling regimes, who used the principle of *sobornost* to justify a 'symphony' between secular and spiritual aims. The Tsar controlled the Church's Holy Synod and approved all senior appointments. He received a loyalty oath from priests and personally blessed the troops under his command. Unofficial Orthodox groups, such as the Old Believers, or *Raskolniki*, who had broken away in the seventeenth century, faced regular harassment. So did newer sects who proliferated in the nineteenth century. Circulation of the Bible was banned until the 1870s because of fears that it would fuel subversion.

The Vatican had maintained respectful relations with the Tsars, despite the repression regularly meted out to the Russian Empire's Catholic minorities. Nicholas I had visited Gregory XVI in 1845 to discuss a common stand against revolution, signing a temporary accord two years later. The popes declined active support to the Polish uprisings of 1830 and 1863. They were apparently rewarded when Nicholas II's

Toleration Manifesto in 1905, the year of France's much-resented Separation Law, gave Catholic and Orthodox Christians equal rights.

In practice, however, the picture was different. Russian Orthodox leaders distrusted Rome's intentions after the proclamation of papal infallibility, while the Vatican feared a new wave of Russian expansionism to unite Eastern Europe's Orthodox territories. Meanwhile, efforts continued to Russify predominantly Catholic Poland and Lithuania, and to suppress the empire's Greek Catholic, Protestant and Jewish communities. 'A third will emigrate, a third will convert to Christianity and a third will die out,' the procurator Konstanty Pobedonostsev said of the Jews in 1905, the year of a savage pogrom in Kiev.[54]

Whatever its reactionary political associations, the Orthodox Church had preserved Russian unity during the Napoleonic invasions. It permeated society and culture at every level. Orthodox spirituality and devotion reached their highpoint in the work of the ascetic St Serafim of Sarov (1759–1833), and in a monastic revival which more than doubled the number of Russian religious houses by 1914. They also inspired Russian writers from Leo Tolstoy to Fyodor Dostoevsky.

Dostoevsky, the son of a landowner murdered by his serfs, gave up religious beliefs under the influence of socialism and liberalism, but returned to Christianity after four years' hard labour in Siberia. Unlike Tolstoy, who rejected traditional Christianity after renouncing his literary works, Dostoevsky remained loyal to Orthodoxy. In his major works – *Crime and Punishment* (1866) and *The Brothers Karamazov* (1879–80) – he showed with uncompromising realism how the deification of man in place of God had unleashed the primal instincts of destruction and death.

Dostoevsky's *sobornost* meant spiritual togetherness – 'responsibility of each for all'. He sensed where the rejection and destruction of religion were leading. 'The preachers of materialism and atheism, who proclaim man's self-sufficiency,' the Russian warned, 'are preparing indescribable darkness and horror for mankind under the guise of renovation and resurrection.'[55]

Dostoevsky was not alone. At the First Vatican Council, the German bishop of Mainz described how Cardinal Manning had 'made our hair stand on end' with his apocalyptic vision of the violence and bloodshed likely to ensue in an atheistic twentieth century. Pius X blamed European governments, predicting that God would send war as an atonement for the continent's sins. 'You are lucky indeed, my friend, to be leaving Europe at this moment,' he told a Brazilian ambassador in 1914, a few days before shots rang out in Sarajevo. 'You will thus avoid the greatest war of all times, which is just about to break over us all.'[56]

They were prophetic words. The Pope could look back over a century which had seen belief invested in the power of humanity to master the world and correct the errors of history, in which the river of Christianity had been buffeted on all sides by fast-flowing brooks and tributaries. The ideological currents unleashed in their wake – nationalism, liberalism, socialism, Marxism – would all have an impact, creative or destructive, on the century that followed. But it would be the great Church-secular divide which had the most dramatic consequences. This would take decades to heal. Rival theories and programmes would have to be tested first under pressure for miracle solutions and instant improvements. Yet the ensuing conflict would also teach much-needed lessons about nurturing human development from a firm foundation of faith principles and ethical values.

CHAPTER 3

Death of a Continent

Everything is modern – that is what one must see. And everything is completely un-Christian. Alas, if it were merely bad Christianity, one could see a way out, begin to talk. But when we talk of de-Christianisation, when we say there is a modern de-Christianised world, we mean it has given up the whole system altogether, that it moves and has its being outside the system ... We, the first since Jesus, have seen and see every day a whole world, if not a city, a wholly un-Christian, post-Christian society, being born and growing, rather than decreasing, prospering rather than perishing. And between the two there is a chasm.

The spiritual desolation captured by the French mystic Charles Péguy, four years before his own death at the Battle of the Marne, expressed a pessimism which was widely shared on the eve of the First World War. Péguy's Irish contemporary, W.B. Yeats, called it the 'crowning crisis of the world', while philosophers talked about Christianity's extinction, the 'death of God'.[1]

The war was, for many, the ultimate negation of Christian values – the culmination of the nineteenth century's religious-secular divide, and the final petering out of the Christian river which had flowed through European history. Although priests and pastors supported their own nations, the four-year cataclysm eroded faith and brought a moral revolution in its wake. 'When war had broken out, religion capitulated,' noted the Protestant theologian and missionary, Albert Schweizer. 'It became demobilised. In the war, religion lost its purity and lost its authority.'[2]

Europe's Churches nevertheless survived. Having cold-shouldered the papacy for two decades, the liberal Entente powers woke up to its importance. The Vatican was well-informed about the stance of neutral states. It also had close ties with Germany and Austria-Hungary. By contrast, despite a growing Catholic population around its empire, Britain had had no relations for four centuries, while ties with countries from Portugal to Russia had been disrupted by the anti-Catholic climate. European governments scrambled to reopen contacts. Having hosted ambassadors from just six countries in 1914, the Vatican would have thirty-five accredited by 1922.

Despite this, Christian voices were to be systematically excluded from the decision-making process. Benedict XV became Pope in September 1914, a month after the start of the war, when the Russian Army had already been annihilated by the Germans at Tannenberg after invading East Prussia. By the year's end, he had made his first peace proposals, deploring the 'horrible carnage that dishonours Europe'. The Vatican was urged to condemn the German occupation of Belgium. But the Pope insisted on his impartiality. He resisted attempts to legitimise the conflict with the Just War notions of Aquinas. Meanwhile, he also rejected the view of belligerent bishops that the conflict offered an opportunity for ethical and spiritual regeneration. This was, he objected, 'a childish morality in an adult age'.[3]

In this way, Benedict XV alienated both sides. The French premier, Georges Clemenceau, suspected him of pro-German sympathies and dubbed him 'le Pape Boche'. The German chief of staff, Erich Ludendorff, believed he counted on Germany's destruction and called him 'der französischer Papst'. The Pope was doomed to fail when he came up with a major peace plan in 1917. This outlined a peaceful organisation for international life after the war. Territorial questions would be settled with Germany's withdrawal from France and Belgium, the Allied evacuation of German colonies and the restoration of independence to Poland and the Balkan states. Meanwhile, military service would be abolished and war damages paid by all sides. The fundamental aim, the Pope stressed, was to stop the 'useless massacre' by ensuring that 'the material force of arms should be substituted with the moral force of law'. 'Will the civilised world then become nothing but a field of death?' he asked. 'And will Europe, so glorious and so flourishing before, rush to the abyss, as if driven on by a universal folly, and be the agent of her own suicide?'[4]

Yet the plan was ill-timed. With the tide about to turn in their favour after the US entry to the war, the Allies were confident of victory. Instead of sitting over a negotiating table with Germany, they preferred to settle the conflict on the battlefield. The accusations came thick and fast. Britain's Prime Minister, David Lloyd George, accused the Pope of 'plotting a German peace', while the Communist-controlled International Socialist Congress in Stockholm branded the plan 'a typical example of religious-capitalist hypocrisy'.[5] In the US, the Wilson Administration was sure the Vatican was siding with the Central Powers to preserve the Catholic Austro-Hungarian monarchy under the saintly Karl I. Not surprisingly, it disagreed vigorously with Rome over the future map of Europe.

It was said that the Kaiser had invited the Pope to chair a peace conference after a German victory, whereas Britain, France and Russia had promised to exclude him as a price for Italy's entry into the war on their side. In the event, the Vatican was left out of the Versailles Treaty of 1919, which declared Germany guilty of causing the war and imposed heavy territorial and financial reparations. Benedict XV and his Secretary of State, Cardinal Pietro Gasparri, had grave doubts about the new European order. It was, the Pope said, only 'peace of a sort'. It would not eradicate Europe's ancient rivalries or achieve the 'fraternal reconciliation of the peoples'.

> It is the teaching of history that when the Church pervaded with her spirit the ancient and barbarous nations of Europe, little by little the many and varied differences that divided them were diminished and their quarrels extinguished. In time they formed a homogeneous society from which sprang Christian Europe which, under the guidance and auspices of the Church, whilst preserving a diversity of nations, tended to a unity that favoured its prosperity and glory.[6]

Besides the restrictions imposed on Germany, the Pope deplored the dismembering of Austria-Hungary at the Treaty of Trianon a year later, and warned of the dangers of leaving the small states of Eastern and Central Europe open to Russia, now under Communist rule. He appeared to have foreseen the alternative society now being imposed there. 'If this war continues much longer,' Benedict XV told the leader of Germany's Catholic Centre Party, Matthias Erzberger, in 1916, 'we shall have such a social revolution in Europe as the world has not seen since 1789.'[7]

Ironically, the new revolution had happened not in industrialised Germany or Bohemia, as Marx had prophesied, but in backward, under-developed Russia, sweeping away three centuries of rule by the Romanov dynasty. Initially, the Vatican had kept diplomatic contacts open with Lenin's Bolshevik regime, sending aid to victims of post-war famine and expressing optimism about church life. As Ukraine and Belarus were swallowed up into the new Soviet Union, however, after just a few months of notional independence, it became clear that something truly calamitous was afoot. In May 1920, en route west towards war-weakened Germany, the Red Army was turned back by Marshall Józef Piłsudski's Polish legions at the 'Miracle on the Vistula'. The dramatic rout was personally witnessed from nearby Warsaw by the Vatican's Nuncio, Archbishop Achille Ratti, the future Pope Pius XI.

By then, the Bolsheviks had made clear what Christians could expect. The Russian Orthodox leader, Patriarch Tikhon, had denounced the murder of Tsar Nicholas II and his family in 1918, and excommunicated the 'godless rulers of the darkness'. A new law had promised freedom of religion, but also of 'anti-religious propaganda', while church rights had been summarily curtailed and church properties confiscated without compensation. Orthodox priests, monks and nuns – those 'agents in cassocks', in Lenin's words, who had been used by the Tsar to 'sweeten and embellish the lot of the oppressed with empty promises of a heavenly kingdom' – had been taken out and massacred in their tens of thousands, often in the most brutal ways.[8]

The exiled writer, Alexander Solzhenitsyn, would later see

Russian Orthodoxy's weakness as a key factor in the 1917 revolution. The Bolsheviks saw themselves as heirs to the secular republican ethos born in the French Revolution and believed their successful seizure of power would be heeded by revolutionaries across Europe. Lenin himself had studied western intellectual traditions from Hegel to Fichte, as well as furious arguments over the Church and Christianity among thinkers from Nikolai Gogol to Bakunin, Anton Chekhov to Dostoevsky. Although baptised and married in church, Lenin had left Christianity behind, in an extreme version of the anti-clerical mindset of nineteenth-century secular radicalism. To call religion the 'opium of the people' was too kind, Lenin had quoted Marx back in 1909. It was, in fact, 'a kind of spiritual vodka, by which the slaves of capital blacken their human figure and their aspirations for a more dignified human life'.[9]

There would be something more complex about communist attitudes to religion. Religious Russians knew the meaning of 'red' – a traditional synonym for blood and beauty, redemption and resurrection. Bolshevik poets such as Alexander Blok used messianic Christian imagery in their work, while many Communist leaders had deeply religious backgrounds. The man who would succeed Lenin at his death in 1922, Josif Stalin, won a scholarship to Georgia's Orthodox seminary in Tbilisi and would have become a priest had he not been expelled in 1899, just before his final exams. As ruler, Stalin used catechetical language in his speeches and writings, and could quote extensively from the Bible.

Such paradoxes were not unusual. Although determined to destroy the Church as a social force, Europe's would-be Communist dictators recognised the value of metaphysical symbols and invented their own quasi-religious rituals. The effects were captured by the Russian writer, Mikhail Bulgakov, in his allegorical 1938 work, *The Master and Margarita*, in which the Devil makes his appearance in Moscow. By promising a perfect society, Stalin's system created a world of dark absurdity, in which the moral infra-structure provided by religion and culture broke down, leaving individuals at the mercy of an all-powerful state – and of their own confused, embattled consciences.

There was no ambiguity, however, about the regime's attitude when it came to organised religion and Churches. They were all, Lenin said, 'organs of bourgeois reaction'. Soviet propagandists spoke of Vatican support for a 'Black International', which was intent on propping up reactionary capitalist states. A League of Militant Godless was established on Easter Day 1925. Four years later, all religious instruction was banned by decree, unleashing a violent programme of atheisation, which would see most of Russia's 57,000 Orthodox churches closed, and ninety per cent of its 54,000 priests jailed or exiled.[10]

With its traditional subservience to the state now turned against it by hostile rulers, the Orthodox Church would be kept alive by the dogged faith of its peasant masses against the urban atheism of the Communist Party, as well as by the persistent work of exiled writers such as the Marxist-turned-priest, Sergei Bulgakov. Yet the regime's anti-religious savagery found emulators elsewhere. In Munich, communist groups proclaimed a Soviet government during the 'Red Days' at the end of the war, while Berlin and Vienna looked set to follow suit. In Estonia, a communist coup was attempted in 1924. In Hungary, Béla Kun's 'Republic of Councils' imposed a Soviet dictatorship before being brutally suppressed by the Habsburg 'regent', Admiral Horthy.

On the other side of Europe, a Spanish republic was declared in 1931 after the abdication of King Alfonso XIII. Church property was attacked, pilgrimages banned and Catholic schools taken over. 'With these measures,' the socialist premier, Manuel Azaña, told parliament, 'Spain ceases to be Catholic.'[11] Hatred of the Church reached unparalleled ferocity during the Civil War which ensued in 1936–9. Churches were systematically torched and ransacked around the country, leaving twelve bishops and over 8,000 priests, monks and nuns dead. After the persecutions in the East, it seemed a warning of what the Church could expect wherever modern anti-clerical parties came to power.

* * *

Writing before the war, Charles Péguy had seen the new anti-Christian climate as a positive challenge. 'Once Catholics have consented to see, measure and admit the disaster,' the mystic predicted in 1910; 'once they have given up their cowardly diagnosis, then and only then will they perhaps be able to work usefully.'[12] Yet Pope Pius XI had been right to agree with his predecessor that the post-war settlement had failed to extinguish the 'seeds of discord, broadcast and sown in a soil so ready to receive them'. Instead, it had 'fostered ever more violence, bloodshed and hatred among the peoples, and even more among the various classes of society'. The 'habit of religion and moral life of the peoples' had been ruined in the process.[13]

So had any hope of accomodation between the forces of extremism in Europe. In Italy, Mussolini's Fascists took power in 1923 and began constructing a new type of one-party state, mixing nationalism with social collectivism. In Germany, Hitler's Nazis repudiated the tolerance of the post-war Weimar Republic and proclaimed an ideology which combined socialist and fascist elements, with racist demagogy and corrupted religious imagery.

Though raised as a Catholic, Hitler had long since channelled his faith in an Aryan, anti-Semitic direction. In 1873, the theologian Paul de Lagarde had concluded that both Catholicism and Protestantism were a 'distortion of the Bible', imposed on humanity by the 'Judaised Christianity' which St Paul had invented to bring down the Roman Empire. Such theories fed Hitler's paranoia. He knew the work of the philosopher Oswald Spengler, whose *Decline of the West* (1918) showed how nations and cultures rose and fell. He was also familiar with the ideas of Friedrich Nietzsche (1844–1900), who saw traditional Christianity as a debasement of human ideals – 'the one important blemish of mankind' – and blamed its Jewish apostles for elevating the 'slave morality' of humility, compassion and self-denial to a supreme virtue. It was this, Nietzsche concluded, which had sapped the will of superior humanity, the *Übermensch*.

> The fact that the strong races of northern Europe did not repudiate this Christian god does little credit to their gift for religion – and not much more to their taste. They ought to have been able to make an end of such a moribund and worn-out product of the *decadence*. A curse lies upon them because

they were not equal to it; they made illness, decrepitude and contradiction a part of their instincts ... The whole of Judaism appears in Christianity as the art of concocting holy lies, and there, after many centuries of earnest Jewish training and hard practice of Jewish technic, the business comes to the stage of mastery. The Christian, that *ultima ratio* of lying, is the Jew all over again.[14]

Nietzsche had gone mad by 1897, when Theodore Herzl's *Der Judenstaat* proposed establishing the Jewish people in a national state. The Zionist movement, holding its first congress in Basle the same year, had been formed against a background of growing anti-Semitism in Germany and Austria-Hungary. Many Jews had opposed it, believing Europe's Jewish communities should continue seeking assimilation in societies which appeared to be offering them civil equality. By the 1930s, however, hopes of tolerance and fairness were dwindling fast.

Although Nietzsche had been the son of a Lutheran pastor, Hitler was also full of contempt for Protestants – those 'insignificant little people, submissive as dogs', who 'have neither a religion they can take seriously, nor a great position to defend like Rome'. But Judaism, Bolshevism and effete Christianity were linked together. 'Conscience is a Jewish invention, a blemish like circumcision,' Hitler declared in *Mein Kampf*, his 1924 political testament. 'I am acting in accordance with the will of the almighty Creator. By defending myself against the Jews, I am fighting for the work of the Lord.'[15]

There were those who saw ideologies of this sort as a logical consequence of the decline of Christianity. 'A drama will be enacted in Germany compared with which the French Revolution will seem like a harmless idyll,' the Jewish poet, Heinrich Heine, had predicted a whole century earlier. 'Christianity may have restrained the martial ardour of the Teutons for a time, but it did not destroy it. Now that the restraining talisman, the cross, has rotted away, the old frenzied madness will break out again.'[16]

Christianity was, in fact, under continual pressure everywhere. In Britain, the prevailing Anglican ethos was predominantly middle-class and male-dominated, despite efforts by a new Archbishop of Canterbury, William Temple, to bring church life up to date with modern culture. Smaller Churches were less hidebound by class associations. But in their first yearbook, the country's Free Churches had urged members to face up to a 'startling reality' – that the 'educated middle class, especially the young, are losing touch altogether with the House of God'.[17] The Anglican and Protestant establishments of England, Germany and Scandinavia had accepted the onset of Biblical criticism more easily than the Roman Catholic Church. But the development of physics, astronomy, psychoanalysis and the natural sciences posed problems for theologians everywhere. So did the increasing internationalisation of science symbolised by great names such as Freud, Einstein, Rutherford and Planck. So too did advances in relativity and quantum theory, the discovery of the neutron in 1932 or the splitting of the uranium atom in 1939.

Although restricted to a narrow elite, scientific knowledge raised questions about the meaning of life and objective values. Traditional morals and aesthetics had been under threat since the nineteenth century. Against this unstable background, the horrors of the Great War bred cynicism and disillusionment with the social order and its liberal culture. It pointed to the existentialism of Martin Heidegger, with its focus on the individual's quest for sense and understanding, as well as to the sense of alienation and estrangement reflected in the works of Marcel Proust, Thomas Mann and Franz Kafka. It also provoked irrationalism and fragmentation in art, typefied by Cubism and Surrealism.

With the economic shock waves of the Great Depression still felt, political polarisation was placing democracy under pressure, along with its rights and freedoms. The Popular Front movement, beginning in 1930s France, tried to rally Europe's radical Left against an emerging confraternity of authoritarian governments. There were those, like the French writer, Julien Benda, in his *Trahison des clercs* (1927), who reminded educated western contemporaries that their commitment to truth should never be compromised by politics and ideology. But idealistic intellectuals were tending to look in one of two directions – Moscow or Berlin. Both shared an impatience with the liberal capitalist system which had survived the 1914–18 conflagration, with its dull rationalism and individualism. Both offered a dynamic revolutionary programme. Both exploited the same grievances and insecurities.

The atmosphere was much the same in Eastern Europe. For intellectuals raised in countries which had been condemned to backwardness by 150 years of foreign imperial rule, the new ideologies were attractive. They appeared to offer a real possibility of accelerated development, a great leap forward to parity with the West. Their atheistic pretensions found echoes too. The loosening of imperial rule had accentuated political and social divisions, leaving education, art and literature dominated by secular perspectives. Reforming priests lower in the Church's ranks had helped bring Enlightenment ideas to the region. They had also supported the national reawakening in the nineteenth century and backed calls for the redistribution of Church wealth. But the Church's upper echelons were hostile to social emancipation. 'Give us clerics who identify with the poor, whose apostolic life leaves no room for doubt!' pleaded the Hungarian Catholic social reformer, Ottokár Prohászka. 'For the Gospel, with its resignation and suffering, is but an empty shadow.'[18]

By the 1930s, the whole of Eastern Europe, from Estonia to Albania, was ruled by authoritarian regimes. Only Czechoslovakia still had a democratic constitution. Even here, however, the Communist Party had become Europe's largest after that of France. The playwright, Karel Čapek, deplored the 'pessimism and dismal hatred being pumped artificially into the working class'.[19] But Czech intellectuals had acquired radical sympathies, which were to be spurred on by the 1938 Munich debacle. In neighbouring Slovakia, the Catholic Church had helped preserve the national identity under Hungarian rule. Among Czechs, by contrast, the Church had been seen as a tool of Habsburg rule. Although the 1930s witnessed a Catholic revival in the Czech Lands, the political and cultural establishment had inherited anti-Catholic reflexes from its founding father, Masaryk.

In Hungary, similarly, the 1930s brought a proliferation of Catholic social initiatives. Yet these offered few real answers to the great questions of the day. Catholic periodicals multiplied too, such as the *Vigilia* monthly, which published western philosophers and claimed links with great Hungarian literary figures such as Endre Ady and Mihály Babits. But Leo XIII's *Rerum Novarum* was left unpublished for four decades in Hungary. Here too, Christian Churches were powerless to prevent a drift to extremes.

In Poland, a gap had opened up between the Church and intelligentsia in the late nineteenth century, between the traditional popular Catholicism of the countryside and the secularism of an educated city elite. There were priests, such as Władysław Korniłowicz, who attracted intellectuals seeking an opening to the Christian faith, and renewal movements such as Odrodzenie which proclaimed a 'Christian humanism' to heal the rift between reform-minded Catholics and socialists. But these initiatives had little visible impact. If the Church's hierarchy championed the national identity, it also defended its own rights and privileges. Its philanthropic and charitable efforts, though extensive, barely touched the surface of current needs. Since secularisation was less advanced here than in Czechoslovakia and Hungary, the Church remained Poland's only coherent source of moral authority. But it was an authority tainted with intolerance, which was incapable of assimilating new Catholic thinking from the wider world.

Could the Church have resisted the slide to chaos? In later years, the Vatican would be criticised for failing to encourage a tactical alliance between Catholic politicians and moderate socialists, which might have diluted communism and fascism. Germany's Centre Party, formed in response to Bismarck's *Kulturkampf*, had enjoyed strong public support in the 1920s. So had Catholic parties from Italy to Czechoslovakia. In 1927, Pius XI had quashed claims that the Church automatically sided with right-wing forces by condemning Charles Maurras's monarchist, anti-Semitic *Action Française* movement and rejecting its claim to stand for Christian values. It was the Church's final accomodation to France's republican order, as heralded by Leo XIII's Ralliement of 1889. But it came late in the day. Within six years, the German Centre Party had been dissolved after the burning of the Reichstag. The political options were narrowing.

The Pope made clear he had no objection to necessary social and economic reforms. 'The Church is never bound to one form of government more than to another, provided the divine rights of God and human consciences are safe,' Pius XI reaffirmed in 1933. 'She does not find difficulty adapting herself to various civil institutions, be they monarchies or republics, aristocratic or democratic. Evident proof of this lies in the numerous Concordats and agreements concluded in recent years, and in the diplomatic relations the Holy See has established with different states since the Great War.'[20] While deploring the anti-Church excesses in Spain, Pius XI declined to condemn the Spanish republic, and even gave the impression of favouring a moderate Catholic republicanism against Church objections. General Francisco Franco styled himself 'El Generalissimo Cristianissimo de la Santa Crusada'. But his requests for the Pope to bless his anti-communist campaign were repeatedly ignored.

Yet Pius XI could see Europe's vulnerablity to the radical politics of the new epoch, and their link to the 'idols' of liberalism which the popes had repeatedly warned against. In a new encyclical, marking the fortieth anniversary of *Rerum Novarum*, he recognised that many Christians believed 'the tenets of a mitigated socialism' were compatible with 'the just demands of Christian social reformers'. They were mistaken. 'Religious socialism, Christian socialism, are expressions implying a contradiction in terms,' Pius XI insisted in *Quadragesimo Anno*. 'No one can be at the same time a sincere Catholic and a socialist properly so called.'[21]

The Pope saw parallels with the social and economic conditions which had confronted the Church in Leo XIII's day. On the one side, the 'growing division between two classes' had spurred a yearning for socialist solutions which would expose society to even graver dangers. On the other, liberal dogmas had prevented 'effective interference' by governments and shown their 'utter impotence' in solving social problems. When it came to cause and effect, the Church was clear. Socialism and communism were the offspring of liberalism. They represented misguided reactions to the abuses of modern capitalism; and their appeal would not be defused until these abuses had been neutralised. The Church regretted the 'indolent apathy' of governments who allowed the propagation of socialist doctrines – 'which seek by violence and bloodshed the destruction of the whole of society'. But it condemned 'even more severely' the failures of those 'who neglect to remove or modify such conditions as exasperate the hearts of the people, and so prepare the way for the overthrow and ruin of the social order'.[22]

Unfortunately for Europe, the Pope had little to offer by way of solutions. The encyclical called for a 'community of communities' free of both liberalism and socialism, which would ensure a living wage and improved conditions for employees and their families, and be buttressed by voluntary associations and vocational groups all interacting in the cause of social reconstruction. This dreamy, paternalistic vision clearly under-estimated the radical forces which were seizing the initiative by the 1930s. It could hardly be expected to compete for secular allegiances with the rhetoric coming out of Berlin and Moscow. Pius XI spoke vaguely of 'social justice'. But its 'soul' must be 'social charity', he insisted, and a sense of common good.

For all its limitations, *Quadragesimo Anno* proved influential. In Austria, an attempt was made to apply Catholic social principles by the authoritarian regimes of Chancellors Kurt von Schuschnigg and Engelbert Dollfuss, although this was disrupted by rival Nazi and socialist revolts and terminated by the 1938 Anschluss with Germany. In Portugal, where a socialist premier, Alfonso Costa, had boasted that Catholicism would be 'eradicated entirely within two generations', a similar programme was put forward by the authoritarian António de Oliviera Salazar and lasted longer.[23]

In Ireland, by contrast, Catholic teachings inspired a successful democratic constitution under Eamon de Valera's Fianna Fáil government. This began with an invocation, 'In the name of the Most Holy Trinity, from Whom is all authority and to Whom, as our final end, all actions of men and states must be referred.' Its guiding principles – the common good, family rights, individual freedom defined by moral duties – could be traced back to Aquinas. They fulfilled the dream of Ireland's nineteenth-century Catholic 'Liberator', Daniel O'Connell.[24]

Pius XI's condemnation of socialism was balanced six

weeks later by *Non abbiamo bisogno*, which denounced the 'pagan worship of the state' in Mussolini's Italy, as well as the brutality of the Fascist regime. Although totalitarian threats were growing in both directions, the Pope believed Christianity had more to fear from communism. He was aware of its attraction to western intellectuals – to people like André Gide and George Bernard Shaw, who returned from stage-managed visits to Moscow lauding Soviet humanitarian achievements, while millions of Russians and Ukrainians were dying in a Soviet-engineered 'terror famine' or in Stalin's 1936–7 Great Purge. Lenin had had a term for fellow-travellers like this – 'useful idiots'. But the Pope knew communism offered a 'pseudo-ideal of justice, equality and brotherhood', as well as a 'counterfeit mysticism' which thrived in the current climate of disillusionment. It advocated class warfare and a 'godless human society'. But it also worked through a 'diabolically efficient system of propaganda, probably unparalleled in history', and made use of philosophies which had 'long sought to set up a barrier between science and faith, and between human life and the Church'.[25]

Initially at least, Mussolini had attempted to accommodate the Catholic Church. In 1929, the 'Roman Question' had finally been settled after sixty years of uneasy stand-off by a Lateran Treaty (also invoking the Holy Trinity) and Concordat, which proclaimed Catholicism the 'sole religion of the Italian state'. Hitler had also been cautious towards the Church. A Concordat in 1933 presaged the dissolution of all non-Nazi groups, but also promised the Church important concessions. None of these promises were kept in practice. Clergy were harassed, Christian ceremonies replaced with Nordic rites, and attempts made to ban the Cross and Christian prayers from schools. Between 1933 and 1936, the Vatican sent over thirty formal protests to Berlin.

By the mid-1930s, however, it was clear that Germany's Christian leaders had knuckled under to Hitler. There were voices of dissent from Catholic figures such as Bishop Clemens von Galen of Münster, as well as from the Protestants Martin Niemöller and Dietrich Bonhoeffer, who opposed the Aryan Laws in 1933. But neither the Catholic nor the Protestant Churches offered effective opposition to Nazi crimes such as the 1938 Krystallnacht, when 400 synagogues and thousands of Jewish homes were torched and ransacked. By contrast, forced labourers were put to work on Church lands, as well as on government projects. 'We have learned from Martin Luther to distinguish clearly between the spheres of Reason and Faith, Politics and Religion, and State and Church,' Lutheran leaders declared in 1939. 'The Evangelical Church holds the state in reverence as an order set up by God, and requires loyal service from its members within that order.'[26]

* * *

A new 'German Christian' movement, formed among Protestants, went along with Hitler's campaign to purge Christianity of the 'Jewish servility' fostered by St Paul and St Augustine. But it was fear of communism which also impelled Church subservience. 'We consider it our duty to support the head of the German Reich by all means at the Church's disposal,' Germany's Catholic bishops noted in a 1937 pastoral letter. 'The Führer and Chancellor of the Reich, Adolf Hitler, has sighted the advance of Bolshevism from afar. His thoughts and aspirations aim at averting the horrible danger to our German people and the entire West.'[27]

The Vatican did not share this view. In September 1936, its newspaper, *L'Osservatore Romano*, warned again that historic international enmities were being exacerbated by the 'war of ideologies'. Half a year later, Pius XI set the record straight with two new encyclicals, issued within five days of each other. The first, *Mit Brennender Sorge*, reaffirmed Christian teachings against the corruptions of Nazi ideology. The 'iron language of facts' had already 'worn away the veil' of Nazi intentions, the Pope said. The second, *Divini Redemptoris*, did the same with communism. The 'revolution of our own time', Pius XI noted, was 'now either already raging or else frowning its menace in nearly every part of the world, exceeding in violence and magnitude any persecution which the Church has ever sustained, and threatening to reduce whole nations to a state of barbarism'. Communism was 'intrinsically evil'. The sovereign reality of God offered an 'utter and complete refutation' of communist theories, and no one wishing to 'save Christian civilisation from extinction' should offer assistance to it.[28]

Despite everything, Pius XI still believed, like his predecessors, that it was the 'policies of economic liberalism' which had caused Communism's rise in the first place. There could be no hope of saving Europe, he insisted, unless its economic and social order returned to Christian precepts. A new Pope, Pius XII, went on trying to defuse tensions until German armies crossed the Polish border on 1 September 1939. But his eve-of-war broadcast, with its famous appeal – 'Nothing is lost by peace; everything may be destroyed by war' – illustrated how far Christianity and the prevailing ideological order had been driven apart.

* * *

In a broadcast to the defeated Germany in 1945, T.S. Eliot argued that cultural and ideological assaults on Christianity had weakened European civilisation by closing its 'mental frontiers'. Christian tradition had incorporated 'the legacy of Greece, of Rome and of Israel', the poet pointed out. Only a Christian culture could have produced a Voltaire or a Nietzsche. 'I do not believe that the culture of Europe could survive the complete disappearance of the Christian faith,' Eliot continued.

> I am talking about the common tradition of Christianity which has made Europe what it is, and about the common cultural elements which this common Christianity has brought with it ... It is in Christianity that our arts have developed; it is in Christianity that the laws of Europe – until recently – have been rooted. It is against a background of Christianity that all our thought has significance. An individual European may not believe the Christian faith is true; and yet what he says, and makes and does will all depend on the Christian heritage for its meaning.[29]

It was arguable when Europe's division was finally sealed. Perhaps it was with the Nazi-Soviet pact of 1939, which divided Poland into rival 'spheres of influence' and allowed the Soviet Union to expand westwards into the Baltic States and south 'towards the Persian Gulf'. Perhaps the moment came at the December 1943 Teheran conference, when the British Prime Minister, Winston Churchill, ceded territory to Stalin by agreeing to allow Poland's borders to be shunted 150 miles towards Germany. Perhaps it was confirmed in 1944, when the battles of Kursk and Stalingrad turned the tide of the war and launched the Red Army on its triumphant drive to Berlin, and when Stalin refused to allow aid to reach the embattled anti-Nazi insurgents of the Warsaw Uprising.

Attitudes to the heroic Uprising, which left 200,000 Poles dead, highlighted similarities between the secular mentalities of East and West. Soviet, British and American leaders spoke in the same language of power politics. They also shared the same disdain for the Christian nations of Eastern Europe. 'The eagle should permit the small birds to sing, and care not wherefore they sang,' Churchill reputedly told Stalin flatteringly at Yalta.[30] Yet the wartime alliance between the three leaders caused an imbalance in western thinking. Communist misdeeds, however abhorrent, could henceforth never be as bad as the crimes of the Nazis and fascists.

It was at the Crimean resort of Yalta on 4 February 1945 that Europe was given its shape. The statement signed by Churchill, Stalin and the US president, Franklin Roosevelt, confirmed plans for a final four-sided assault of the doomed Nazi Germany, followed by its partition into occupation zones and free elections in liberated territories. Yet these provisions were never honoured. For later generations, 'Yalta' would come to symbolise western connivance in Stalin's conquests. 'I feel no doubt whatsoever in saying that Stalin has been sincere,' Churchill told Britain's parliament after returning from the conference. But *realpolitik* had been decisive, Churchill admitted, in creating the new international system. If Hitler had invaded Hell, he wrote later, 'I would have made at least a favourable reference to the Devil in the House of Commons.'[31]

The greatest war in Europe's history had cost 50 million lives and inflicted continent-wide devastation on an unprecedented scale. Six years of Nazi occupation had cost Poland alone a third of its national wealth and a fifth of its population, including ninety per cent of its once-vibrant Jewish minority. Six million Jews had been wiped out in the Holocaust, in the greatest single blow ever inflicted on European culture. Whole cities lay in ruins, along with their social structure and historic patrimony.

Communism reached Eastern Europe with Stalin's Red Army and was imposed over the years 1946–50 with ruthless inexorability. The Baltic States of Lithuania, Latvia and Estonia were reincorporated into the Soviet Union, after just two decades of independence. So were western Ukraine and Romania's northern Bessarabia province. Up to twelve million German civilians were expelled from their homes in Silesia and the Sudetenland to seal the new borders, with hundreds of thousands dying en route. Poles were deported from Ukraine and Ukrainians from Poland, while Russian cossacks and Yugoslav royalists were forcibly repatriated by Allied forces. As the silent terror campaign continued, disorientated intellectuals and impoverished workers were drawn to the new communist programme, with its seductive promises of a world of peace and justice.

The post-war period brought a political shift to the Left in Western Europe too, thanks in part to the discrediting of right-wing ideas. Under the Bretton Woods agreements of 1944, the United States and its European allies had set up an International Monetary Fund to stabilise exchange rates and promote free trade. But economic policies would be dominated by the theories of John Maynard Keynes, with their emphasis on government interventionism. Like other prominent Europeans, Keynes had attacked the war reparations imposed on Germany at Versailles a generation earlier, seeing these as a barrier to the continent's economic reconstruction. Keynesian economics saw the route to recovery this time as lying through central control and nationalisation.

There were darker threats at work. Powerful Communist parties were poised for power in Greece and Italy. They too saw Yalta as a sell-out, in this case of socialism to capitalism. It was largely to prevent parties like this from gaining ground on the back of Soviet expansionism, that an ambitious plan for political and economic reconstruction was launched by the US Secretary of State, George Marshall, in 1947. Under the

European Recovery Programme, or Marshall Plan, \$12.5 billion in aid were disbursed over the next three years, to combat 'hunger, poverty, exploitation and chaos'. East European governments would gladly have participated. But they were barred by Stalin, who saw the Marshall Plan as a plot by 'dollar imperialism'. The ensuing division between Europe's richer and poorer halves would deepen steadily for the next half-century.

Meanwhile, 1949 saw the creation of NATO, embracing Britain, Belgium, Denmark, France, Iceland, Italy, Luxembourg, the Netherlands, Norway and Portugal, as well as Canada and the US. Its aim was to 'restore and maintain the security of the North Atlantic area', by committing signatory states to protect any member who came under attack. Greece and Turkey joined in 1952, followed by West Germany in 1955. Moscow responded the same year with the Warsaw Pact, incorporating the Soviet Union, Bulgaria, Czechoslovakia, Hungary, Poland, Romania and (till 1968) Albania.

When Churchill spoke of a new 'Iron Curtain' between democratic and communist Europe in a famous 1946 speech, it evoked dismay among Church leaders. But Christian representatives had again been excluded from the post-war settlement. Pope Pius XII had made mistakes in his response to the Holocaust, by placing his trust in diplomacy, rather than in forthright testimony and witness. Vatican diplomats would later cite evidence that he had saved at least 15,000 Jews in Nazi-allied Hungary, as well as tens of thousands through Church channels in Italy. But the real question was whether he had done all he could. That could be asked of every wartime leader. But the Pope's moral standing made open and clear condemnations especially important. The resulting uncertainties touched off a debate which would still be acerbic six decades later.

Pius XII had done other controversial things too. In particular, he had antagonised the Roosevelt Administration by refusing to endorse the British-US alliance with Moscow, despite preposterous claims of religious tolerance in the Soviet Union. 'So far as I am informed, churches in Russia are open,' Roosevelt wrote to Pius XII in 1941. 'I believe the survival of Russia is less dangerous to religion, to the Church as such, and to humanity in general than would be the survival of the German form of dictatorship.'[32] It was a contentious opinion. The Vatican had a representative in Moscow throughout the war, as well as scattered observers in Ukraine and Belarus, who agreed there were signs of change. But Vatican officials were shocked that Roosevelt apparently took Stalin's benign claims at face value.

These were the reasons why the Church was not consulted about the post-war settlement – its relevance dismissed by Stalin's trite question at Yalta, 'How many divisions has the Pope?' The Church had, indeed, taken a decisive step away from the institutional power it had once enjoyed. In so doing, it had gained the possibility of emerging for the first time as a purely moral and spiritual force. There would be much in the new post-war order which Pius XII applauded. When the United Nations was founded in October 1945, with a charter pledging 'human rights and fundamental freedoms for all, without distinction as to race, sex, language or religion', the Pope praised it as an achievement of 'unprecedented experi-ence, goodwill, political wisdom and organising power'. When a Paris conference was convened to draw up a European response to the Marshall Plan, its objective of 'economic soli-darity' was eagerly supported by *L'Osservatore Romano*.[33]

But the Pope believed, like Benedict XV before him, that a stable Europe needed, despite everything, a strong, united Germany. Without it, Communism could only benefit from the defeat of Nazism and Fascism. What he found instead was the Yalta Agreement's provision for Germany's 'complete disar-mament, demilitarisation and dismemberment'. The negotiators who carved up Europe had predicted 'a continuing and growing understanding between East and West'.[34] That 'lasting peace' had turned out to be an unjust and unstable international order, achieved at the cost of humane principles.

Speaking in October 1945, Pius XII set out two principles for Church–State relations. First, it was the state's duty to secure the common good by allowing unity through diversity – something impossible under totalitarian or authoritarian regimes. Second, the Church's own structure of authority derived from divine precepts and could not be compared to

that of secular states. The Church would henceforth always
opt for democracy. But the fate of pre-war Europe had shown
that democracy was far from foolproof. It required, at the
very least, a secure foundation in the Christian faith.

> Certainly, the Christian Middle Ages, which were particularly
> imbued with the spirit of the Church, proved by the abundance
> of their flourishing democratic communities not only that the
> Christian faith is able to produce a genuine and true democ-
> racy, but also that it is the only durable foundation for
> democracy. A democracy without an accord of spirits, at least
> as to the fundamental maxims of life – and, above all, as to
> the rights of God, the dignity of the human person and the
> respect due to the person's honest activity and liberty – would
> be defective and unsound ... Even democracy is easily altered
> and deformed, and in the course of time is liable to fall into a
> one-party totalitarianism or authoritarianism.[35]

* * *

The Pope was not alone. Other Church leaders had reached
similar conclusions. The Anglicans William Temple of
Canterbury and George Bell of Chichester had done their best
to restrain crusading nationalistic impulses during the war,
criticising the saturation bombing of German cities and
demands for unconditional surrender. No nation, no church,
no individual was without guilt, Bishop Bell warned. The
principal goal of the war had to be 'the recovery of
Christendom'. There would be no regeneration 'without
repentance and without forgiveness'.[36]

Bell had links with Germany's Confessing Church, the only
Christian body to have publicly protested the mass-killing of
Jews, and with Dietrich Bonhoeffer, its best-known theologian, who paid with his life at Flossenburg concentration camp
for criticising Nazi methods. In its Stuttgart Confession of
October 1945, the month of Pius XII's allocution, the
Confessing Church admitted the Germans' need for a 'solidarity of guilt'. However, it too stressed that the recovery of
Christianity would be crucial to the country's future. 'We
accuse ourselves of not having made our avowal more
completely,' the statement continued – 'of not having prayed

more faithfully, not having believed more joyfully and not having loved more ardently.'[37]

Despite everything, the Pope still hoped to hold Europe together, by defending the rights of citizens against the *machismo* of geopolitics. Vatican nuncios remained at their posts in parts of Eastern Europe, and contacts remained open. Meanwhile, the Catholic Church encompassed a range of political options. At one extreme, the Czech 'peace priest', Josef Plojhar, willingly served the Communist regime as Health Minister. At the other, the American Cardinal Francis Spellman supported Senator Joseph McCarthy's purge of Communists – those 'God-hating lustful beasts masquerading as men'.[38]

With its own members divided, efforts were made to safeguard the Church's independence as a spiritual force above the East–West division. The encyclical *Humani Generis*, published when millions of Catholics were flocking to Rome for a Holy Year, strengthened the authority of the Church's central Magisterium, or teaching office. The Dogma of the Assumption (1950), establishing the Virgin Mary's bodily translation to Heaven, appealed to the loyalty of the Catholic masses.

The Pope resisted attempts to gain his personal backing for NATO. Although the Vatican shared the interest of the US in containing communism – a concept outlined in the 1947 Truman Doctrine – it did so in the name of Christianity, Pius XII made clear, not of 'western' or 'liberal' values. The Vatican had never acted against Russia, he insisted in a letter to 'the most dear Russian peoples' in 1952. 'When in 1941 some people tried to persuade us to approve war against the Russian people, we never did,' the Pope added. 'Our office compels us to condemn and reject the errors preached by atheistic communism. But we have your good in mind in doing this. We know how many of you still nourish the Christian faith in your hearts.'[39]

This needed stressing. In the Pope's native Italy, the Communist Party had become Western Europe's largest and best-disciplined. It viewed the Church and Vatican as enemies – as reactionary forces, in the words of the PCI leader, Palmiro Togliatti, 'poisoning, perturbing, lacerating mankind with their empty controversies, ridiculous condemnations and senseless persecutions'.[40] Armed communist bands killed 52 priests in the Emilia-Romagna province alone between the 1944 liberation of Rome and the declaration of an Italian republic in 1946. Having been attacked by Mussolini's Fascists in the 1930s, the clergy were now being targeted by his opponents. The estimated million workers on Catholic trade union books in 1948 were outnumbered six-to-one by communist-backed labour organisations. There were fears that the Communist Party could attempt a coup like that staged in Czechoslovakia during February.

In the event, the combined forces of Communists and Socialists were defeated convincingly in April 1948 elections by Italy's Christian Democrats, suggesting the 'Red Italy' scare had been exaggerated. Even then, there was talk of the Pope fleeing Rome, of 80,000 young Catholics preparing for armed resistance, of gun-running across the Adriatic, Soviet infiltration and US intervention. The Vatican maintained its fear of social movements and was unwilling to sanction Christian Democrat attempts to generate mass pro-Church pressure. But Togliatti claimed to have abandoned the idea of seizing power through violent revolution. The aim now would be a 'long march through the institutions' to the 'progressive democracy' envisaged by Antonio Gramsci. The PCI leader still insisted on seeing Italian Communism as a 'complete religion of man' – a 'counter-church' with the historical mission to bring about a new social order. But he was convinced his party could win power without help from Moscow. Some kind of expedient relationship with the Church was inevitable. 'Even in the Communist Party, there are Catholic citizens – perhaps even the majority,' was Togliatti's explanation. 'There is no contrast between a socialist regime and religious freedom, particularly of the Catholic Church.'[41]

Pius XII thought otherwise. It was against the backdrop of events in Italy that his Holy Office issued in decree in 1949, excommunicating all Catholics who 'profess, defend or propagate' communist doctrines. 'Communism is materialistic and anti-Christian,' the decree insisted; 'and the leaders of the Communists, although they sometimes profess in words that they do not oppose religion, do in fact show themselves, both in their teaching and in their actions, to be the enemies of God, of the true religion and of the Church of Christ.'[42]

The document was dated 14 July, the anniversary of the fall of the Bastille. It was prompted in part by a call that February by the international Communist Information Bureau, or Cominform, for an offensive to break Church links with Rome. This had raised fears of subversion from within. Despite this, the decree received a mixed response in France and Germany, where there had been calls for co-operation between Catholics and moderate Communists. But the most acerbic reactions came, predictably, from Eastern Europe, where it was seen as effectively debarring Catholics from any social involvement. It encouraged the kind of polarisation which communist regimes needed. In Czechoslovakia, a new law annulled all previous Church-related legislation and transferred all 'rights of patronage' and institutional control to the state. Henceforth, all clergy would require state approval. It would only be given to people deemed 'politically reliable and morally irreproachable, who fulfil in all other respects the general conditions required for candidates to state offices'.[43]

The Vatican decree succeeded in deterring some priests from active collaboration. But it generally made little difference. Church leaders faced limited options anyway. It was naive to imagine a choice existed between co-operation and confrontation.

After 150 years of foreign partition, Poland's Catholic Church had had barely two decades to reorganise itself before losing a third of its clergy and much of its infrastructure in the war. In the eyes of many, it had been compromised by pre-war nationalism and intolerance. It now faced an ideologically hostile state, which would use any means to undermine and destroy it. Across the border in the Czech Lands, the Church was still widely viewed as an intrument of Austrian imperial imposition. In Slovakia and Croatia, it was tainted with failure to stand up to wartime Nazi-allied regimes – headed, in the case of Slovakia, by a priest, Mgr Josef Tiso. In Ukraine and Romania, a savage campaign was underway against Greek Catholic communities, who were viewed as a westernising fifth column for combining the eastern liturgy with loyalty to Rome.

As it happened, there were contrasts in the way Church

leaders faced up to the challenge of Communist rule. But there were no obvious conclusions to be drawn. Two confrontational cardinals, József Mindszenty of Hungary and Alozije Stepinac of Croatia, ended up in prison. But so did their more conciliatory Czech counterpart, Cardinal Josef Beran. In the end, there was only one figure who showed true statesmanship – Cardinal Stefan Wyszyński of Poland. Far from rejecting communism a priori, Wyszyński claimed to have studied Marx's *Das Kapital* three times, beginning in his seminary days. He knew the Church had to offer alternatives to Communism, rather than just attacking it. 'Together with many others who had long fought for social justice, I came to consider that altering the socio-economic structure was a necessity,' the Cardinal recalled in his memoirs. 'Had it not been for its narrow atheism, which carried us to the brink of religious war, Polish society, with its cultural, historically democratic tendencies, would have been a most fertile field for a wise government to work with . . . If Marxism had come directly from the West, without eastern intervention, it would undoubtedly have been accepted with greater trust.'[44]

It was thanks to Wyszyński's indefatigable readiness to negotiate, while rallying Catholics behind him, that the Polish Church was able, in the Cardinal's words, 'to gain time to build up strength to defend God's positions'. In 1950, Wyszyński defied Vatican disapproval and signed an 'Understanding' with the Communist government, which promised the Church institutional protection in return for encouraging 'support for national reconstruction and respect for the State authorities'.[45] Most of its provisions were soon broken. But Wyszyński was right to hold the regime to its word. When Stalin died in March 1953, conditions for Church life showed signs of easing; and in 1956, after Stalin's crimes had been denounced by a new Soviet Party boss, Nikita Khrushchev, a new Church-State agreement was signed in Poland. This too was distrusted by the Vatican, which rightly viewed Communist 'concessions' with suspicion. But Wyszyński's painstaking negotiations and accords created an infrastructure for Church-State relations, which gradually, through trial and error, created the basis for a fractious but lasting stand-off.

However tentative and problematic, this was better than nothing. When a Hungarian Uprising was crushed in November 1956, it revealed the apparent futility of hoping Communist power might be overcome with popular resistance, or the countries of the Warsaw Pact allowed to break free from Soviet domination. The Hungarians were, in effect, the first victims of the new *realpolitik*. Pope Pius XII responded with three encyclicals in the space of a week, urging prayers and solidarity with people who were 'moving the hearts of all those attached to the rights of civilisation, human dignity, and the freedom due to persons and nations'. As a new Hungarian Party boss, János Kádár, declared the 'counter-revolution' suppressed, the Pope proclaimed that 'the blood of the Hungarian nation cries out to God for vengeance'. But it was clear that there would be no western backing for attempts to overturn the status quo decreed at Yalta. In his Christmas 1956 broadcast, Pius XII attacked the 'softness' of the UN and western powers, and the 'false realism' conjured up by 'peace at any price'. No one expected the impossible, he conceded. But the fitting UN response should have been to strip the Soviet Union and Hungary of membership. 'It is manifest that in present circumstances, once all other efforts have proved vain, a war of effective self-defence with hope of success against unjust attacks could not be considered "illicit",' the Pope went on. 'The sad reality obliges us to define the terms of struggle in clear language. No one can honestly reproach us for wishing to harden the opposing fronts. If we remained silent, we would have far more to fear from God's judgement.'[46]

The Church had always avoided calling Christians to an anti-Communist crusade, Pius XII continued. But where religion was long-established, it was natural that people should view the struggle unjustly imposed on them in these terms. Christians could not sit at the table of God and His enemies simultaneously. 'What aim can be served by reasoning where there is no common language. How can divergent paths be reconciled, when on one side absolute common values are rejected, making "coexistence in truth" impossible?'[47]

The suppression of the Hungarian Uprising was followed by a clampdown on Christianity too. Here as elsewhere, the regime's aim was to promise the Church a 'secure future' after permanently emasculating it as a social force. Despite the Pope's strictures, it continued to seek out 'progressive' Christians who could be made to serve Party aims. In East Germany, where Christian churches had not yet been separated by the Berlin Wall, the Party leader, Walter Ulbricht, believed he could use them to enhance the Communist image. 'It seems to me that capitalism and basic Christianity are irreconcilably opposed,' Ulbricht told Church leaders. 'I am increasingly concluding that socialists, communists and Christians, despite differences in philosophy, must work together in shaping society and ensuring peace.'[48]

There would be many who accused Pius XII of identifying the Church too closely with western interests, to the extent of becoming a proponent of Cold War confrontation. 'Catholic Europe had ended up becoming nothing but Atlantic Europe,' was the view of one Roman Catholic critic. 'Christianity was identified with western civilisation; and the marriage of religion and politics became once again very close, while the condemnation of atheist communism served the interests of capitalism, imperialism and colonialism.'[49]

It was an understandable view. But it was also one-sided. The Vatican had signed Concordats with Salazar's Portugal in 1950, and with Franco's Spain three years later – a clear sign, critics insisted, of its enthusiasm for authoritarian governments. By 1955, helped by Church support, Christian Democrats held up to two-thirds of parliamentary seats in Germany, France, the Netherlands and Belgium, and were edging on communist rivals in their ties with organised labour. Given the Vatican's previous disdain for Christian Democratic parties, critics believed the Pope had only approved them to hold back communism.

But Pius XII could plausibly contest this. He had also viewed the Christian Democrats as a necessary check on the re-emergence of pre-war economic and social injustices. These were the very abuses which had spurred the rise of extremism in the first place. 'We warn Christians in an industrial era not to be content with an anti-communism based on the defence of a liberty empty of content,' the Pope had warned a year before the Hungarian Uprising. 'They should rather build a society in which man's freedom rests on the moral order.'[50]

Certainly, with the experience of Eastern Europe in mind, the Pope distrusted any talk of a Catholic opening to the Left; and there were *bona fide* Catholic initiatives which fell foul of this. One of the best known was the 'worker priests' movement inspired by France's 'red cardinal', Jean Verdier of Paris. This had sent specially trained pastoral teams to tackle working class alienation in the new industrial communities as part of a new Mission de France initiative. Movement activists could cite Pius XI's summons to priests in *Divini Redemptoris* to go 'among the workers and the poor, and put them on their guard against prejudice and false doctrine'. But some went further, arguing that the Church needed *désembourgeoisement* and should learn from Marxist analysis.

In 1950, the Pope deplored the 'alarming spread of revolutionary ideas' among the worker priests. He followed this up with a decree three years later, which allowed the movement to continue but barred union membership and restricted those involved to part-time work only. Meanwhile, he took steps to rein in the theologians who had inspired it, such as the Jesuit Dominique Chenu, whose talk of 'liberating Christianity from the Church' had become a radical catchphrase.

Supporters of the worker priests, who had built on the experience of clergy in Nazi forced labour camps, blamed right-wing pressure on the Vatican. Yet a compromise of sorts was not long in coming. Over half the movement's members chose to remain in factory work, while just a year later, in 1954, the Mission de France was honoured with a personal prelature at its centre in Pontigny.

The *'Nouvelle Théologie'* represented by the worker priests survived and prospered. Christians remained at the centre of reform programmes throughout Europe, and there was no shortage of radical priests, or *prêtres contestataires*, to give their efforts a religious sanction.

The Catholic Church would continue to be burdened by its response to the twin ideologies of fascism-Nazism and communism. Both had been essentially anti-Christian. But both had approached religion in different ways. Communism had rejected Christianity and tried to impose its own belief system instead. Nazism and fascism, by contrast, had sought to harness Christianity and obtain Church support. This helped explain the Church's confusion, and why it appeared to condemn communism more severely. The Church was destined to play its part in the collapse of communism. But had it contributed enough to the collapse of Nazism and fascism? That question would keep historians busy.

Having come close to stagnation in the early twentieth century, however, after decades of storm and tempest, the river of Christianity was flowing again. It was a Christianity, furthermore, which had been purified by its experiences, and which was now ready to be shaped and applied in creative new directions.

CHAPTER 4

Rebirth and Recovery

*Our religion, as it mixes with events of the world, gener-
ates new things – now a kind of art, now a form of
science, now liberty, now a theory of egalitarianism.
Above all, throughout our history, it has been of the first
importance that our church has not merely launched or
inspired great human enterprises, only too often to watch
them break away and sail off on their own account; it has
not merely leavened society generally with its principles
of Christian charity, for example, so that the enemies of
religion have owed more to it than they have ever been
able to recognise; but, by being here, the church stands
as a perpetual centre from which the whole process can
be forever starting over again.*

The optimistic words of Herbert Butterfield, an English historian, caused surprise in 1950. Amid the destruction of war and
revolution, it was easy to believe Christianity had run its
course. Yet the world and humanity were more complex.
Butterfield's much-quoted advice, 'Hold to Christ, and for the
rest be totally uncommitted', suggested there was still a place
for Christian conviction in a Europe grown coldly cynical
towards great ideals. 'Those who preach the Gospel, nurse the
pieties, spread New Testament love and affirm the spiritual
nature of Man,' he was sure, 'are keeping open the spring
from which new things will still arise.'[1]

New and hopeful things were indeed on the way. Although
the Second World War had left deep geopolitical divisions in
its wake, the first moves were also being made towards a new
international system. The United Nations and its agencies
were at the centre. But eleven separate fora for regional inte-

gration, from Latin America to Asia, were also in the making. If security and economics were the driving force, efforts were also underway to define common values on a wider scale.

That was particularly true in Western Europe. When a European Coal and Steel Community was founded in 1952, it was a risky but imaginative initiative. The stated aim was to neutralise traditional inter-state hostilities, especially between France and Germany, by placing strategic coal and steel industries under a single co-ordinating authority. The heavy industries of the Ruhr Valley had been the motor for pre-war German power, while both countries had fought over the coal resources of Alsace-Lorraine. But Italy signed up to the Community too. So did Belgium, the Netherlands and Luxembourg, who had formed their own Benelux customs union in 1948. The goals, in short, were a lot wider. The Treaty of Paris which launched the ECSC set out the central theory behind it. By establishing 'common bases for economic development', the Community would 'raise the standard of living and further the works of peace'. Integration in one area would encourage integration in others – where economics led, politics would follow. Governments were resolved, the Treaty noted, 'to substitute for age-old rivalries the merging of their essential interests; to create, by establishing an economic community, the basis for a broader and deeper community among peoples long divided by bloody conflicts, and to lay the foundations for institutions which will give direction to a destiny henceforward shared'.[2]

The Community's mastermind, Robert Schuman (1886-1963), believed the project would make future wars between France and Germany 'not merely unthinkable, but materially impossible'. 'Europe will not be made all at once, or according to a single plan,' the French statesman noted in his 1950 Declaration. 'It will be built through concrete achievements which first create a *de facto* solidarity.'[3]

This was highly idealistic. While recognising the importance of economic co-operation, critics dismissed Schuman's deterministic assumptions, insisting the realities were a lot more complex. Schuman conceded that political and cultural animosities could not resolve themselves – decades of single-minded effort would be needed. But it was worth starting that effort now, he insisted, with some visible, measurable tasks, which might, over time, build up into a workable long-term strategy.

Talk of a united Europe was nothing new. In 1942, the British prime minister, Winston Churchill, had proposed a 'United States of Europe', functioning under a 'Council of Europe' with shared armed forces and judicial authorities, and a joint commitment to the free movement of people, goods and services.[4] The Organisation for European Economic Co-operation, which disbursed Marshall Plan aid from its Paris headquarters, had provided a test-case by promoting a free trade federation. Yet there were historic precedents as well. Some of these were hardly encouraging. Charlemagne, the Habsburgs and Napoleon had tried in their time to 'unite Europe,' while even Hitler had talked of a 'European house'. But a Europe without conflict, freed from the dominance of any single power, had long been the dream of intellectuals.

As long ago as 1306, a French diplomat, Pierre Dubois, had advocated a 'Christian Republic' under a permanent assembly of princes, with the papacy as a final court of appeal. In the fifteenth century, the Bohemian king, George of Podebrady, had called for a European confederation against the Turks, governed by a rotating assembly and majority decision-making. In the early seventeenth century, the Duc de Sully had come up with a 'Grand Design' for a new balance of power, involving a European senate and continent-wide administration. Meanwhile, European unity had been taken up by thinkers from Rousseau and Bentham, to Kant and Saint-Simon, all chiming in with their own proposals for lasting peace and stability. Most had been religiously inspired. 'Without losing their glorious individuality, the nations will merge closely into a higher unity and form the fraternity of Europe,' Victor Hugo predicted optimistically in 1848, the year of revolutions. It was, Hugo had insisted, 'a necessity on which all philosophers agree'. 'Two huge groups will be seen, the United States of America and United States of Europe, holding out their hands to one another across the ocean.'[5]

The quest for unity had become especially urgent after the Great War (1914–1918). The League of Nations, founded in 1920, had acted as a magnet for regional initiatives. One of these, the Pan-European Union, worked for a settlement of outstanding disputes, arguing the case for a customs union and federal constitution. It failed to gain a mass following. But the initiative attracted the interest of cultural figures from the German composer, Richard Strauss, to the Spanish philosopher of 'vital reason', José Ortega y Gasset, as well as from politicians from Eduard Herriot to Tomáš Masaryk. With the Second World War exposing the weakness of the previous inter-state order, the search for lasting solutions now became a top priority. Having dominated world trade and finance since the nineteenth century, in empires stretching across the globe, Europe had been brought down twice by its own internal conflicts. The costs of nationalism and xenophobia were obvious.

Even after the war, interests and perspectives remained far apart. There had, in reality, been no winners from the six-year conflagration. Territorial borders had been redrawn, industry destroyed, identities and loyalties severely shaken. At such a fraught and fragile moment, few Europeans had the energy and vision for grand ideas which would yield no immediate benefits. Spain was under the dictatorship of Franco, Portugal under Salazar. Austria, like Germany, was divided into separate occupation zones and would declare neutrality in 1955. The Scandinavian countries had set up a Legislative Co-operation Committee and were gearing up to a full-scale Nordic Council in 1953. France was preoccupied with involvements from Algeria to Indochina and uneasy about its role in NATO. Britain had seen its national wealth slashed by three-quarters during the war and was busy phasing out its empire and introducing programmes of nationalisation and social welfare under a new Labour government.

Schuman's vision of the European Coal and Steel Community as 'a first step in the federation of Europe' generated little public enthusiasm. As the advantages became clear, however, support for the project picked up. By 1958, when a European Economic Community (EEC) was founded, the whole European project was being conceived on a much broader scale. Several continent-wide initiatives occurred in parallel. A European Defence Community attempted to bring German forces into an integrated European army in 1952, giving way two years later to a Western European Union committed to a joint defence, as well as 'unity and progressive integration'. In the meantime, ten European countries formed a Council of Europe in 1949, with a statute envisaging 'common action in economic, social, cultural, scientific, legal and administrative matters'.[6]

None of these would have as much practical impact as the new EEC. In 1955, the six original member-states had promised to work for a 'united Europe' by developing common institutions, fusing national economies, creating a common market and progressively harmonising their social policies'.[7] The 1955 Treaty of Rome set a timeframe of twelve years to achieve this.

*   *   *

Had Christianity played its part, as Butterfield claimed, in inspiring this 'great human enterprise'? Could it still lay claim to being the 'perpetual centre'? In its Catholic, Orthodox or Protestant forms, it was still firmly present as a religion in Europe. State Churches were established in Britain and Scandinavia, while several countries, from Ireland to Greece, reserved a special place for churches in their constitutions. Yet in cultural and moral terms, Christianity would now be competing with new secular mentalities and ethical attitudes. On the public scene, it had withdrawn from its once-established institutional position. It was represented now, if at all, as a source of authority above political divisions.

In short, Christianity's role was changing. Yet it was still present. The ECSC's Paris Treaty had contained traces of the social teaching set out in Pius XI's *Quadragesimo Anno* in the 1930s. Article 1 stressed the need for states to act 'within the limits of their respective powers' and to ensure improved working conditions and 'equal access to the sources of production'. Such formulations owed much to Robert Schuman, a devout life-long Catholic.

Born in Luxembourg, Schuman had been educated in Alsace as a German, changing his nationality after the Great War but continuing to speak with a German accent. He had escaped from a German prison in 1942 after resigning from France's collaborationist Vichy government and, when the war ended, had been elected to parliament for France's Mouvement Républicain Populaire, a party formed largely by Catholic fighters from the Resistance. He became France's premier in 1947, later serving as Foreign Minister and first president in 1958–60 of the EEC Assembly.

In his testimony, *Pour l'Europe* (1963), Schuman claimed to have gained inspiration for a new geopolitical vision of Europe from the 'universality of the Christian faith', and acknowledged his debt to Catholic thinkers from Maurice Blondel to Jacques Maritain. He paid a price for his Christian convictions. The German chancellor, Konrad Adenauer (1876–1967), recognised that the European Coal and Steel Community belonged 'to the moral order', noting how Schuman lived a celibate, ascetic life, attending Mass daily – a 'saint in an official's suit'. But his fellow-German, the Socialist leader Kurt Schumacher, condemned the united Europe project as a mix of 'Kapitalismus, Klerikalismus, Konservatismus, Kartelle'. France's own future president, Charles de Gaulle, concurred with the doubters. What would such a 'Community' mean, de Gaulle wondered, but 'giving modern economic, social, strategic and cultural shape to the work of the emperor Charlemagne'?[8]

It was a fair comment. The territory covered by the EEC's six member-states did indeed closely correspond with the early medieval ruler's dominions. Yet Schuman was not alone. The united Europe's other founding fathers shared the same Christian outlook.

The first president of the ECSC's High Authority, Jean Monnet, had been a deputy secretary-general of the inter-war League of Nations when his fellow-Frenchman, Aristide Briand, had called for a European confederation to ensure the Continent's 'rational organisation'. In a 1930 memorandum, Briand had used terms such as 'European Union' and 'Common Market' while outlining proposals for regional and social policies. Although thrown aside in the rush to war, such ideas had lived on in Monnet's mind. Of course, these were complex issues – 'Europe' had any number of definitions. Alongside every enthusiast for unity, there was a sceptic who questioned whether unity was possible or desirable. By 1945, however, France had gone to war with Germany three times in seven decades. It was worth making sacrifices, even great ones, Monnet concluded, to ensure against a repeat of such catastrophes in future. 'Europe will rediscover the leading role she used to play in the world, which she lost because she was divided,' the French statesman told Adenauer in 1949. 'Europe's unity will not put an end to her diversity – quite the reverse. That rich diversity will benefit civilisation.'[9]

Adenauer shared Monnet's vision. He had started his political career with Germany's Catholic Centre Party, which had emerged in the inter-war Weimar Republic as a central force between extremes. As mayor of Cologne from 1917, the year of the Bolshevik revolution, he had opposed the rise of Nazism, hiding out in a monastery at Maria Laach when opposition groups were suppressed in 1933. It was here, reading *Rerum Novarum* and *Quadragesimo Anno*, that Adenauer claimed to have discovered 'a comprehensive and coherent programme' inspired by 'belief in an order willed by God which was perfectly practicable in terms of modern society'.[10]

Narrowly surviving arrest after Klaus von Stauffenberg's bomb plot against Hitler in 1944, Adenauer went on to found Germany's Christian Democratic Union amid the shame and bitterness of 1945. When a Federal Republic was founded three years later out of the US, British and French occupation zones, he led the CDU to victory over Schumacher's Social Democrats in Bundestag elections. As Chancellor for the next fourteen years, he presided over the restoration of West German sovereignty under a 1954 constitution, as well as over his country's admission to NATO and the rebuilding of international links. He also spearheaded Germany's economic recovery, using the 'social market' models pioneered by a fellow-Christian Democrat, Ludwig Erhard.

Like Schuman and Monnet, Adenauer drew energy and inspiration from his Christianity, seeing this as the utimate source of political coherence and moderation. The Christian *Weltanschauung*, or worldview, meant 'support for human dignity, combating totalitarianism and advancing integration'. The central remaining question was whether Europe would be characterised by a Christian or non-Christian vision. 'A Christian view of life must once more take the place of materialist beliefs,' Adenauer wrote in the CDU's programme. 'Christian ethics must become the determining factor in the reconstruction of the state and the delimitation of its powers and authority. It must be the guiding principle for defining the rights and duties of the individual, as well as for economic and social life and relations between the nations.'[11]

Adenauer's Italian contemporary, Alcide De Gasperi (1881–1954), would have agreed wholeheartedly. Coming from the deeply Catholic Trentino region, which had been Austrian-ruled before the war, De Gasperi's first experiences had been with Church-related youth groups and newspapers. In 1919, he had co-founded Italy's Catholic Popular Party, only to find himself arrested when the party was suppressed by Mussolini's fascists seven years later. Released from prison at Pius XI's intervention, De Gasperi joined the anti-fascist resistance while working as a Vatican librarian. He became secretary-general of a newly formed Christian Democratic party in 1943 and Italian premier from 1945 to 1953.

The Christian Democrats inherited the old Partito Popular's peasant and lower middle-class constituency. But they were suspected by Church leaders of seeking tactical political compromises. In the run-up to Italy's election in 1948, an alternative *Comitato Civico* was set up by a Catholic medical doctor, Luigi Gedda, to oppose De Gasperi and build a *unione sacra* of right-wing forces. Using Catholic Action networks set up in the 1860s to oppose Garibaldi's *Risorgimento*, Gedda's movement quickly gained two million members and was active in two-thirds of Italy's 27,000 parishes. The evils of the day, Gedda argued, were all traceable to a basic flaw in European civilisation which had led from Protestantism, via the French Revolution, to liberalism and communism – a communism now poised to 'cross the borders of Italy and poison our people'.[12]

De Gasperi was unperturbed. A limited *apertura a sinistra*, or opening to the left, he insisted, was essential for an effective coalition. It could achieve crucial political results without requiring any sacrifice of principle.

In the event, Italy's Communists were not readmitted to De Gasperi's government. But the politician continued to resist pressure to join forces with Gedda's movement. When the

Christian Democrats triumphed in the elections of 1948 and 1952, his stance seemed to have been vindicated. At a Catholic conference in Brussels in 1948, De Gasperi championed the cause of European unity as the best defence against Soviet domination. But his Christian motivation went much deeper. In letters to his wife during his four-term prison sentence in the 1920s, he had described his spiritual odyssey via the biblical psalms to St Augustine and St Thomas à Kempis. Europe, he had no doubt, had been shaped by Christianity. But Christianity had also created conditions for pluralist democracy. It had provided the impulse for a new generation to rally around the ideals of peace, fraternity and co-operation. In 1954, De Gasperi succeeded the Belgian Socialist and Catholic, Paul-Henri Spaak, as chairman of the ECSC's Council of Ministers. When he died the same year, the future Pope John XXIII described him as a politician 'inspired by a biblical vision of life, by service to God, Church and homeland'.[13]

* * *

It was thanks to the personal convictions of the EEC's founding fathers that Christianity's influence became tangible in Community affairs. The British historian, Arnold Toynbee, recalled conversations with Schuman, Adenauer and De Gasperi during a meeting of the Council of Europe in 1953. 'These two great pioneers and architects of European unity told me about the common experiences which had helped them rise above national grievances and discover wider horizons of thinking and feeling,' Toynbee noted. 'It became clear to me that what brought them together was their religion. Catholics simply cannot concentrate only on the affairs of their own nation.'[14]

The Council of Europe's 1949 statute recorded the devotion of member-states 'to the spiritual and moral values which are the common heritage of their peoples'. These values were 'the true source of individual freedom, political liberty and the rule of law', the statute added; and it was these very principles which formed 'the basis of all genuine democracy'.[15] The Council's European Convention on Human Rights, signed in

Rome on 4 November 1950, described fundamental freedoms as the 'foundation of peace and justice in the world'. Every European had a 'right to freedom of thought, conscience and religion', the Convention noted, including 'freedom to change his religion or belief, and freedom, either alone or in community with others, in public or private, to manifest his religion'. Citizens also had a right to refuse to act against their own consciences. The Convention set up a Court of Human Rights, with a judge from each member-state. In 1952, its religious freedom clause was extended to enshrine the right of parents to educate their children 'in conformity with their own religious and philosophical convictions'.[16]

Three years later, the Council adopted the flag which would later be taken over by the European Union, a circle of twelve gold stars on a blue background. Designed by Paul Levy, it was chosen over several others, apparently evoking the twelve stars around the head of the Virgin Mary in St John the Divine's prophecy – 'a woman clothed with the sun, with the moon under her feet, and on her head a crown of twelve stars, who was with child and cried aloud in her pangs of birth' (Revelation 12:1–2).

Christian influences were also evident in the Treaty of Rome which set out the EEC's common policies in commerce, agriculture, transport, social affairs and the environment. The text made no reference to religion. But its stated objectives – 'common action to eliminate the barriers which divide Europe', 'steady expansion, balanced trade and fair competition', 'pooling resources to preserve and strengthen peace and unity' – were Christian priorities too. So was the Treaty's overall aim – 'to lay the foundations for an ever closer union among the peoples of Europe.'

The Vatican welcomed the Treaty of Rome as the dawn of a new era. Key aspects of the document reflected Christian social teaching even more directly. One was its concept of sovereignty, inherited from Aquinas, a sovereignty which resided in the people and was merely 'expressed' through governments and institutions. Another was its stress on subsidiarity, a notion elaborated in *Quadragesimo Anno*. The EEC's institutions – its European Commission, Council of Ministers, Court of Justice and Parliamentary Assembly –

derived their authority from governments, rather than citizens, the Treaty made clear. But authority and power were to be exercised at the lowest possible level. Member-states would keep their own identities, laws, military forces, taxation systems and symbols.

* * *

If there was a school of Christian philosophy which most inspired the founding fathers, it was the Personalism associated with Jacques Maritain (1882–1973) and Emmanuel Mounier (1905–1950). As the grandson of France's anticlerical ideologue, Jules Favre, Maritain came to Catholicism via circuitous paths. One was the philosopher and psychologist, Henri Bergson, who had attempted to resolve the conflict between free will and determinism by stressing the role of personal intuition. Another was the theological and philosophical system of Aquinas, and the search for ways of applying this to modern life. An early association with the extremist Charles Maurras had ended abruptly with Pius XI's condemnation of *Action Française* in 1927. Thereafter, Maritain had vigorously opposed any Church accomodation with the authoritarian, anti-Semitic regimes of Germany, Italy and Spain. His aim, he said, was to reconcile 'the vision of Joseph de Maistre, the Catholic arch-reactionary, with that of Lamennais in the higher unity of the supreme wisdom of which St Thomas Aquinas is the herald in our time'.[17]

Maritain's key work, *L'Humanisme Intégrale* (1936), appeared amid the sense of impending crisis reflected in the agonising of Martin Heidegger, Karl Jaspers, Karl Barth and Edmund Husserl over the 'soul of western man'. Against this troubled backdrop, Maritain saw the roots of contemporary malaise in a shift away from Christianity – from a 'God-centred culture' to an 'anthropocentric humanism' obsessed with personal liberty. History's revolutionary movements had appropriated the Christian ideals of freedom and dignity. Like all revolutionary initiatives, however, they had fatally strayed from their first positive impulses, unleashing the de-humanising forces which had led inexorably to the atheistic materialism of Left and Right. It was a case, Maritain argued, of 'Christian impulses gone astray'. What was needed now was a 'new historical ideal', a reborn humanism under the sovereignty of God.

> Is it not a sign of the confusion of ideas which today extends over the whole world that we see such one-time Christian impulses aiding the propaganda of cultural ideas which are diametrically opposed to Christianity? The time is ripe for Christians to bring things back to the fount of truth, reintegrating in the plenitude of their first origins those desires for justice and that nostalgia for communion (now so misdirected) in which the world finds comfort for its sorrow; thus raising a cultural and temporal force for Christian inspiration able to act in history and come to the aid of men ... Then we could work to substitute for the inhuman system which is dying before our eyes a new form of civilisation which would be characterised by an integral humanism, and which would represent the outline of a new Christian order no longer sacred but secular in its forms.[18]

This 'integral humanism' was Maritain's master-concept. It had to be one which rejected the theocratic politics of the Middle Ages, where the sacred dominated everything and left little room for personal freedom. But it had to shun bourgeois individualism as well. The only outcome could be a new philosophy of the human person – a philosophy suited to democratic, pluralistic societies, in which politics, economics and social life were animated by Christianity.[19]

Maritain's younger protégé, Emmanuel Mounier, founded a journal, *L'Esprit*, in 1932, a year after *Quadragesimo Anno*, with a programme which rejected both Marxism and capitalism. 'Capitalism reduces the person to a state of servitude irreconcilable with the dignity of man,' the manifesto explained. 'It orientates all classes and the whole personality towards the possession of money, the single desire for which chokes the modern soul. Marxism is the rebel son of capitalism.'[20] Mounier gave credit to communism for rejecting exploitation and attempting a planned economy. But the answer to both communism and fascism, he believed, lay in a 'communitarian Personalist revolution', which would counteract the spiritual and moral bankruptcy of the West. His vision was of a new civilisation in which both Christians and non-believers could find their place by giving primacy to the spiritual. He rejected the atheistic existentialism of his fellow-Frenchman, Jean-Paul Sartre, believing it cut away the ground for any morality, just as Marx's historical materialism had done. But he also concurred with Nietzsche that Christianity had become a 'religion of the weak', of listless people cowed by moral intimidation and authoritarian demands for humility. If Christians were encountering contempt, it was because they failed 'to realise the truth of which they are the bearers'.

The work of Maritain and Mounier laid the groundwork for a new and effective social Catholicism with the capacity to bring Christians back into an active engagement with modern society. Their Personalism appeared to provide the longed-for Christian answer to liberalism and socialism, by upholding the dignity and value of the human person against all systems which diminished them. But it also meant extending the individual's role in the world to a responsibility for others and the problems of contemporary society. Withdrawing from the world was no longer a valid or realistic option.

This kind of Personalism was open to ideas and activities outside the Catholic Church. *L'Esprit* had Jewish and Orthodox collaborators, such as the Russian-born sociologist Georges Gurvitch and writer Nikolai Berdyaev, whose *Nouveau Moyen-Age*, published in 1922, the year he was exiled, called for Orthodoxy to be renewed through an encounter with European culture.

The rebuilding of Europe was a preoccupation of *L'Esprit* contributors too, from the Swiss Denis de Rougemont to the French Gabriel Marcel and Jean Lacroix. Maritain had supported federalism in Europe, seeing a rediscovered Christianity as its best means of defending human values. This was a platform, Maritain was certain, which non-Christians could support too. As Charles Péguy had argued, the social revolution would be 'a moral revolution, or none at all'. It could go further and deeper than the secular radicalism currently on offer, whether via the anti-capitalist revolution preached by Lenin, or the welfare revolution advocated by Keynes.

Maritain's metaphysical explorations gained a wide readership among students and intellectuals, and attracted the interest of theorists across the political spectrum. They also provided an important Christian justification for emerging European priorities. As for democracy, Maritain believed this owed its very premises to Christianity: brotherhood and equality, the inherent dignity of the person, concern for bettering the human condition. Without Christianity's values, furthermore, democracy would quickly degenerate into extremes. Maritain blamed Descartes for forcing a distinction between the human mind and body; it had encouraged materialistic individualism by separating man's spiritual and material identities. He blamed Rousseau for making matters worse by viewing the individual as no more than an atom in a society ruled by the general will. In this way, democracy had fallen short of its promises. The political democracy which predominated in contemporary Europe needed to be transformed into a social democracy founded on Gospel precepts.

Mounier went further. In the Cold War atmosphere after the War, he moved closer to Marxism, believing the communist movement could be an agent of positive resistance to US capitalism. Visiting Warsaw in 1946, he regretted that Polish Catholics remained 'sunk in bourgeois traditionalism' and had not used their 'historic opportunity to reconcile the Church with socialism'. Mounier believed in communism's *mystère* – 'the central force which established its power in men's hearts'. It had brought a possibility of redemption, thanks to the faith in man and history which it shared with Christianity. The two were, in fact, bound together – 'with a rigour and fraternity which goes well beyond class struggles'. Communism was devalued by its narrow, stultifying atheism. It needed Christianity to give it the *intériorité* which it lacked. Yet it was important to realise that the Christianity which communists rejected was not authentic Christianity, but the corrupted, complacent 'bourgeois Christianity' represented by the forces of wealth and power. In its place, there was a 'true Christianity' which had retained its 'sense of Being' and commitment to love. This was the Personalism which communists could work with as they embarked on their 'great and total exploration of the new man', in whom eternal values could be 'saved and transfigured'.[21]

*   *   *

Unfortunately for Mounier, events soon told against the notion of a humanised communist order. When the Communist Party seized power in Czechoslovakia through a coup in 1948, he was forced to admit he had encountered an 'iron curtain of ideas and feelings' instead. Far from embracing dialogue, the Communist regimes had hardened themselves into an 'airtight system'.[22] The French writer had not been alone in hoping for a very different outcome.

When the World Council of Churches was founded at Amsterdam that same year, incorporating 200 Protestant, Orthodox, Anglican and Old Catholic Churches, it was in an atmosphere of intense debate over the social priorities facing contemporary Christians. This occupied many inter-church meetings. One of the most incisive took place in Amsterdam between the future US Secretary of State, John Foster Dulles, representing the US Presbyterian Church, and Josef Hromádka, the Protestant dean of Prague's Theology Faculty. Hromádka had welcomed the imposition of communist rule, seeing it, not unlike Mounier, as the culmination of a historic struggle for freedom. As for the ruthless repression now being meted out in his own country, this was a necessary price, Hromádka believed, for laying the foundations of a just society. Communism embodied, 'although under an atheistic form, much of the social impetus of the living Church'. Once it was secure, humane principles would be observed. The challenge of the 'Church in socialism' was to ensure this happened as soon as possible. 'Many barbarians are coming of age through the Communist movement and aspiring to a place in the sun,' Hromádka told delegates in Amsterdam. 'The Church must make a new beginning, start from the bottom up and work for a new society, a new order.'[23]

Hromádka was never a simple collaborator. But he misjudged the workings of communist power and became one of Lenin's 'useful idiots'. Such delusions were commonplace. Russia's Orthodox Church joined the World Council of Churches in 1961, the year the Soviet Communist Party listed the qualities expected of good Communist citizens: patriotism, honesty, moral integrity, protection of the family, conscientious work for the community. Were these not also the virtues of democracy, the very same Christian values underlying European civilisation? One man who apparently thought so was Patriarch Justinian Marina of Romania, who urged Orthodox followers to undertake a 'social apostolate' while thousands of Greek Catholics and other minority Christians were languishing in Communist prisons. 'Christ is a new man,' the patriarch told his flock in the 1950s. 'The new man is a Soviet man. Therefore Christ is a Soviet man.'

> Can we not see in the present social order the most sacred principles of the Gospel being put into practice? Is not the sharing of goods, thus excluding them from the exploiters, better? Do we not recognise that for 2000 years the Church has counselled men with riches to lay up their treasure in heaven and not on earth? Have we not told them they are but administrators of their weath, and not its masters? Let us therefore be loyal and recognise that the state leadership has brought peace to men.[24]

It required an awareness of the ways of disinformation to grasp that such communist ideals, however high-sounding, had no grounding in objective laws and ethics. They were mere words; and their meaning and sense depended on the ideological whims of Communist officials.

The WCC's grand inter-church pretensions were criticised as little more than a cosmetic surface gesture. Opponents accused it of pursuing a selective moral agenda and failing to represent Christian opinion. When it came to justice and peace, they argued, practical ecumenical links at local level were of much greater importance. It was largely at Orthodox insistence that the Council systematically ignored the persecution of Christians in Eastern Europe. At the same time, it criticised western governments and supported liberation movements in Africa and Asia, fuelling suspicion that it had become a tool for Soviet interests. The cause of ecumenism was tarnished by the Council's political and ideological accents.[25]

* * *

It did not, however, die completely. Attempts had been under-way to bring churches together since the late nineteenth century, and missionary work had been a key impulse. The first World Missionary Conference at Edinburgh in 1910 had been attended by 1,200 Christians from 160 organisations, and had brought pledges of greater inter-church co-operation in spreading the Gospel. Holding back Islam had been a shared interest at the time, whereas the concern had widened by the 1950s to finding a united, coherent Christian response to current dilemmas in the wake of the destructive nationalism unleashed by two world wars. It was a largely Protestant matter. Orthodox Churches continued to have doubts, while Roman Catholics remained aloof. But Pope Pius XII allowed dialogue to happen and showed a tolerant attitude to modern theological and scriptural research.

However problematic, ecumenical initiatives took place against a background of renewed church membership, coupled with attempts to update structures and liturgies. In England, where the Anglo-Catholic ascendancy was slowly passing to Evangelicals, the Anglican Church set up specialist ministries as part of a wave of reforms. Greater concern was being shown for social issues, while a new generation of Christian writers such as C.S. Lewis and Dorothy L. Sayers rose to the intellectual forefront.

The most seismic changes, however, were about to occur in Catholicism. Here too, it was widely believed that hostility to Christianity was not necessarily an integral feature of new ideologies. The Church had condemned the French Revolution and aspects of Enlightenment thought. The ideological move-ments generated by both had, in turn, viewed the Church as a hostile force. But had the Church not itself exacerbated this confrontation? Had it not embroiled itself in areas where it should not have been present, proffering solutions to earthly problems where it could claim no special insight? The result had been a spiral of misunderstandings and conflicts. But did the humanistic ideals of the radicals not have something in common with Christianity after all?

Questions like these would prove bitterly divisive. But it would be thanks to a new pope, John XXIII, drawing on the work of Maritain and others, that Europe's Roman Catholic

Church completed its transition from conservative paternalism to social humanitarianism, positioning itself for a final healing of the rift between Christian social teaching and modern democratic values. Perhaps that healing could have been attempted earlier, when humanity plunged to its lowest level in the atrocities of the Holocaust, and came to realise with the clarity of penitence that ideal societies were a utopian illusion. Yet the shock had made Christianity more open to dialogue. The first fruits of that new openness were about to be seen.

As a Vatican nuncio, Pope John had followed Pius XII's hard line on Communism. In his first encyclical, *Ad Petri cathedram* (1959), eight months after his election, he warned Christians to avoid errors which entered 'the bloodstream of society as would a plague', and to shun the 'false principles' which threatened to 'destroy the basis of Christianity and civilisation'.[26] There were, nevertheless, immediate hints of a change in style and direction. Another encyclical the same year, *Princeps Pastorum*, acknowledged that Church leaders had themselves at times committed faults. 'There would be no need for sermons if our lives were shining; there would be no need for words if we bore witness to our deeds,' the document quoted St John Chrysostom. 'There would be no more pagans if we were true Christians.'[27]

The next major text, *Mater et Magistra* (1961), appeared on the seventieth anniversary of Leo XIII's *Rerum Novarum*, and contained enough sharp language about injustices and inequalities to suggest a real shift in the Vatican's position. This time, the emphasis was on structural solutions, much more than the charity and goodwill urged by previous popes. *Mater et Magistra* reaffirmed Pius XII's condemnation of communism and socialism. But it also recalled Marx's contemptuous charge that the Church took no interest in social concerns 'other than to preach resignation to the poor and generosity to the rich'. A radical transformation had occurred in the past twenty years, John XXIII said. This made it essential to reflect on how Catholic social principles were being applied.[28]

The Pope's conciliatory tone drew positive reactions from the Soviet Union. At a 1961 Communist Party Congress, the new general secretary, Nikita Khrushchev, insisted 'peaceful coexistence' was the main aim of Soviet foreign policy. The creation of NATO and rearming of Germany, he added, had made war with the West no longer inevitable. Communism's ultimate victory remained assured. But care had to be taken to prevent capitalism from unleashing a nuclear conflagration in its death throes. Budding anti-war movements in Western Europe and the US offered an opportunity. So did the Catholic Church under an 'anti-Western pope'. Khrushchev wondered whether 'fervent Catholics' like Adenauer and the US President, John F. Kennedy, would grasp the Pope's 'admonition' to peace and disarmament. 'The head of the Catholic Church takes into account the feelings of millions of Catholics in all parts of the world who are uneasy about the military preparations of the imperialists,' the Soviet Party boss added. 'John XXIII honours reason when he exhorts governments against a general catastrophe and makes them aware of the immense responsibility they have towards history.'[29]

When a Soviet threat to deploy missiles in Fidel Castro's Cuba brought the Soviet Union and US to the brink of war in October 1962, the Pope sent appeals to both in a much-reported peace initiative. Khrushchev backed down and pulled the missiles out. John XXIII's intervention, he claimed, had been 'the only gleam of hope. It demonstrated that the Church's aim was truly to 'serve all humanity'. Because of this, Khrushchev now wished to 'extend contacts' with the Vatican.

There were other benefits from what John XXIII called these 'unmistakeable signs of deep understanding'. When a new Vatican Council was convened that October, the Pope made clear that restoring Christian unity would be its key objective. A specially created Vatican secretariat approached the Russian Orthodox Church about participating. The Moscow Patriarchate refused, insisting the Pope had no right to call an ecumenical council, and that sending Orthodox observers would wrongly imply recognition of his primacy. When the Council opened, however, two Russian Orthodox representatives suddenly showed up. The Kremlin had pressured Patriarch Alexei I to change his mind.

Of the 2,449 bishops who attended Vatican II to map out future Catholic priorities, fewer than half were from Europe, a sign of the Church's shifting demographic balance. Despite

this, the Council played a vital role in fostering and highlighting links between East and West. With other Communist
regimes also allowing Church leaders to participate, the
Council was used as an occasion for concessions, including
the appointment of new bishops and release of imprisoned
prelates. When the Pope received Khrushchev's daughter and
son-in-law at the Vatican in March 1963, their meeting faced
strong opposition within the Church. But for all its nebulous-
ness, John XXIII's charm offensive put East-West unity firmly
on the Church's agenda, at a time when the attention of
secular governments was restricted to their own halves of
Europe.

When a new encyclical appeared that April, nine-tenths of
its references were to the teachings of Pius XII. But *Pacem in
terris* showed the Church's position had changed. The Pope
had strong words about the East-West military confrontation,
demanding that the arms race be stopped and nuclear weapons
banned. But disarmament, he added, must reach 'right down
into men's hearts'. Inter-state relations must be settled 'in a
rational way by appealing to truth, justice and the spirit of
brotherhood'.[30]

The encyclical condemned the violation of human rights
and endorsed freedom, self-determination and democracy.
'The age-old ideas,' it noted, 'which led to some men being
given second-class citizenship whilst others were allotted a
privileged rank because of their economic and social status,
their sex or their position in the state, are now outdated.' In
its most famous passage, the document then demonstrated how
Catholics could co-operate in useful causes with non-
Christians – those who retained a 'natural moral integrity':

> We must make a clear distinction between false philosophical
> theories about the nature, origin and purpose of the universe
> and of man, and the practical measures that have been put into
> operation as a result of these theories, in social and economic
> life, in cultural matters and in the management of the state. For
> whereas theories, once formulated, remain unalterably fixed
> and frozen in the words that express them, the measures to
> which they give rise are constantly subject to alteration as
> circumstances change. Besides, who will deny that good and
> praiseworthy elements can be found in such measures in so far

as they conform to the rules of right reason and reflect the lawful aspirations of men?[31]

This was certainly a long way from the formulations of John XXIII's predecessors. The encyclical's distinctions – error and victim, theory and practice – could be traced back to St Augustine. But the influence of Personalism was visible, too. It would be acknowledged directly in future Vatican texts.

* * *

Vatican II went on to set a baseline for Catholic thinking in the modern age. The Church's Dogmatic Constitution, *Lumen Gentium*, spoke of a 'pilgrim Church' ready to enter communion with all forms of culture which were based on authentic values. Meanwhile, its Pastoral Constitution, *Gaudium et Spes*, spoke of a 'new age of human history', of moral extremes and sharp dichotomies, in which the social order would require constant improvement if it was to 'grow in freedom towards a more humane equilibrium'. People were repudiating political systems which hindered liberty and abused authority for the benefit of 'governing classes'. Today's Church, the 'people of God', proclaimed the rights of man. It knew true peace could only be assured when human welfare and dignity were recognised and protected. Yet it also had to undergo changes to fulfil its 'earthly responsibilities', recognising that it had faults too, and could not answer every question.

> Whatever history's judgement on these shortcomings, we cannot ignore them and must combat them earnestly. The Church also realises how much it needs the maturing influence of centuries of past experience in order to work out its relationship with the world ... By reason of her role and competence, the Church is not identified with any political community nor bound by ties to any political system. It is at once the sign and the safeguard of the transcendental dimension of the human person.[32]

There was much else which seemed to confirm the historic shift in the Church's centre of gravity. Vatican II's Decree on

Ecumenism, *Unitatis redintegratio*, recognised the rich heritage of Christianity's eastern Churches, to which Catholicism was indebted in liturgy, spirituality, jurisprudence and monasticism. After all, the very dogmas of the Trinity and Incarnation had been defined by ecumenical councils held in the East. The eastern Churches had suffered to preserve their faith, and were still suffering today under Communist rule. Thanks to their shared apostolic succession, however, they already enjoyed the 'closest intimacy' with the Catholic Church.

The Decree urged a rediscovery of the 'communion of faith' of the First Millennium. It was followed up in 1965 by the lifting by Pope Paul VI and Patriarch Athenagoras of Constantinople of the mutual excommunications imposed 911 years earlier. In a poignant, symbolic declaration, both leaders regretted 'the offensive words, the reproaches without foundation and the reprehensible gestures' exchanged by their predecessors in past centuries.[33]

Unitatis redintegratio called for dialogue with the Protestant Churches, too. Meanwhile, a separate declaration, *Nostra aetate*, called for closer ties with Jews, Muslims and non-Christian faiths. The Church rejected 'nothing of what is true and holy' in other religions, the declaration noted. On the contrary, it had a high regard for their 'manner of life and conduct, precepts and doctrines'. Christians should 'acknowledge, preserve and encourage the spiritual and moral truths found among non-Christians'.

> Over the centuries many quarrels and dissensions have arisen between Christians and Muslims. The sacred Council now pleads with all to forget the past, and urges that a sincere effort be made to achieve mutual understanding ... The Church reproves every form of persecution against whomsoever it may be directed. Remembering then her common heritage with the Jews and moved not by any political consideration, but solely by the religious motivation of Christian charity, she deplores all hatreds, persecutions, displays of anti-Semitism leveled at any time or from any source against the Jews.[34]

Another Decree on Religious Liberty, *Dignitatis humanae*, defended 'free enquiry' in matters of faith, and gave the green light to previously contested practices ranging from Bible analysis to the use of vernacular languages. It ruled out all discrimination against religious minorities and promised greater 'collegiality' between the Pope and local bishops in the running of the Church. There were echoes here of the Conciliar movement of the fifteenth century, which had been so decisively rejected by the Council of Trent during the Catholic Counter-Reformation. Opinions would differ sharply in years to come over what 'collegiality' should mean in practice. But an immediate consequence was the summoning of a permanent synod of bishops, which began meeting regularly to debate pastoral strategies.

Vatican II even had conciliatory, self-critical things to say about communism. Atheism often found roots, the Council acknowledged, in a 'violent protest against the evil of the world', which saw Christian 'hopes in a future life' as a barrier to human autonomy and emancipation. 'Believers can thus have more than a little to do with the rise of atheism,' *Gaudium et spes* warned. 'To the extent that they are careless about their instruction in the faith, or present its teaching falsely, or even fail in their religious, moral or social life, they must be said to conceal rather than reveal the true nature of God and religion.' Christians should learn from this. Although the Church demanded religious freedom, it also saw the value of a 'sincere and prudent dialogue' between believers and non-believers, who could work together to 'establish right order' in the world. With this in mind, the Church invited atheists 'to weigh the merits of the Gospel of Jesus Christ with an open mind'.[35]

* * *

The Second Vatican Council's summons to renewal and dialogue would be open to rival interpretations. For some Roman Catholics, it would point to ever more liberal reforms, such as the abolition of priestly celibacy. To integrists such as the French Archbishop Marcel Lefebvre, by contrast, the very call to be open to the modern world was deeply suspect. Set against a background of East-West tension and growing social fragmentation, however, the Council was a major bridge-building exercise. The Berlin Wall, built in 1961, symbolised the permanence of Europe's division. Vatican II seemed to have challenged this. In Italy, the Communist leader, Palmiro Togliatti, rejected the 'naive and erroneous conception' that religiousness would wither with the advance of knowledge and social change, and called for a 'reciprocal understanding and search for common goals' with the Catholic Church. In France, the Marxist philosopher, Roger Garaudy, saw Vatican II as a seminal event. Through dialogue with Christians, Garaudy argued, Marxists could 'rediscover beneath the myths the aspirations that brought them forth'. Through an encounter with Marxism, Christians could transform their faith from Nietzsche's 'Platonism for the masses' into a vehicle for social and political commitment.[36]

Of course, these were just words. The Church's Secretariat for Unbelievers acknowledged that differences over religion need not rule out practical agreements. But dialogue was a two-way process. It required an 'open and benevolent mind', which acknowledged 'the dignity and worth of the other person'. Whatever Communist spokesmen might say about co-operation with Catholics, their actions told a different story. As one Soviet ideologist cautioned in 1965, it certainly did not mean 'ideological compromise'.[37]

Yet it did signify a readiness on the Church's part to think beyond conventional categories and engage in debate with Christianity's opponents. John XXIII's successor, Pope Paul VI, would take this further. In 1967, a new encyclical, *Populorum progressio*, rejected systems based on 'atheist or materialist philosophy', but talked again of the need to tackle social unrest and inequality. Paul VI followed Maritain in offering a 'new humanism' – a 'solidarity in action' to counter 'the material poverty of those who lack the bare necessities of life, and the moral poverty of those crushed under the weight of their own self-love'. The encyclical 'gladly commended' trade unions, noting that free trade could be called just 'only when it conforms to the demands of social justice'. The *New York Times* called *Populorum progressio* 'strongly leftist, even Marxist in tone'.[38] However exaggerated, it was another indication of how far the Church had travelled.

Not everyone was happy with the new tone of Church documents. Catholics in Eastern Europe, knowing their own geopolitical realities, believed Vatican II reflected western perspectives. The Council had rightly spoken up for equality and social justice in the Third World. But it had said very little about the human rights violations occuring daily under communist rule in the heart of Europe. There was concern too about the Vatican's new diplomatic contacts with Eastern Europe. By the 1960s, the Catholic Church in Poland had re-emerged as a formidable force in national life, with over 60 bishops, 18,000 priests, 28,000 nuns and 4,000 students at 70 seminaries – twice the numbers of 1945. It had also risked Communist wrath by keeping East-West links open. At the close of Vatican II in 1965, the country's Roman Catholic bishops sent a letter to their German counterparts, calling for the rebuilding of friendship and trust. The text deplored the wartime crimes of the Nazis. But it also acknowledged for the first time the post-war sufferings of German civilians and ended with the much-quoted words, 'We extend our hands to you, pledge forgiveness and ask for it.'[39] The text provoked furious regime reactions. But Poland's Lutheran bishops had made a similar call for reconciliation the same year with Germany's Evangelical Church, the EKD, which had not yet been divided East and West. These were signs of the positive role religious communities could play in maintaining bonds of fraternity in a divided Europe.

Against this sensitive background, local Church leaders feared Rome's new diplomatic approaches could undermine their position. The Vatican had disapproved of Cardinal Wyszyński's accords with the Polish regime in the 1950s. In 1964 and 1966, however, it went ahead and signed its own agreements with the Communist bosses of Hungary and Yugoslavia, after no more than symbolic consultation with the local Church. A year later, Paul VI personally received the Soviet president, Nikolai Podgorny, using the tentative thaw to make conciliatory gestures to the Russian Orthodox Church.

Despite this, rights violations continued on a massive scale. All Communist regimes relied on social divisions to maintain their power. In 1968, the year protesting left-wing students were dispersed by baton-wielding police on the streets of Paris and Berlin, the Polish Party forced 20,000 surviving Jews to flee the country during an anti-Semitic campaign against 'Jews, Zionists and revisionists'. That same year, a communist-led reform movement in Czechoslovakia, the Prague Spring, was crushed by Warsaw Pact tanks. The Church and Vatican reacted late to the ensuing repression in Czechoslovakia, which saw borders closed and 1.5 million people sacked from their jobs. The 'Brezhnev Doctrine' had been unveiled, giving Communist states the right to intervene in each other's affairs. 'What the powers that be call "consolidation and normalisation" of our national life in fact brought about its utter stultification,' recorded the Slovak 'reform communist' philosopher, Miroslav Kusý. 'Anyone who does not prove suitable becomes an outsider, a person without a future. This inevitably means that the vast majority resort to hypocrisy, a "double face", the schizophrenic upbringing of their children. It leads to apathy and cynicism, the disintegration of the nation's moral fibre.'[40]

* * *

Eastern Europe's 1968 was, in most senses, the opposite of 1968 in the West. While western middle-class students discovered ideology and raged against capitalism and bourgeois lifestyles, their impoverished Eastern counterparts rejected ideology and asked for democracy and basic rights. Yet there were common elements too. Both episodes symbolised the erosion of post-war hopes in a perfect society. Both ended in a parallel disillusionment with both the capitalist and the communist systems.

By the late 1960s, western debate had intensified over the desirable shape of a united Europe. The European Economic Community had fallen short of the targets set by the 1957 Treaty of Rome. The visionary optimism of the 1950s founding fathers had dissipated. It was generally accepted that the EEC needed a common policy for economic development, environmental protection and security. From there on, however, the views diverged. There were those, such as the European Commission's first president, the German Walter Hallstein, who shared Monnet's commitment to federalism. But there were many shades of grey when it came to how that federalism – or confederalism – should be expressed. Most Europeans believed state sovereignty should be pooled rather than surrendered. But many also agreed with De Gaulle that, rather than seeking ever closer integration, Europe must remain a *Europe des patries*, or nation-states. Supranational organisations, the French president had warned in 1960, tended to become 'irresponsible super-states'.

> What are the pillars on which Europe can be built? In truth, they are the states, states that are certainly very different than one another, each having its soul, its history and its language, its glories and ambitions, but states that are the only entities with the right to give orders and the power to be obeyed. To fancy that one can build something effective in action, and acceptable to the peoples, outside or above the states, is a chimera.[41]

Even then, the challenge remained the same: how to establish shared values, interests, identities and priorities in a region with contrasting histories, cultures and social structures, in which there were at least thirty-six official languages and an array of different legal systems, planning methods and traditions of governance. In 1960, a European Free Trade Association had been set up as a looser parallel organisation by seven European countries: Britain, Austria, Denmark, Norway, Portugal, Sweden and Switzerland. Yet this had failed to emerge as a rival to the EEC. Britain, Ireland, Denmark and Norway applied for admission to the Community a year later. They were soon joined by Austria, Greece, Malta, Portugal, Spain, Sweden and Switzerland.

In 1965, EEC decision-making was streamlined under a Merger Treaty. Three years later, the Community's position in world trade was strengthened by an industrial customs union and common external tariff. Meanwhile, internal trade expanded rapidly. Gross National Product grew by an average 5.7 per cent during the 1960s, while per capita incomes rose by 4.5 per cent. There was steady standardisation in areas from health services to labour markets. In 1968, a Common Agricultural Policy created a single market for agricultural products with guaranteed prices. At the same time, governments agreed to earmark a proportion of tax profits for the development of Europe's poorer regions.

Britain's EEC membership was resisted by De Gaulle, who still saw a strong Franco-German axis as the backbone of European unity. In 1963, he blocked a joint membership application by Britain, Ireland and Denmark, and signed a new Franco-German Treaty instead, repeating his refusal when Britain reapplied four year later. The French leader's insistence on the right to a national veto of Community decisions was enshrined under a 'Luxembourg Compromise' of 1966 and prevented majority voting for two decades. Yet the integration continued. His successor, Georges Pompidou, finally consented to British, Irish and Danish accession; and in January 1973, the EEC duly expanded from six to nine members.

Steps to a full monetary union were initiated under a British Commission president, Roy Jenkins, with backing from President Valéry Giscard d'Estaing of France and Chancellor Helmut Schmidt of Germany. When a European Monetary System was launched in 1978, Britain opted out. Yet the Community had gained greater stability, with regular summits of a European Council of heads of government from 1974.

* * *

By then, East-West détente was in full swing too. The Soviet Union had assumed superpower status and the balance of forces seemed to be shifting in its favour, aided by a nuclear stalemate which held military confrontation in check while communist influence was extended in the Third World. The Vietnam War had ended in a humiliating US defeat in 1975, while a Four-Power Agreement on Berlin in 1971 and an East-West German Basic Treaty in 1973 had all indicated final acceptance of Europe's bi-polar division. With hopes of change now more remote than ever, opportunities for East-West co-operation were increasing. East-West trade had expanded twenty-five-fold in a decade; President Richard Nixon had visited Moscow; and a US-Soviet SALT 1 agreement had been signed on strategic arms limitations.

Western Communist parties were growing in strength too, gaining fifteen per cent or more in elections in at least a dozen countries by the early 1970s. In Italy, a new Communist boss,

Enrico Berlinguer, talked of a 'historic compromise' with 'anti-bourgeois' Catholics and Christian Democrats. This would stall with the May 1978 murder of the Christian Democrats' pro-compromise leader, Aldo Moro, by the country's Red Brigades terror group. But if Communist power was to be permanent in Eastern Europe, some Church leaders reasoned, it was necessary to make the best of a bad situation. That was the thinking which now predominated in contacts with communist regimes. One senior Vatican negotiator, Archbishop Agostino Casaroli, travelled regularly to Moscow and other capitals in the hope of 'saving what could be saved'. Like western governments, Casaroli concluded that too vigorous a defence of rights and freedoms would merely incite worse repression. Communism would surely evolve, like all ideological movements. So it was essential to maintain contacts and pursue co-operation, however meager the initial results might be.

This was widely disputed. There were many prominent Church figures, like the exiled Hungarian cardinal, József Mindszenty, who believed the Vatican was wrong to seek compromises – especially over the heads of East European Church leaders who had a far better grasp of the local situation. Despite this, the Vatican went ahead and became a party to East-West negotiations. Addressing the opening session of a Conference on Security and Co-operation in Europe in 1973, Casaroli conceded that human rights abuses would lead 'sooner or later, somewhere in Europe, to grave internal disorders' which threatened international peace. But the Vatican maintained a 'respectful discretion', the Vatican diplomat added, in areas outside its competence. It would gladly support any negotiating process which brought the two sides closer.[42]

The CSCE's 'Final Act', signed by thirty-five participating states at Helsinki in 1975, listed 'respect for human rights and fundamental freedoms, including the freedom of thought, conscience, religion or belief', as one of ten principles which should guide inter-state relations. But the Act's concrete commitments were minimal and the text was 'politically binding' only. The point of the three-year Conference had been to sanction Europe's new geopolitical order.

Casaroli's approach was cleverer and more nuanced than that of other Christian East-West fora, such as Josef Hromádka's Prague-based Christian Peace Conference, which had attempted to rally Church support for Moscow's 'peace offensive'. On paper at least, it was also more productive, gaining regime acceptance for occasional episcopal appointments and other concessions. Doubts about the Vatican's diplomatic stance nevertheless multiplied. Another veteran cardinal, Franz Koenig of Vienna, deplored the 'confessional state of atheism' which, for all the 'professions of intent' about human rights, still reigned in the East. Koenig had spent a quarter of a century rebuilding Church links with Eastern Europe, as well as with Bruno Kreisky's Austrian Socialists. He could claim a deep knowledge of contemporary East-West politics. But Pope Paul VI saw the contradictions too. In October 1975, he spoke of Christians 'oppressed by systematic persecution'. 'The drama of fidelity to Christ and of freedom of religion continues,' the Pope warned, 'even if it is disguised by categorical declarations in favour of the rights of the person and life in society.'[43]

Pope Pius XII had coined the term 'Church of silence' as long ago as 1951, to describe the suppression of East European Christians under communist rule. The western 'Church of privilege' was being challenged by a hostile secular culture too. But its weapons were indifference and apathy, rather than harassment and repression. In France, where contraception and abortion were legalized in 1967 and 1974, Mass attendance had dropped to ten per cent in Paris and fewer than five per cent in other industrial centres, alongside a sharp fall in clergy numbers and religious order membership.[44]

There were some bright lights on this otherwise bleak horizon, such as the Taizé Community, founded by the Protestant Roger Schulz in 1940, which attracted young people of all denominations and none from all over Europe. Europe's great Christian shrines – Lourdes, Fatima, Loreto, Altotting – continued to draw pilgrims too, while renewal movements were springing up in an effort to provide a more dynamic alternative to traditional parish life.

Ecumenical achievements between churches were adding a

spiritual and cultural dimension to European unity as well, such as in 1977 when Paul VI met the Anglican Archbishop of Canterbury, Donald Coggan. 'Many in both Communions are asking themselves whether they have a common faith sufficient to be translated into communion of life, worship and mission,' noted their common declaration, *After Four Hundred Years*. 'Only the communions themselves through their pastoral activities can give that answer. When the moment comes to do so, may the answer shine through in spirit and truth, not obscured by the enmities, prejudices and suspicions of the past.'[45]

Meanwhile, new forms of Christian reflection, both liberal and conservative, gave an important boost to contemporary thought. In Protestantism, the influential work of Karl Barth sought to uphold the absolute primacy of God in human life and history. In Catholicism, the German Jesuit Karl Rahner tried to adapt the scholastic system of Aquinas to modern theological needs in the form of a 'transcendental Thomism'. His Swiss contemporary, Hans Urs von Balthasar, a one-time exponent of the *nouvelle théologie*, championed spiritual renewal – a 'kneeling theology' – as a means of regenerating the Church and the world.

Balthasar rejected the 'anonymous Christianity' which had sought in the 1950s and 1960s to 'baptise secular and religious movements outside the Church'. In the era of the common man, the Church had to return to its biblical simplicity, and find new prophetic ways of spreading its message and inculcating its values. All that was needed was a spark of inspiration to give this dynamic challenge shape and direction – to bring the age-old Christian river back to its authentic wellsprings.

CHAPTER 5

The New Spring of Nations

We cannot forget or fail to criticise the Church's relationship with the forces which generated the formula of human rights in modern times. At certain times in history, human freedom was asserted against Christianity, making the Church treat liberating tendencies as a sign of rebellion against religion and God ... But today, a crucial change appears to be occurring: a shift from the defence of Church and religion to the defence of human rights.

The confidence of a Polish dissident, Tadeusz Mazowiecki, summed up how Christianity's prophetic message seemed to have evolved.[1] For many, the spark of inspiration came precisely on 16 October 1978, when a Polish archbishop, Karol Wojtyła, became head of the Roman Catholic Church. John Paul II was the first non-Italian pope since Adrian VI in the early sixteenth century, a Renaissance figure in whom poetry, theatre, sporting prowess and prayer were fused in a heady mixture. His election was a tribute to the religious spirit of his native Poland, unquenched after three decades of communist rule. It was also a visible rebuttal of the East-West division symbolised by the Berlin Wall. In the Church at least, there was still an institution which could unite the Continent behind coherent values and principles.

In an article before his election, Wojtyła had insisted Europe's frontiers were 'more contractual than natural'. There was a much deeper border, he added, which ran through people themselves; so it was in the hearts and minds of people that 'captivity and subjugation' would be overcome.[2]

The vision of a Europe of multiple identities – from Greek

and Latin, to Germanic and Slavic – would be a constant theme of John Paul II's pontificate. So would the conviction that Christianity held the key to Europe's reunification. 'Europe is not all Catholic – but it is almost all Christian,' the Pope told the Continent's Catholic bishops soon after his election. 'It has become, over two millennia, like the bed of a great river, from where Christianity has spread out, creating a fertile earth from the spiritual life of its peoples and nations.' The Church's task, he added, was to foster 'not just an awareness of what Christianity was in the past – but also a sense of responsibility for what it must be tomorrow'.[3]

In Wojtyła's homeland, Mazowiecki saw the coming of a Polish pope as 'a kind of compensation for history'. The Rome election did, indeed, arouse great expectations. Poland's Communist rulers tried to calm the fears of their Soviet minders. But an exiled Ukrainian cardinal, Iosif Slipyi, was sure the new Pope would 'reach out a helping hand to the oppressed, and not limit himself to words of consolation and patience, as his predecessors did'.[4]

John Paul II made clear the Vatican's 'small steps' diplomacy would continue under its architect, Archbishop Agostino Casaroli. But there would be no more superficial accomodations. The Church remained 'open to every country and regime', the Pope told Vatican-accredited diplomats. But it also welcomed 'authentic representatives of peoples and nations'. If essential rights were respected, the Church could coexist 'without inherent contradiction' with any political, economic or social order. It reserved the right to speak out, however, in defence of what it believed. 'There is no longer a Church of silence,' John Paul II explained. 'She now speaks with the voice of the Pope.'[5]

Having lived through Nazi and Communist rule, Wojtyła knew totalitarianism from the inside. He could see its weaknesses – and the strengths of the Christian culture Poland shared with its neighbours. But he also knew Christianity had to offer convincing answers to the claims of Marxism. Even in the western Church, it was widely believed that Marxism had eradicated injustice and exploitation by destroying the structures of capitalism. In reality, it had imposed its own structures, through a 'totalitarian bureaucracy' which captivated and abused human beings 'even more severely'. True liberation would come through rediscovering the values – love and selflessness, trust and forgiveness – which these structures had attempted to destroy. Christianity had to have its own *praxis*, something which could provide a meeting-point with other humanistic philosophies.[6]

The Pope's first encyclical, *Redemptor hominis*, published in March 1979, read like a personal manifesto. The Church approached all cultures and ideologies with a deep esteem for human capacities, the Pope reiterated. As a guardian of human freedom, though, it had to be faithful to Christ's words: 'You will know the truth, and the truth will make you free' (John 8: 23). This meant distinguishing between genuine and illusory freedoms. 'We are not dealing with the "abstract" man, but the real, "concrete", "historical" man,' the Pope continued. 'Man is the primary route the Church must travel in fulfilling her mission.'

This struggle for the soul of contemporary man was an innovation in *Redemptor hominis*. But the encyclical went further, highlighting the contradiction between human rights in letter and spirit. It was this contradiction which most called in question the legitimacy of power, the Pope said. It risked dissolving society into 'oppression, intimidation, violence and terrorism.'

> The essential sense of the state, as a political community, consists in that the society and people composing it are master and sovereign of their own destiny. This sense remains unrealised if, instead of the exercise of power with the moral participation of the society or people, what we see is the imposition of power by a certain group ... The Church has always taught that the fundamental duty of power is sollicitude for the common good of society; this is what gives power its fundamental rights. Precisely in the name of these premises of the objective ethical order, the rights of power can only be understood on the basis of respect for the objective and inviolable rights of man.[7]

People wanted to hear Christianity's message of redemption, *Redemptor hominis* noted, since they wanted 'justice, peace, love, goodness, fortitude, responsibility and human dignity'. The atheism which had been superimposed on 'the map of the world's religions' could only be understood 'in relation to the phenomenon of religion and faith'. This was why the denial of religious freedom in the name of atheism was such a 'radical injustice'.[8]

* * *

The Pope could claim to be building on the dialogue between dissident intellectuals in Eastern Europe, who had looked increasingly to Christianity for a unifying ethos. In the 1960s, Poland's Cardinal Wyszyński had sought out critical Communist Party insiders for an exchange of views. So had the Catholic journals, *Więź*, *Znak* and *Tygodnik Powszechny*. The Personalism of Maritain and Mounier had offered a point of contact. Its 'axiology' was similar to Marxism: social justice, human emancipation, engagement with the world. But it gave these values a Christian meaning and offered real ideas about the Church's place in modern society.

Exchanges like these were not to be confused with the official discussion platforms arranged by groups like Pax in Poland, which were ostentatiously Catholic while obsequiously supporting communist aims. Nor did it touch the trickle of progressive western theologians who journeyed periodically to Moscow in search of 'Christian-Marxist dialogue'. Meanwhile, not all Marxist 'revisionists' were interested. Hungary's leading philosopher, György Lukács, had castigated Roger Garaudy for his dialogue with Christians in the 1960s. Yugoslavia's showcase Praxis Group had been thrown out of Belgrade University in 1975 for advocating a 'critical Marxism'. But it continued to pour scorn on churches.

Yet some Marxists were. Czechoslovakia's academic elite – Karel Kosík, Milan Machovec, Václav Černý – had admitted communism's failures and begun debating the values to be found in Christianity. Poland's most talented Marxist thinker, Leszek Kołakowski, had also re-evaluated Europe's debt to Christianity. Supporters of social justice were no longer obliged to oppose the Church, Kołakowski concluded. They could act within a Christian framework.

Polish dissidents talked of creating 'democratic spaces', of living freely under Communist rule. Dietrich Bonhoeffer's *Letters from Prison*, published in Polish in 1970, suggested Christian principles could be used in the struggle for justice without necessarily 'retreating into prayers'. In a 1971 letter, *Octogesima adveniens*, Paul VI had predicted a 'retreat from ideologies' would create a new opening to Christianity. What was occurring in Poland was not the *metanoia*, or general conversion, some had hoped to see. But many intellectuals who had abandoned communism were looking to the Church as an ally. It was the only social entity which remained independent and uncompromised. When the regime of Edward Gierek announced plans in 1975 to amend the constitution and declare Poland a permanent 'socialist state', it triggered a coalition of protesters ranging from former Party members to Catholic priests. People like this were united on the need to reject the fake reality and discredited relativism of communism.

In Czechoslovakia, a 5,000-word declaration, 'Charter 77', called on Gustáv Husák's regime to honour its human rights commitments. As in Poland, its signatories came from many backgrounds: Catholic and Protestant Christians, Masarykian liberals, 'reform communist' veterans of the 1968 Prague Spring. The Charter's architect, Jan Patočka, died after a police interrogation in March 1977, but not before setting out its aims. The movement was not questioning state prerogatives, the blacklisted philosopher argued. It merely believed the state should uphold moral principles and observe its own laws.

In his writings, long banned by Communist censors, Patočka had resurrected natural law as a unifying thread between ideologies. Christians and ex-Communists could not wish away their differences, he pointed out. But they could learn to trust each other and engage in constructive moral thinking together. 'It does not speak about God or God's kingdom', a group of clergy signatories explained of Charter 77. 'But it is fighting for freedom in religious matters and thus serving God's purposes. In this we glimpse the future universality of Christ's kingdom.'[9]

In the Soviet Union too, the human rights movement was broad-based, especially in predominantly Catholic Lithuania. Not all dissidents agreed with the Church. But religious rights provided a catalyst. A *Chronicle of the Catholic Church in Lithuania* became the republic's best-known *samizdat* journal. In 1977, almost half of all Catholic priests signed petitions against a new Soviet constitution. 'We need to unite currents of thought which regard Catholicism as the key to national salvation, with those who favour a nationalistically inclined atheism,' commented another underground title in 1978. 'No other force in today's world can help Lithuanians remain Lithuanian as much as religion.'[10]

Church leaders were cautious about opposition initiatives like this. But they knew they held the moral high ground. Research data in 1978 suggested religiousness was growing among Poland's traditionally secularised groups, as forms of identity re-emerged with a stronger integrative capacity than communist culture. The lack of mediating institutions between state and society had strengthened local group loyalties. But they were defined less by age or social background than by ethos and religious belief. This was where the Polish Church's real power lay as an alternative system of authority.

* * *

Like other Catholic bishops, the Pope could see Poland's Communist bosses were kept in power only by external force. With that force now mired in its 'era of stagnation' under Leonid Brezhnev, the geriatric Soviet Party leader, it was not unrealistic to believe Communist rule would one day end. Arriving home in Poland in June 1979 on his first pilgrimage, he left no doubt that the Church would help this happen. The Soviet regime had opposed the visit. Events would justify its misgivings.

In the course of a week, John Paul II preached thirty-two sermons in six cities before thirteen million people. He spoke up for Eastern Europe's 'often forgotten nations and peoples' and urged Europe to rebuild its unity through shared Christian values. What other unity was there, if not this? The Second World War had left the Continent torn apart. It would only come together again by rediscovering the Christian heritage of Czechs and Slovaks, Croats and Slovenes, Bulgarians and Lithuanians – by 'opening the frontiers' to the Holy Spirit. 'Is it not Christ's will,' the Pope declared at Gniezno, Poland's oldest Christian see, 'that this Polish Pope, this Slav Pope, should at this very moment manifest the spiritual unity of Christian Europe?'[11]

While Gierek evoked thirty-five years of Communist Poland in his speeches, the Pope appealed to a Polish identity which was infinitely richer and deeper. Poland's own baptism in 966, he recalled, had also marked the creation of an independent Polish state, at a time when Christianity's expansion was creating the first cultural links between European nations. Peace could only be assured if the nation was able to remain true to its thousand-year Christian tradition. It was Christianity which had given Europe its fundamental unity, a unity which lived on regardless of 'regimes, ideologies and economic and political systems'.

The Pope had come with a new language of rights and freedoms, and with a message of optimism and endurance which was relayed to other East European countries too. Vatican II had talked about 'acculturating' Christianity in different contexts. In the Pope's hands, culture became a word for national identity, history and spirituality put together. 'Culture is, above all, a common good of the nation,' the Pope explained. 'It was decisive for us throughout history, more decisive than material power, more decisive than boundaries ... In the works of Polish culture, the soul of the nation is reflected.'[12]

In future years, the pilgrimage would be best remembered for the Pope's invocation at an open-air Mass for 300,000 people on the eve of Pentecost in Warsaw's Victory Square: 'Let Your Spirit come down! And renew the face of the earth. This earth!' Many Poles would look back on this as the moment when Communism's fate was sealed.

* * *

All of this lay in the future, though. The Soviet Foreign Minister, Andrei Gromyko, compared the Pope's Polish visit to Ayatollah Khomeini's return to Iran in early 1979. The Czechoslovak regime ridiculed his 'audacious' appeal to Europe's Christian roots. The Church was attempting to make up for its past hostility to the working classes, the regime hit back – a glance at Czech history showed it had always been 'on the side of our enemies'. All over Eastern Europe, however, small dissident groups felt emboldened by the Pope's challenge. 'It is obvious that we have experienced an event whose importance will continue to grow,' Poland's opposition Workers Defence Committee (KOR) enthused in a statement. 'For many in Poland and beyond its borders, listening to the Pope has posed a moral obligation to intensify a struggle for rights.'[13]

The stress on human rights reflected the general theological climate worldwide, which had been marked by the advance of Liberation Theology in the Third World and attempts by Protestant thinkers such as Jürgen Moltmann to bring Christian ideas up to date with modern society. Atheists claimed to have rejected God, Moltmann maintained; in reality, they had failed to encounter God as He really was. Like the Pope, Moltmann taught that the Christian faith must have practical consequences – it carried a duty to take responsibility for the world. Unlike the Pope, his own ideas never achieved a mass audience.

This was a far cry from the fate of the Church in Russia, which was all but ignored by dissidents. Small Christian groups – Baptists, Adventists, Mennonites, Old Believers – had shown remarkable resilience under Soviet rule, often in remote parts of Siberia. But the Orthodox Church was in a sorry state. Half the 20,000 places of worship still open at the war's end had been closed by the 1970s, along with five of the Church's eight surviving seminaries and half its sixty-seven monasteries and convents.

In an open letter to Patriarch Pimen in 1975, a year after he was exiled to the West, Alexander Solzhenitsyn had rejected the familiar argument that subservience was the price of the Church's survival. All it had gained, Solzhenitsyn argued, was a landscape of destroyed churches, of people condemned to material and spiritual poverty, deprived of any hope for the future. He contrasted the situation with the Church's defiance in Poland. 'A Church dictatorially ruled by atheists is a sight not seen in two thousand years,' the writer commented acidly. 'What sort of reasoning can convince us that the consistent destruction of the spirit and body of this Church by atheists is the best means for its preservation? Preservation for whom? Certainly not for Christ.'[14] Some fellow-dissidents thought Solzhenitsyn's attack was unfair. Orthodox Church leaders were doing their best, they argued, in an impossible situation. Yet it was a reminder of the comparative coherence and vitality of Catholicism in Eastern Europe.

These qualities were about to be tested. When 17,000 shipyard workers began an occupation strike in Poland's northern Baltic ports in August 1980, Communist power seemed to have been challenged head-on. Although triggered by price rises, the strikes quickly became much more than an industrial protest. Solidarity called itself a union. With 9.48 million members enrolled within weeks, however, it was really a social movement.

The upheaval came at the end of a year which had seen East-West detente collapse with the Soviet invasion of Afghanistan and a growing nuclear confrontation. It also came as an embarrassment for western diplomats, whose East-West policy was premised on the assumption that Europe's division was immutable. Unlike their American counterpart, West European governments had not made human rights central to their foreign policy. The 1975 Helsinki Final Act had tried to forge an East-West consensus on the civil and political rights which most concerned the West, and the economic and social rights held up in the East. No conditions had been attached, however, and the Act was not legally binding. The resulting gap between rhetoric and reality was quickly seized on by the new tough-talking Reagan Administration. When the Polish strikes erupted, Europe's stability began to look shakier.

The Pope had used the word 'solidarity' in *Redemptor hominis*, and his authority was invoked by the Gdansk strikers. There was, indeed, clearly a link between the protest and John Paul II's 1979 visit, with its message about upholding the truth against the forces of power and coercion. The pilgrimage had begun to look like a dress rehearsal. Poland's Communist rulers mere confused – they had no answer to industrial protests which evoked the teachings of a church.

From the Church's viewpoint, Solidarity's demands were legitimate. Vatican II's Pastoral Constitution had listed 'degrading working conditions' as offences against human dignity (alongside slavery and prostitution). It had also enshrined the rights of workers to form unions and go on strike. With the Polish Communist Party's economic monopoly causing wastage, inefficiency and poverty, these criteria plainly applied. Here at last was the kind of movement Pius XI had dreamed of in *Quadragesimo anno* – a movement defending workers' rights, but also steered by Christian principles.

Solidarity's leader, Lech Wałęsa, recounted how Christianity seemed to have replaced Marxism as the ally of working people. It was 'a kind of revolution on the knees', Wałęsa wrote later, 'in which prayer protected us against a totalitarianism limited by the existence of the Church, private individual farms, the historical consciousness of the population, and the presence in the Vatican of a Polish Pope with an explicit reminder that Poland was a part of Europe and its Christian heritage'.[15] Despite this, Poland's Catholic bishops had no more idea than the Party how to handle an 'independent self-governing trade union' in the geopolitical conditions of Eastern Europe. Although Church rights were strengthened under the Gdańsk Agreement of 31 August 1980, Cardinal Wyszyński advised extreme caution. 'Remember the heart, though very important, is somewhat lower than the head,' he told Solidarity leaders. 'Achieving even reasonable rights demands a hierarchy of values, and patience.'[16]

With fears of a Soviet invasion running high, Wyszyński's misgivings were understandable. Poles had had enough, he insisted, of noble but quixotic rebellions which merely brought worse repression. The Pope counselled 'circumspection and moderation' too. He had demonstrated where communism was weak. But the path to freedom would be lengthy, he cautioned Wałęsa. When the invasion scare resurfaced in March 1981, as Solidarity threatened a general strike, John Paul II exchanged messages with Brezhnev and helped ensure the strike was called off. The following September, he set out the Church's latest thinking on workers' rights in a new encyclical.

Published during Solidarity's first congress, *Laborem exercens* brought the Catholic 'theology of work' up to date with contemporary economic thought. Human work, it pointed out, provided a key to understanding humanity. God had made man disobedient to worldly powers, but obedient to values. It was through work that man served these values and gained control over his destiny. The world was living through a new phase of development comparable to the Industrial Revolution, and this was fuelling even graver injustices. What was needed now were 'movements of solidarity' which could unite all those facing poverty and exploitation. The Church was no longer afraid of social movements like this. It saw them as allies in the godly cause of human rights and social justice.

Popes from Leo XIII to Pius XII had talked complacently about Christian charity, while John XXIII and Paul VI had gone to the other extreme and demanded structural transformations. By contrast, Wojtyła saw the problem in anthropological terms. The 'great conflict' of labour and capital still dragged on. It was being expressed in an ideological contest between liberalism ('understood as the ideology of capitalism') and Marxism ('understood as the ideology of scientific socialism and communism'). But its root cause was really the 'error of economism', which had subordinated the spiritual and personal to 'material reality' under both capitalism and communism. This 'error' had its origins in theories which had laid the philosophical foundations for industrialisation in the nineteenth century. But it was in danger of being repeated whenever efficiency and production were given priority over social justice and the primacy of labour.

Whereas Marx had viewed the human person as no more than a minor extra in the historical drama of economic competition, *Laborem exercens* placed him centre-stage. It was the working person, linked to God by conscience and will, who was history's prime mover, not the external forces of wealth and class struggle.

Laborem exercens vigorously defended the rights of workers, describing unions as an 'indispensable element of social life'.[17] What it seemed to sketch out was a 'humanistic' market economy, checked and balanced by moral principles. Fighting communism was unnecessary. It could not be intimidated by confrontation or appeased by diplomacy. But it could be undermined through the power of values – by a moral victory over fear and hatred which ultimately became a political victory.

* * *

The Pope's reassuring message was eagerly seized on in Eastern Europe. 'In so far as we can speak of a workers' revolution, Solidarity was the first workers' revolution in history; the Bolshevist coup of 1917 has no claim to this title,' the ex-Marxist, Leszek Kołakowski, wrote from exile in Oxford. 'It follows that the first workers' revolution in history was directed against a socialist state, and has proceeded under the sign of the Cross with the blessing of the Pope. So much for the irresistible laws of history discovered scientifically by Marxists.'[18]

Back in Poland, the Church's cautious mediation efforts failed to head off a confrontation, as power appeared to slip from the Party's hands. The result, on 13 December 1981, was the imposition of martial law. Its architect, General Wojciech Jaruzelski, claimed to be saving from Poland from 'catastrophe, chaos, poverty and famine'. But Soviet propagandists had no doubt about who was to blame. Solidarity had been born, the TASS newsagency insisted, 'in the bosom of the Catholic Church', which had demoralised and humiliated the ruling Party.[19]

The use of military force to reimpose control nevertheless widened the division in world communism. In Western Europe, electoral support weakened for Eurocommunist parties. There was no more talk of a 'historic compromise' with Christian Democrats. The dialogue pioneered by Mounier and others appeared to have reached its limits. Christians might still co-operate with Marxists in practical tasks, as Pope John XXIII had conceded. But if Marxism still had uses as an analytical tool, its ideological precepts seemed irreconcilable with Christianity.

When the Pope returned home in June 1983, after tough bargaining with Jaruzelski's regime, he assured Poles their struggle was not in vain. The moral victory was still possible, he insisted. It would come from 'uprightness of conscience, love of neighbour, ability to forgive'. A state was genuinely sovereign only when it served the common good and allowed the nation to express 'the whole of its historical and cultural identity, to be sovereign *through* the state. In a 'brutally frank' meeting with Jaruzelski, John Paul II said his image of Poland was of a 'vast concentration camp, full of hungry, shoeless, ill-clothed people'. An internal Party memo confirmed that the government had protested about the Pope's 'aggressive statements' and threatened to curtail the visit.[20]

In reality, the pilgrimage had highlighted the gulf separating the *realpolitik* of the state from the aspirations of society. Asked in a 1983 survey who deserved public trust, eighty-two per cent of Poles cited the Church, while only thirty-seven per cent chose the ruling Party. Fewer than half wanted the Church to be more assertive in public life: religious sympathies did not necessarily translate into political loyalties. But the survey indicated the paradoxes at work. Half of Party members admitted to being practising Catholics, while over ninety per cent believed only the Church could 'guarantee the nation's moral education' and favoured the teaching of religion in state schools.[21] When an outspoken Catholic priest, Jerzy Popiełuszko, was kidnapped and murdered by Communist agents in 1984, it dealt another massive blow to the regime's hopes of regaining the initiative.

* * *

The case of Poland demonstrated how hopelessly outdated had become any surviving stereotype of a Church allied to conservative, privileged establishments. The East-West conflict was a conflict of power, Europe's Council of Catholic Episcopates, the CCEE, later recalled. But it was also a conflict over truth – the truth about man and his place in society. No socio-political system had ever fully realised this truth. The current confrontation was only the latest in an age-old battle to define it.[22]

Conceived during Vatican II, the CCEE reflected the need for what Paul VI had called 'pastoral solidarity' in tackling the common challenges thrown up by Europe's integration: marriages and families, refugees and migrants, youth work and tourism. Although its first president was a French cardinal, Roger Etchegaray, it included several Bishops Conferences from Eastern Europe. As such, it was a visible reminder that the Church embraced the entire continent – East and West, North and South – over and above political and ideological divisions.

From 1971 onwards, the Council had met yearly to debate Vatican II themes. Its main focus, however, was on tackling secularisation. Distinctions were drawn between the 'acceptable' secularisation which came from recognising the autonomy of secular life, and the 'unacceptable' secularisation reflected in outright hostility to Christianity. Whichever form it took, most bishops agreed that criticism was not enough. 'Deep and complex transformations in the cultural, political, ethical and spiritual order have given Europe's social fabric a new configuration,' the Pope told the CCEE in 1986. 'The new quality of evangelisation must correspond to this. It must reformulate the imperishable message of salvation in a convincing way for contemporary man.'[23]

In September 1980, a month into the Solidarity uprising in Poland, Europe's Catholic bishops had met at Subiaco to mark the 1500th anniversary of the birth of St Benedict, whose monastic movement had profoundly marked European history. Their message made no mention of the East-West division. Instead, it addressed Europe as a whole. It was the Church's task, the bishops said, to be a 'communion surpassing all frontiers', to create 'a Europe of peoples, not just a Europe of material and technical progress'. Growing East-West contacts and exchanges were making this possible. At one time, Christians had exported their divisions around the world. They could now make amends by working together.

> Christians are attesting that faith and spiritual values are not only compatible with human and historical progress, but actually promote integral development ... Many people who do not recognise Jesus Christ as Saviour are travelling with us on the world's pathways. Many believe, like us, in a personal, creative God, including Jews and Muslims. We are ready to work with them and all people of goodwill in building peace and asserting the rights of man. Profoundly human values, nourished in the soil of a common past, are binding Europeans

together over and above the frontiers of religion and ideology.[24]

By the 1980s, the Roman Catholic Church had other continent-wide organisations with an outreach into Eastern Europe, including religious orders, laity committees and priests' assemblies. Relations with Islam – now Europe's second religion, with twenty-three million adherents – were a pressing concern. So were ties with Judaism. As the veteran Austrian Cardinal, Franz Koenig, pointed out, the Church would go on reminding Europe of its Christian roots – expressed by the churches and cathedrals in its cities, the crosses and statues in its cemeteries, the customs and traditions of its inhabitants. But it was well aware that, without the Jews, the people among whom Christ was born, European culture would have been incomparably poorer. 'When the Church speaks of Europe, it isn't referring to just one part – the Europe of the EC, the Europe of the free trade zone, the Europe of the Council of Europe, still less of the military blocs,' Koenig told the CCEE's Rome colloquium in October 1982. 'It still sees a Europe in its totality ... from Portugal to the Urals, from Iceland to Malta. For us, Europe cannot be restricted to military frontiers, or to political and social boundaries.'[25]

Were Roman Catholics pursuing a purely Catholic vision of Europe, to the exclusion of other Christian voices? The CCEE vigorously denied this. Catholics made up fewer than half the baptised Christians of Europe. In declaring solidarity with people under every regime, the Council emphasised, the Church was standing up for everyone. The post-war division sealed at Yalta had merely reinforced the old East-West rift between Rome and Byzantium. The restoration of Christian unity was a condition for overcoming it.

By the 1980s, the CCEE was co-operating closely with the ecumenical Conference of European Churches, which grouped over 120 Orthodox, Lutheran, Anglican, Calvinist, Methodist, Baptist and Pentecostal denominations from twenty-six countries. Founded in 1957, CEC had held its first four assemblies at Nyborg Strand in Denmark. Its constitution required it to discuss 'questions concerning the churches in Europe', which were bound to 'assist each other' in Christian service. With half CEC's member-churches coming from Eastern Europe, it too highlighted Christianity's potential as an East-West link and gave the lie to suggestions that 'Europe' was a western affair. The same could be said of other church organisations too, such as the Baptist Union, Lutheran World Federation and World Alliance of Reformed Churches.

Addressing the European Parliament in April 1979, six months after his election, the Pope had cautioned MEPs not to think 'they constitute Europe by themselves'. Europe's borders, he added, had been shaped by the spread of the Gospel. The Church's purpose was not to confer privileges on Christianity – only to recreate the Christian culture which all Europeans possessed as a common heritage.[26]

On the last day of 1980, John Paul II had declared the eastern saints, Cyril and Methodius, co-patrons of Europe with St Benedict. Coming from Thessaloniki, where St Paul had lived and taught, the two brothers had undertaken a mission sometime around AD 863 to the Slavs of the Danube and Balkans. By translating the sacred texts, they had created a Slavic alphabet, becoming not just Christian apostles, but fathers of Slavic culture and literature too. Though sent by the Church of Constantinople, Cyril and Methodius had also been supported by Rome. They had worked at the East-West cross-roads long before the Great Schism. This made them a 'sign for the times' when steps were being taken to reunite eastern and western Christianity. If Benedict represented the logical, rational culture of the West, Cyril and Methodius embodied the mystical, intuitive culture of the East. Taken together, they personified a common spiritual patrimony.[27]

The symbolism was important. Catholic-Orthodox relations had seen no real development since Russian Orthodox observers had arrived at the Second Vatican Council back in 1962. The Moscow Patriarchate had sent a delegation to John Paul II's inauguration, and Vatican and Orthodox theologians had reopened a commission at Patmos in 1980. But relations remained tense. In 1979, the Pope had written to Ukraine's Cardinal Slipyi, supporting the rights of his outlawed Greek Catholic Church. By combining the eastern liturgy with loyalty to Rome, he argued, Greek Catholics had built a church in which East and West enjoyed 'full and visible unity'. As such, they could act as a bridge between Catholicism and Orthodoxy.

Such talk was anathema to the Russian Orthodox Church. It viewed the 'Uniates' as a fifth column whose very existence appeared to call in question the validity of Orthodoxy. Patriarch Pimen hit back, accusing the Pope of 'cancelling' the ecumenical openness heralded by Vatican II. Such tensions suited the Soviet regime, which frowned on ecumenical ties unless they directly served its objectives. Communist propagandists responded accordingly. The Slavic alphabet had predated St Cyril, the Soviet press insisted, while Benedict's monasteries had been 'seedbeds of obscurantism'. 'Christian Europe' was just a ploy by western powers to stir up political opposition.[28]

The Pope was undeterred. Cyril and Methodius had truly been 'precursors of ecumenism', he insisted in a new encyclical, *Slavorum apostoli*. Instead of imposing Latin or Greek, the saints had rooted the Gospel in the language and mentality of the Slavs, thus enabling them to defend their identity. They had made a 'decisive contribution to the building of Europe' and their heritage remained 'deeper and stronger than any division'. It was indeed a 'spiritual bridge'. The Pope looked ahead to the 1988 millennium of the baptism of Prince Volodymyr of Kiev, whose Christian kingdom had stretched from Ukraine to the Baltic. Like the two saints, Volodymyr had maintained ties with both Rome and Constantinople. His adoption of the faith had initiated the 'original form of European culture' embodied in eastern Christianity.

> Europe is Christian in its very roots. The two forms of the great tradition of the Church, the Eastern and the Western, the two forms of culture, complement each other like the two lungs of a single body ... In the differing cultures of the nations of Europe, both in the East and in the West, in music, literature, the visual arts and architecture, as also in modes of thought, there runs a common lifeblood drawn from a single source.[29]

* * *

The 'two lungs' metaphor was not new. The Russian poet, Vyacheslav Ivanov (1866–1949), had used it in the 1930s to convey the spirit of European unity. So had the nineteenth-century Russian mystic, Vladimir Soloviev, in his dream of a single universal Church. Visiting France in May 1987, the Pope spoke of his vision of a 'Europe united from the Atlantic to the Urals'. On another pilgrimage to his native Poland a month later, he again challenged the view that change was impossible. It was still a question, he told fellow-Poles, of thinking 'in a long-term perspective' with the patient self-confidence supplied by Christianity.

The true meaning of solidarity, Wojtyła told a Mass for workers outside Gdansk, was bearing each other's burdens. No social or political theories could be invoked against it, and there would be no going back on the ideals invoked by the movement which had taken the name seven years before. He had special words for intellectuals too. 'We realise that people of culture and creativity, often coming from afar, have rediscovered their bond with the Church to an unprecedented degree,' the Pope told writers and artists in Warsaw. 'They have found in the Church a dimension of freedom they could not find elsewhere, discovering also its spiritual essence and reality, which they once saw only from outside.'[30]

There were moments during his third Polish visit when the Pope spoke as if Communism was already over. As a challenge sent by Providence, it had purified and mobilised Christians for new tasks, he told Poland's bishops, enabling the Church to 'give witness to the truth about God, Christ and man with new depth and force'. Sure enough, within twenty months, after a new wave of failed reforms and strikes, Jaruzelski's regime would finally sit down to 'Round Table' talks with Solidarity.

In a new encyclical that December, *Sollicitudo rei Socialis*, John Paul II denounced the whole 'logic of blocs'. Both rival concepts of development – the East's and the West's – needed 'radical correction', he said. Each harboured 'in its own way, a tendency towards imperialism'. It helped explain why the Church was critical of both. 'The Church's social doctrine is not a "third way" between liberal capitalism and Marxist collectivism, nor even a possible alternative to other solutions less radically opposed to one another: rather, it constitutes a category of its own,' the Pope explained. 'Its aim is to interpret realities, determining their conformity with or divergence from the lines of the Gospel.'[31]

This moral equivalence was the most controversial aspect of *Sollicitudo rei socialis*. But it represented a vigorous attempt to reassert the Church's independence from rival powers. The encyclical condemned the 'absolutising of human attitudes' through the desire for profit and lust for power, and the 'structures of sin' which assisted them. By stressing human responsibility for the world's injustices, it avoided both utopian hopes of structural change and a disembodied, nebulous anthropocentrism.

* * *

John Paul II's polemic against the East-West division had found echoes not only in Poland. All over Eastern Europe, underground Church activities were proliferating. In Ukraine, ten Greek Catholic bishops and at least 500 priests were said to be ministering in secret. In Lithuania, an unofficial Catholic Committee thanked the Pope for 'reminding the forgetful West that this is a European country'. 'History will forgive no one who has helped the atheist government destroy the Church,' a Lithuanian *samizdat* journal warned. 'Whatever one's view of religion, everybody who considers himself Lithuanian must realise that contributing to atheist propaganda amounts to a national betrayal.'[32]

The Soviet authorities were uneasy. Having been separated from the Church by modernity, one Soviet academician argued, the bourgeoisie were seeking a new alliance with it. The Church itself, thrown into crisis by a century of social and scientific revolutions, had now turned to political extremism and nationalism to maintain its position. Unofficially, however, Communist officials conceded that religiousness was feeding on genuine problems – labour hardships, inequalities and shortages, lack of identity and repression. The Soviet Party's youth paper, *Komsomolskaya pravda*, disclosed that some of its readers had taken to attending church, while Bulgaria's Academy of Sciences reported that eighty per cent of adult citizens now wanted church funerals. More than a third of Hungarians were attending church weekly – a rate far beyond anything in Western Europe.[33]

All Communist regimes took steps to combat the Christian revival. The East German Stasi had run an agent in the Vatican during the 1978 election and made attempts to infiltrate the Pope's entourage. When the Pope was shot in St Peter's Square in May 1981, the hand of Soviet and Bulgarian agents was detected. Yet the revival continued. In 1985, when 150,000 Czech and Slovak Christians descended on the shrine of Velehrad for their largest religious gathering in four decades, it was a sign that, here too, the Church had re-emerged as a social force.

Speaking to the European Court in October 1988, Wojtyła reiterated the 'common good' of human rights. Wise states had discarded the illusion, he said, that they could embody their people's interests without them. The Church would remain in the vanguard when it came to asserting them.

> The Church vigorously defends human rights because it considers them a necessary part of the recognition that must be given to the human person's dignity ... Human rights draw vigour and effectiveness from a framework of values, whose roots lie deep within the Christian heritage which has contributed so much to European culture. These founding values precede the positive law which gives them expression. They also precede the philosophical rationale that various schools of thought are able to give them.[34]

There were still uncertainties about the legal position of human rights in Europe. The European Convention of 1950 had required states to secure rights and freedoms 'to everyone within their jurisdiction', while the European Court had promoted the idea that there were universal principles of law to which all Europeans could appeal. In 1977, the European Community had declared maintenance of human rights to be an 'essential element' of EC membership. But it had not formally signed up to the Convention, and it was unclear how far this was binding. Pressure from the Church was clearly important.

The Church could claim to be at the forefront in its vision

of Europe too. If the Berlin Wall had condemned East Europeans to poverty and repression, it had also freed West Europeans to become stable and prosperous. As the East-West confrontation eased, however, so did the cold *realpolitik* calculations of the past. 1987 saw a summit between US and Soviet leaders in Rejkjavik and an INF Treaty limiting the deployment of intermediate nuclear weapons. Having shunned contacts with East European dissidents, western governments grudgingly began to see them as partners in dialogue. Yet their notion of Europe remained fundamentally political and economic.

In March 1985, Mikhail Gorbachev had taken over as Soviet Communist Party general secretary, ending the gerontocracy of Brezhnev's successors, Yuri Andropov and Konstantin Chernenko. Gorbachev had risen as a hardliner, declaring war on 'reactionary nationalist and religious survivals' at the CPSU's 27th Congress in 1986. Once in control, however, he began to put out feelers towards Patriarch Pimen and other religious leaders.

Gorbachev's book, *Perestroika* (1987), spoke of a 'democratised' communist order, purged of its failures by 'new thinking'. Socialism would still triumph, the Soviet boss insisted. But it would do so peacefully, as capitalism was forced to accomodate the righteous demands of the world's downtrodden. In the process, East Europeans should be free to 'consider their own specifics'. Soviet leaders would no longer act as 'sole guardians of truth'.[35] The Brezhnev Doctrine, allowing Moscow to intervene in its client-states, was apparently being revoked, calling in question the assumption that significant reforms would always be blocked by Moscow.

Eastern Europe had become a cauldron of ideas anyway.

The idea of Central Europe had been rediscovered by writers such as the Hungarian György Konrád and Romanian Emil Cioran, in a bid to reassert the identity of a region stretching from the Baltic to the Black Sea. 'Central Europe' had various meanings. Some saw it as a synonym for the old Habsburg dominions, others as the 'New Europe' of nation-states proposed by Tomáš Masaryk in 1918, still others as the German-centred *Mitteleuropa* conceived by Friedrich

Naumann. For the Czech Milan Kundera, a man who had defended his country's Communist system before the 1968 Prague Spring, the reborn 'Europe' could not include Russia. To the Russian Josif Brodski, 'Europe' was unimaginable without Dostoevsky and Chekhov, or the dissident Andrei Sakharov. For the French Edgar Morin, or the Swede Hans Magnus Enzensberger, the test of 'Europeanness' was found elsewhere, in an attitude of 'critical rationality' which allowed a civil society to survive, unbowed, beyond the control of states and empires.[36]

Whichever conceptions of Europe came into play, none could claim as much comprehensiveness as that of the Church. A sense of nationhood had been reviving in Eastern Europe since the mid-1980s. Its enthusiasts looked to the Church as a natural advocate, just as Basque or Irish patriots had done in Western Europe. The Pope had been invited unofficially to Lithuania for the sixth centenary of its Christian conversion, and Church leaders were giving moral support to calls for Soviet withdrawal from all three Baltic republics. In Hungary, where large demonstrations marked the anniversaries of the 1848 and 1956 uprisings, the writer Mihály Vajda observed that the rebellions against Communist rule were not just political events. They were also acts of cultural assertiveness, Vajda said, which 'made Europeanness possible'.[37]

* * *

Yet they would carry a price too. When Church representatives from East and West met at Basle in May 1989 for a European Ecumenical Assembly, they welcomed the Continent's latest 'providential moment'. But they also urged Christians to work against a revival of regional conflicts. Devoted to 'Peace with Justice', the Assembly's final document recognised past Christian failures: persistent divisions, support for war, indifference to discrimination and suffering. But Christian hope, the document added, constituted 'a resistance movement against fatalism'. Small nations had a right to their own culture, religion and democracy. The process of transformation should also be a process of reconciliation.

If Europe was to be a 'common house', the Assembly went

on, there must be 'house rules': a positive attitude to different religions, cultures and world views, 'open doors and open windows'. These were best protected by common Christian values. But this did not mean restoring the 'models of the past'. It meant being guided by a spirit of co-operation, and criticising the 'walls, barriers and ditches' which got in the way.[38]

The Assembly brought all Christian denominations together under the joint auspices of CCEE and CEC. A previous gathering had been staged a year earlier in the East German city of Erfurt with the theme, 'Thy Kingdom Come'. As 1989 wore on, the prophetic tone of Church pronouncements seemed justified.

Many factors would be cited in the collapse of Communist rule: economic crisis, ideological meltdown, national unrest, western pressure. But none would explain its swiftness and near-total peacefulness. This was the area where the Church's influence was felt most as a catalyst for the forces of revolt. The final *dénouement* took various forms. In Poland, it was a power-sharing contract, negotiated with Church help; in Czechoslovakia, a 'velvet revolution' co-led by Christians. In Romania, it was the toppling of a dictator, Nicolae Ceaușescu. Here too, a Catholic archbishop spoke of 'the presence of God in the streets', of 'a faith which has lived on, through concealment and humiliation, and is now expressing itself in simple, open words and deeds'.[39]

Mikhail Gorbachev visited the Vatican in December 1989, acknowledging that the end of Communism would have been 'impossible' without the Pope. Not only did he now agree with much of the Pope's teaching; John Paul II had also contributed to his 'understanding of Communism'. 'I believe he is the world's most left-wing leader,' Gorbachev went on to say. 'No one else reacts with such pain to poverty, injustice and human misery, to the tarnishing of human life, even though it is a gift from God.'[40]

Poland's General Jaruzelski agreed. The Pope's homecoming visits, he conceded, had imparted much-needed values. 'Whereas earlier popes saw the evil only in one system – the communist, or "collectivist" system – the Polish Pope has also stressed the Church's critical attitude to the other side's system,' Jaruzelski explained. 'In this way, he has attempted to raise the Church above both systems and show a way forward.'[41]

The Pope spoke glowingly of the 'unstoppable drive for freedom, which breaks down walls and opens borders'. What lay ahead, he told young people at the ancient shrine of Santiago de Compostela, a place dubbed a 'symbol of European identity' by the Council of Europe in 1987, was a 'world without frontiers', which proclaimed Christ the 'Redeemer of mankind, the centre of history, the hope of nations, the Saviour of peoples'.[42]

In the first months of the 1990s, that hopeful vision seemed to be fulfilled. Christian life recovered rapidly, as Church-State agreements were signed, long-vacant bishoprics filled, and places of worship crowded with people free to express their faith publicly for the first time. Within a year, the Vatican had diplomatic relations with the Soviet Union, Poland, Hungary, Czechoslovakia, Romania and Bulgaria. 'Our country is entering a new path, leading to the democratic rule of law,' explained Hungary's Bishops Conference. 'The Church will be independent of all parties and respect the state's autonomy. But it will also demand that the political authorities respect its independence, ensuring appropriate conditions for its activity.'[43]

Some East Europeans saw the events of 1989 as a triumph for the 'Liberty, Equality and Fraternity' proclaimed by the French Revolution, and for the spirit of defiance shown by the nineteenth century's national uprisings. In contrast to the bloody events of previous centuries, the Church had unequivocally welcomed the latest spring tide of human liberation. But it had tried to give once-distrusted ideals a deeper Christian interpretation, one which went beyond the secular political dimensions of 1789 and 1848. It had also cautioned against false notions of freedom, and an uncritical acceptance of western norms and values. The words of Christ about the householder who 'brings out of his treasure what is new and old' (Matthew 13:52) were appropriate.

Some of the 'old' quickly made its appearance.

Tensions reignited with Orthodox leaders over the re-legalisation of Greek Catholic Churches in Ukraine and Romania, and the revival of Catholic parishes in Russia. Although

Orthodox hierarchies accepted democracy, the traditional closeness of throne and altar inhibited them more than their Catholic and Protestant counterparts. Nationalist groups looked to Orthodoxy to justify their struggle, while traditional notions of an 'Orthodox Slavic brotherhood' acted as a brake on calls for independence.

At their first united meeting in March 1990, Germany's Catholic bishops demanded a just social order, despite the much lower living standards in the German Democratic Republic. In 1983, the regime of Erich Honecker had celebrated the fifth centenary of Martin Luther's birth in style. But after four decades of Communist rule, barely two per cent of East Germans were even baptised. To allay East European fears, the joint declaration called for recognition of Germany's existing borders. 'During the years of enforced partition, the Church always treated Germany as one single country,' the bishops added. 'Living in a free society presupposes agreement on a scale of basic values, and particularly the personal value of each individual. In this context, the Christian image of humankind offers an incontrovertible opening for the future.'[44]

Polish and German bishops marked a bilateral border treaty that November with a joint appeal for overcoming 'stereotypes and prejudices'. Germans and Czechs exchanged letters of reconciliation, condemning past misdeeds and welcoming the possibility of a 'spiritually united Europe'.

When the Pope visited Czechoslovakia in April 1990, he was welcomed by the new playwright-president, Václav Havel, as the 'living symbol of civilisation'. He listed the Church's priorities in post-Communist Europe: renewing parishes, dioceses and religious orders; reaffirming priestly life and episcopal authority; reviving seminaries and religious education; rebuilding lay participation, ecumenical contacts and family bonds. The Church had been called the 'Church of silence', he recalled. Yet it was not 'the silence of sleep or death', but a silence in which precious values had been born. The Church's solidarity with the persecuted had strengthened its moral authority and contributed to 'healing old wounds in the heart of history'. It had also shown young people that the Church, however 'slandered and ridiculed', was a place of truth.'[45]

*   *   *

The Christian river seemed to be flowing with a new vitality just about everywhere. Over two-thirds of Russians claimed to be religious believers in a 1990 survey, while more than half believed the Churches were 'responding to society's interests' better than other institutions. Confidence in the Soviet Communist Party dropped from thirty-eight per cent to sixteen per cent in a year.[46] There were still serious problems when it came to the public presence of religion. A much-vaunted Soviet freedom of conscience law was implemented patchily. Church-State relations still needed redefining, as did ties between the Churches themselves.

Yet few doubted the Pope had contributed significantly to bringing about the new order in Europe. Benedict XV and Pius XII had been bypassed by the continent's politicians after the two world wars. Their successors in the 1990s could not ignore John Paul II. The Pope had taken his appeal to Europe's inhabitants over the heads of their rulers. He had seen how spiritual loyalties could have political consequences, how the power of the will could prevail over the power of coercion, and how conflicting philosophies and ideologies could be brought together behind a single set of values. In this way, he had helped inspire the social coalition, the 'movement of solidarity', which had ended Europe's East-West division.

It remained to be seen how the 'spiritual inheritance' he had invoked in Prague would fare in the new post-Communist conditions. Utopian programmes were discredited, world views being de-constructed. Greek and Judaic thinkers, from Plato and Aristotle to Martin Buber and Emmanuel Levinas, were back in fashion among Christian intellectuals. The structures of state and society were being re-examined, fundamental questions asked about the meaning of justice, democracy and freedom. While enthusiastic but inexperienced intellectuals seized on fashionable liberal notions, calls for protecting the poor and excluded were viewed as retrograde and communist-tainted. There was talk of a 'return to Europe'. But what kind of Europe had triumphed with the collapse of Communism – a Europe of individualism and consumerism, or a Europe of deeper cultural and spiritual values? How much would Christianity be allowed to contribute if it came to making choices?

When the Continent's Catholic bishops met up again in Rome in November 1991, they were asked how Christians from East and West could best 'exchange gifts'. Conflict in Yugoslavia already threatened, in Cardinal Etchegaray's words, a 'shattered image of Europe and the Church'. Far from just appealing to Europe's 'Christian heritage', urgent resolutions were needed for bringing the Gospel to the Continent's new-look inhabitants.

Putting these fine-sounding injunctions into practice was to prove difficult. The eastern contemplative tradition often sat uneasily with the western rational heritage. There were those, like the Polish bishop Józef Życiński, who believed the new East-West encounter could help distinguish 'real theological problems' from the 'pseudo-theological substitutes' which preoccupied western minds. When Marxist rhetoric was captivating Leftist intellectuals such as Jean-Paul Sartre, Życiński told the assembly, an old Russian *babushka* had often shown a clearer grasp of reality. There were others, such as the Belgian Bishop Paul van den Berghe, who rejected such simplifications. Though often deeply misguided, the Leftist movement had its share of martyrs too, van den Berghe insisted, and the Church should seek reconciliation with it. It would be dangerous and wrong to stake the Church's pastoral strategy on the theoretical benefits of some vague 'post-modernity'.[47]

The Pope had called the Rome assembly while visiting the Czech shrine of Velehrad. In a new encyclical, *Centesimus annus*, he posed the question now on many minds: 'Can it be said that, after the failure of communism, capitalism is the victorious social system, and that capitalism should be the goal of countries now making efforts to rebuild?' The answer was a complex one.

> If by 'capitalism' is meant an economic system which recognises the fundamental and positive role of business, the market, private property and the resulting responsibility for the means of production, as well as free human creativity in the economic sector, then the answer is certainly in the affirmative

... But if by 'capitalism' is meant a system in which freedom in the economic sector is not circumscribed within a strong juridical framework which places it at the service of human freedom in its totality, and which sees it as a particular aspect of that freedom, the core of which is ethical and religious, then the reply is certainly negative.[48]

The encyclical marked the centenary of Leo XIII's ground-breaking *Rerum novarum* and recalled the 'deep chasm' which had separated the classes in the late nineteenth century. It denounced the 'simple and radical solution' offered by Communism's abolition of private property, and praised the free market as the 'best instrument for utilising resources'. But if Communism's collapse had made it easier to tackle exploitation and alienation, it had not removed them. Nor would a 'radical capitalistic ideology' which refused even to recognise them. The Church had no 'models' to offer. But it would go on raising its voice against 'material and moral poverty'.

As for Europe, *Centesimus annus* welcomed the 'peaceful protest, using only the weapons of truth and justice' which had reunited East and West. The post-war period had been one of 'non-war rather than genuine peace'. It had been assumed that some new conflagration would be needed to overcome the Continent's division. Instead, the job had been done by working people, who had rejected an ideology 'which presumed to speak in their name' and found effective ways of 'bearing witness to the truth'. Communist regimes had fallen largely because they violated workers' rights. But the true cause of their collapse had been the void brought about by atheism. Marxism had promised to uproot the need for God in human hearts. Yet the 'struggle born of prayer' which culminated in 1989 had drawn heavily on the Church's social teaching. After a century of Marxist domination, the workers movement had found a new partner in Christianity. The outcome was a warning to those who, 'in the name of political realism, wish to banish law and morality from the political arena'.[49]

A top Soviet ideologist, Vadim Zagladin, described *Centesimus annus* as 'the greatest spiritual document of our time ... deep, rich in content, and looking ahead to the twenty-first century'.[50] There was more to come. Visiting his homeland again in June 1991, on a pilgrimage devoted to the Ten Commandments, the Pope set out the parameters for a new state, recalling Poland's 1791 constitution, Europe's first democratic charter. In Warsaw, he railed against the 'humiliating view' that Poland's 'return to Europe' meant accepting practices like abortion. 'I wish to protest against this – it insults the great world of Christian culture from which we drew,' he added. 'We do not have to become part of Europe, since we ourselves created Europe. We created it, enduring greater hardship than those now credited, or crediting themselves, with being the keepers of Europeanness.'[51]

He had a similar message for Hungarians that August – how to find a new place in Europe without surrendering what was most important. 'A new Europe is struggling to take shape before our eyes,' the Pope told Calvinists in Debrecen. 'The best service we can contribute at this time is a renewed common witness to the Christian values which were its foundation.'[52] It would be an appeal repeated many times over the decade, during visits to Albania, the Baltic states, the Czech Republic, Slovakia and the Balkans.

Addressing 1.4 million Christians from seventy-five countries during a World Youth Day at Poland's Jasna Góra national shrine, John Paul II said he counted on young people from East and West to 'build a common house for a future of solidarity and peace'. The Assumption Day Mass, concelebrated by 2,000 priests, became a spectacular celebration of Europe's reunification. With the borders now open, John Paul II enthused, the Church in Europe could now 'breathe freely with both her lungs'.[53]

Tens of thousands came from the Soviet Union. Just four days later, tanks appeared on the streets of Moscow, as a hardline 'emergency committeee' proclaimed Gorbachev ousted, and his *glasnost* and *perestroika* at an end. The Soviet ruler had been pressing breakaway republics to sign up to a new federation. When the coup collapsed within forty-eight hours, the Soviet Union's disintegration became inevitable. By early September, foreign governments had recognised the independence of Lithuania, Latvia and Estonia. By December, Georgians, Armenians, Belarusans and Ukrainians had followed suit.

* * *

With the straitjacket of the Cold War now removed, conflicts had to be expected. In *Centesimus annus*, the Pope had warned that, for Eastern Europe, 'the real post-war period' was only now beginning. The re-ordering of economies would require sacrifices comparable to those of western countries in the 40s and 50s. But 'hatred and ill-will', he cautioned, had also accumulated in reaction to communist injustices. The international community should prepare itself.[54]

It was anticipated that former Communists would inflame ethnic hostilities to discredit the post-1989 changes. In Croatia's Serb-occupied Krajina and Slavonia regions, an undeclared war escalated into daily atrocities, leaving a death-toll of 5,000. Within a year, an even more vicious conflict had erupted in Bosnia-Herzegovina, which would leave 250,000 dead in three years. Croatia's Roman Catholic cardinal, Franjo Kuharić, appealed for peace with his Serbian Orthodox counterpart, Patriarch Pavle. As the middle ground eroded, however, religious groups came under intense pressure to side with nationalist demands.

Catholic bishops in Czechoslovakia condemned calls for their country to be divided after failed attempts at a new federal union. But they conceded that independence had a moral dimension; and on 1 January 1993, the 'velvet divorce' took place. Czechs and Slovaks could count themselves lucky. In an arc of post-Soviet republics from Moldavia to Nagorno-Karabakh, Chechnya to Tajikistan, disputes over territory and self-rule quickly turned violent.

The Church was embroiled in domestic disputes too – over media rights, religious education and the restitution of Communist-seized Church properties – which would still be flaring a decade later. In Poland, the Catholic Church requested that a constitutional clause declaring Church and State 'separate' be replaced by the more positive term, 'autonomous', found in Vatican II's *Gaudium et spes*. 'In our situation, where the majority belong to both, the necessity of co-operation between State and Church should be stressed for each person's well-being,' the Bishops' Conference explained. 'The time has come to reject the wrongful simplification which has gained acceptance in our social consciousness – that the state's secular character is the fundamental, sole guarantee of citizens' freedom and equal rights.'[55]

In 1993, Polish citizens voted ex-Communists back to power amid frustration at post-Communist inequalities. Opinion surveys showed a sharp deterioration in the Church's public image. But there was no drop in religious participation. There were governments, such as Hungary's, which stood up for Christian values and pledged to help the Church recover. Elsewhere, the Church was forced to contend with reborn anti-clericalism, such as in the Czech Republic, where historical associations between Catholicism and Habsburg rule made a comeback.

There remained the vexed problem of inter-church relations. In *Ut unum sint* (May 1995), the Pope hoped for 'full communion' with Orthodox Christians, and reaffirmed his belief that Sts Benedict, Cyril and Methodius could provide figureheads for ecumenical dialogue. Orthodox leaders continued to accuse him, however, of undoing the conciliatory work of John XXIII and Paul VI by failing to take their complaints seriously.

John Paul II had a flair for grand gestures. During his 1991 Polish pilgrimage, he had become the first pope to pray in an Orthodox cathedral. In 1998, he became the first to visit a predominantly Orthodox country, Romania, following this up in 1999–2002 with pilgrimages to traditionally Orthodox Georgia, Ukraine, Greece and Bulgaria. His hopes of visiting Russia, however, were persistently dashed by the Moscow Patriarchate, which insisted progress should first be made on inter-church grievances. At the 1991 Synod on Europe, the president of the Vatican's Pontifical Council for Promoting Christian Unity, Cardinal Edward Cassidy, had regretted the 'empty seats' left for Orthodox guests. But dialogue could not be used, Cassidy warned, 'as a forum for accusations by one party against another'. Nor could it be entered into 'under constant threat of non-co-operation'.[56]

Of course, inter-faith ties were only part of a wider picture. Former Communist leaders, from President Algirdas Brazauskas of Lithuania to President Edward Shevardnadze of Georgia, had embraced Christianity as bonds between religion

and nationhood were reasserted. Critics saw this as oppor-
tunism; but it was more than that. Both Mikhail Gorbachev
and his successor, Boris Yeltsin, admitted to being baptised as
children, prompting the question whether Communist-era
atheism had ever been more than 'superimposed', as the Pope
had suggested in *Redemptor hominis*. Yeltsin blamed his ideological formation at school for giving him the 'most insulting
opinions' about Churches and religions. 'This was gravely
wrong and seriously unjust,' the former Communist
confessed. 'When I am in a church now, I take a candle. A
religious service lasting four hours bores neither me nor my
wife. And often when I leave church, I feel something new
and luminous has come into me.'[57]

Such views were common. The ideologist, Vadim Zagladin,
admitted the peaceful coexistence of religious faiths had
refuted his Party's claims – a sure sign of the dangers posed
when 'ideological fundamentalists' claimed a 'monopoly on
truth'. As Nikolai Berdyaev had written, communism was
only 'the reminder of an unfulfilled Christian duty'. It was
Christians themselves who had been 'precursors and champions' of the socialist ideal. Zagladin agreed with his Vatican
interlocutors – the affirmation that authority comes from God
provided vital protection against arbitrary power. 'Repression
of spiritual liberty is only a step away from suppression of
physical liberty,' the Soviet went on. 'We have tried to bury
Christianity and religion more than once. With what result?
None at all – except that these attempts introduced a harden-
ing of hearts in our life and inhumanity in personal
relationships.'[58]

Yet there were ironies at work. While top Communists like
Yeltsin and Zagladin seemed, through bitter experience, to
have rediscovered the inherent values of Christianity, liberal
western elites seemed, if anything, to have moved in the opposite direction. If the collapse of communism had healed the rift
between the Church and modern secular democracy, there
were plenty of forces at large who seemed ready to widen it
again.

The Belgian Cardinal, Godfried Danneels of Malines-
Brussels, had observed four types of atheism at work in West
European society. There was scientific atheism, with its

unlimited faith in material progress, which hoped to create a human being guided solely by scientific data. There was humanist atheism, which believed with Feuerbach that God was no more than an external projection of human aspirations. There was also reactive atheism, which could be traced back to anti-clerical stereotypes from the nineteenth century. Finally, there was practical atheism, the atheism of a consumer society which relied on instant gratification and preferred to ignore fundamental questions.

The first three were easy to tackle, Danneels argued, since none could answer contemporary needs. Scientific atheism could describe human phenomena, but could not explain their meaning. Humanist atheism caused 'existential fatigue' by placing an impossible responsibility on the human will. Reactive atheism was superficial and depended on vague, selective memories. The hardest challenge came, as it had always done, from practical atheism. This was not a philosophy, system of thought or secular religion. It was, rather, a spiritual emptiness which penetrated the very tissue of civilisation.[59] How to uphold Christianity in such a climate would be the Church's challenge in the coming decade. If the desire for European unity was increasing, so were the disputes over which values should underpin it.

CHAPTER 6

The Millennium Debate

Some might argue that the decline in religious belief and practice, and the secular character of much of modern culture, makes religion a matter of minority interest. Others might claim that the excesses of the past, and not very distant past, committed in the name of religion, make a secular Europe desirable or even necessary. Others still may argue that the tolerance required of a more pluralist Europe makes our Christian tradition at best problematic ... However, a clear-eyed realism about the past should not allow us to wind up in a situation where our heritage is denied and we are left with no foundation on which to build.

The warning by an Irish minister, Mary Hanafin, speaking for the European Union's rotating presidency, recognised the pitfalls of a purely secular conception of Europe.[1] By 1989, the European Community was generating more than a fifth of global trade and exerting a key international influence. It had expanded southwards with Greece's accession in 1981, and westwards in 1986 to newly democratised Spain and Portugal. With twelve member-states and a population of 322 million, its internal balance had altered, reducing the dominance of France and Germany. But debate continued about its future. Some politicians favoured a closer federal union, others a looser confederation. Some wanted to give priority to internal consolidation, others to further enlargement.

The world energy crisis of the 1970s had highlighted the need for co-operation to protect the West European economies. With different systems from health to taxation, however, economic co-ordination was still difficult. The

European Monetary System, launched under the leadership of Roy Jenkins in 1978, had boosted financial stability. But further progress had been impeded by varying rates of inflation, government subsidy and unemployment. Significant advances nevertheless soon came. In 1985, France, Germany and the Benelux countries agreed to scrap border controls under the Schengen Agreement, which would be adopted by most member-states over the next decade. In February 1986, a Single European Act committed the EC to go ahead and create, within six years, the world's largest single market. This extended the Community's competence into new areas, including environmental and regional policy, and brought the EC closer to a common foreign and security strategy. Fiscal policies were to be co-ordinated, business barriers removed, customs controls eased and monopolies broken up. New powers were also given to the Council of Ministers, Court of Justice and European Parliament, whose representative credentials had been enhanced by the first direct elections in 1979.

As the most important EC document since the 1957 Treaty of Rome, the Act was widely believed to have created a new sense of purpose. It stressed the EC's role in promoting 'freedom, equality and social justice', and claimed support from the 'democratic peoples of Europe'. Europe had a responsibility to 'act with consistency and solidarity' in protecting its common interests while promoting democracy, human rights and the rule of law.[2]

'Cohesion' became a watchword. With the Community's richest countries still five times as wealthy as its poorest, new funds were created for supporting impoverished rural areas, and for job creation and re-training in regions hit by industrial decline. In December 1989, a Charter of Fundamental Social Rights of Workers pledged improved conditions for labourers and employees. Dubbed the 'Social Charter', it was not legally binding. But it imposed a 'moral obligation' to ensure the development of the EC's internal market was matched by the protection of the working population.

Enthusiasts for closer integration had continued to insist that economic union should be matched by political union. This had implications for national sovereignty and was highly controversial. In 1985, however, at the initiative of President François Mitterrand of France, the decision was taken to go ahead with an inter-governmental meeting on the subject.

The resulting Treaty of European Union, signed at Maastricht on 7 February 1992, fell short of agreeing to a federal union. But it renamed the Community the 'European Union', and spoke of 'an even closer union among the peoples of Europe'. Decisions would be taken 'as closely as possible' to the citizens, who now had the right to live, work and vote anywhere.[3] The Treaty extended the EU's powers in justice and home affairs, immigration and asylum, health and social policy, education and culture, transport, police and consumer protection. Meanwhile, it set a timetable of January 1999 for introducing a single European currency, the Euro, backed by a European Central Bank. This had been delayed by monetary instability, as well as by the withdrawal of Britain and Italy from the EU's Exchange Rate Mechanism. But it had been the prime objective of the EU Commission president, Jacques Delors. Mitterrand had supported it too, as a means of anchoring a powerful reunited Germany firmly within the EU, and as the next logical step after the creation of a single market from January 1993.

The Maastricht Treaty faced tough opposition. It was challenged in Germany's Constitutional Court, initially rejected by Danish voters in a referendum and only narrowly approved in France. When it was finally ratified in May 1993, Britain opted out of the planned single currency and the treaty's annexed Social Charter. There were signs of optimism. By the mid-1990s, the EU had pulled out of recession, helped by a US economic boom, bringing annual GDP growth to a respectable average of two and a half per cent. In 1995, Austria, Sweden and Finland joined, swelling the number of member-states to fifteen. Yet the signs were far from consistent. Norway and Switzerland voted against accession, preferring the European Free Trade Association. Despite the proud boast of the Single European Act, public support for the EU appeared to be dwindling.

In 1997, a Treaty of Amsterdam tried to appease the disillusionment by reaffirming the EU's guiding principles of 'subsidiarity and proportionality' and making modest structural changes. The Social Charter was incorporated into EU law and the powers of the European Parliament further strengthened. They were to be used two years later when the whole EU Commission resigned amid corruption allegations with its latest president, Jacques Santer.

Although signatories were unable to agree on political union, an EU commissioner was appointed for foreign affairs and further steps taken towards a common security policy. In the wake of international inertia during the conflict in Bosnia, which had only ended in 1995 thanks to a US-sponsored peace accord, a 60,000-strong rapid reaction force was earmarked for future humanitarian and peacekeeping operations.

These moves faced resistance too. In 1998, it was agreed that all member-states, except Greece, had met the 'convergence criteria' for adopting the single currency. But there were still problems to be sorted out. The Amsterdam Treaty had cited fuller employment and welfare as core EU aims, along with measures to improve living and working conditions and combat social exclusion. It had also envisaged a greater reliance on majority voting, as well as a system of 'enhanced co-operation', allowing a group of countries to take initiatives without waiting for a total consensus. With further enlargement in the offing, this time into post-Communist Eastern Europe, both measures were intended to allay fears that the EU would eventually be dominated by small states.

Yet these changes were controversial too. Although Britain's new Labour government under Tony Blair was broadly sympathetic – even reversing policy to accept the Social Charter – the Conservative opposition was hostile to Europe. It became fashionable to ridicule the EU and scorn any talk of extending its powers.

Ten East European countries had applied for EU membership; and in 1998, formal negotiations duly opened with the Czech Republic, Estonia, Hungary, Poland and Slovenia, as well as with Cyprus. But there was uneasiness about the economic impact of expansion. Many West Europeans – from German steelworkers to Spanish miners – feared cheaper competition from the East. Not all East Europeans were in favour either. In March 1999, after a decade of geopolitical uncertainty, Poles, Czechs and Hungarians were admitted to

NATO, thus securing their defence needs. Joining the EU was a lot more complex. All main parties, from conservatives to former Communists, concurred that it should be an overriding national objective. But they differed over the terms and conditions.

This was hardly surprising. Candidate countries faced twenty-eight negotiating packages, covering everything from taxation and border controls, to transport and fisheries. They had to accept the EU's *acquis communautaire*, an 80,000–page dossier of regulations and procedures, as well as adjusting their domestic laws to hundreds of pieces of EU legislation. As members of the Council of Europe, they had signed up to the 1950 European Convention and accepted the authority of the European courts. Their democratic institutions and free-market economies were now required to meet EU standards. This meant stable laws and accountable office-holders, as well as stringent controls on inflation, budget deficits and interest rates, at a time when average earnings in Poland alone were barely a tenth of neighbouring Germany's.

* * *

The Church had had misgivings about the 'Westernisation' of Eastern Europe. Having survived Communist rule, its leaders were worried that moral and social bonds would be eroded by opening the borders to western influences. Countries which had only recently won independence from Moscow could hardly be expected to surrender it to Brussels, especially when EU membership looked certain, as the Pope had warned, to bring pressure for liberalised abortion and other moral compromises. 'A wave of garbage, a post-modernist, liberal slush of pseudo-values – this is what Europe is offering us today,' Poland's conservative *Nasz Dziennik* daily exploded in 1996. 'Losing sovereignty, surrendering land to foreign hands, cutting a swathe of unemployment, significantly reducing our youth's education levels, universally killing unborn children – this is all too high a price for being together with the West.'[4]

There were worries about the effects on Church life. In the 1950s, when Schuman, Monnet, Adenauer and De Gasperi had placed their Christian stamp on the first European institutions, the churches of Italy and Portugal had been as full as those of Poland, while the Dutch Church had sent as many priests abroad as it employed at home. Since then, the trend in religious observances had been unmistakeably downwards. France's Roman Catholic Church had boasted 45,000 priests in 1945; it now had fewer than a third of that number. The bishops of Spain, a country of transition in the 1980s, had deplored the 'moral deterioration' of society, blaming attempts to 'impose a deterministic conception of life which is laicist and permissive'. Though much-criticised, the blistering critique had expressed a widely shared fear – 'belonging to Europe' spelt the death of religion.[5]

The EU had provided little reassurance. Until the mid-1990s, the words 'religion' and 'church' had not appeared in any of its documents. This might have been justifiable in the early years, given the avowedly Christian vision of the founding fathers. It had now begun to look like indifference, perhaps even disdain.

Yet it could also be seen as a challenge. In the post-war years, western statesmen had busied themselves creating a stable and prosperous alternative to Communism. With Communism now defunct, however, questions of sense and purpose were being posed again. The search for answers was drawing Christians into an ever greater involvement in European issues.

The Vatican had supported the Conference on Security and Co-operation in Europe since its inception in the early 1970s. It was a signatory of the CSCE's 1990 Charter of Paris, which, in language close to Christianity, declared human rights 'the first responsibility of governments' and 'an essential safeguard against an over-mighty state'. When the CSCE, now incorporating fifty-five states, became the Organisation on Security and Co-operation in Europe (OSCE) in 1995, the Vatican was represented on its Vienna-based Permanent Council, as well as on its Parliamentary Assembly in Copenhagen and its many missions and delegations. When an anniversary summit was held at Helsinki, the Vatican's Secretary of State, Cardinal Angelo Sodano, underlined the Church's determination to go on contributing to the 'new

Europe'. Europe's humanistic values were 'imbued with Christianity', Sodano added. As the 'source of its age-old culture', it had 'inspired the genius of its peoples'.[6] There could, indeed, be no doubting western Church support for European integration. The Council of Catholic Episcopates of Europe, or CCEE, had welcomed the EU's steps towards 'better management'. But it had also warned against a 'new demarcation line' between the Union and the rest of Europe.[7] With East European Christians now free to get involved, the Church's importance as a focus of unity could only grow. Post-communist countries accounted for more than half the thirty-four Roman Catholic Bishops Conferences represented at the CCEE, whose president from 1993 was a Czech cardinal, Miloslav Vlk of Prague. They were urged to offer ideas and proposals – not just 'knocking on the door of Europe', as the Pope had complained in 1991, but participating as full members.

A separate Commission of EC Bishops Conferences (COMECE) had been founded back in 1980. Representing over a thousand Catholic bishops from member-states, its statute required it to keep local Church leaders informed of developments, and to maintain contacts with 'competent persons' within the Community, monitoring policy and legislation, and observing 'tendencies and manoevres'. Although independent of the larger CCEE, it co-operated closely with it, as well as with the Vatican's representation in Brussels, which was raised to a full nunciature in 1996.

COMECE saw its role as 'recalling and promoting' the fundamental values set out, as the cornerstone of European unification, in the treaties of Paris and Rome. It sought to make the Christian perspective available to EU policy-makers, and had established working groups with EU officials by the mid-1990s on legal affairs, bioethics, social issues, media policy and relations with Islam. There was a problem here. The past three decades had seen the influence of churches decline in Europe. But was there not a danger that an organisation like COMECE, with the weight of Christian tradition behind it, would define its role in bureaucratic terms, as just one of many non-governmental organisations competing to put its views across? Had the Church not joined the debate too late, thus relegating itself to the ranks of the many groups defending their own agendas?

COMECE was not alone. Around fifty other church organisations had permanent offices in Brussels, including the Jesuit and Dominican orders and the Caritas aid network. The non-Catholic Conference of European Churches (CEC) was also represented, as were Germany's Evangelical Church and the Orthodox patriarchates of Constantinople and Moscow. Despite the obvious Church presence, however, there was still scepticism as to whether the EU was taking Christian voices seriously, amid the cacaphony of contrasting views and perspectives. In 1989, the European Ecumenical Assembly had welcomed the Single European Act as a landmark for improving the well-being of citizens. But the opening of Community borders, the Assembly warned, should not lead to a 'bastion Western Europe', closed to the rest of the world. Attitudes to refugees and asylum-seekers would be a test of the EC's openness. So would a readiness to lessen the economic gaps between East and West, North and South.[8]

The Catholic Church had warned of the dangers of a 'unilateral civilisation' which saw the world in scientific and technological terms and lost sight of humanity's 'transcendental dimension'. Christianity's responsibility, John Paul II told the CCEE, was to 'revitalise a civilisation showing symptoms of a worrying decrepitude'.[9] Against this background, there was disappointment that the 1992 Maastricht Treaty again made no mention of churches, despite 250 pages with detailed provisions covering culture, education and social affairs, as well as fifty attached protocols and declarations on everything from tourism to animal protection.

There were, however, signs of change. German and Polish theologians had warned of a crisis in legitimacy unless the EU set down deeper cultural and social roots. By 1997, there was talk of finding a 'vision', something which might breathe a spiritual impulse into the EU's overwhelmingly empirical and technocratic outlook. EU officials remained uncertain about the place of religion. But Jacques Delors began meeting regularly with Christian, Jewish and Muslim leaders, recognising their potential to enlist public support for EU aims. Step by step, helped by practising Christians among the EU's politicians and civil servants, COMECE became a partner in dialogue.

In his final weeks as EU Commission president, Delors initiated a 'Soul for Europe' programme, to support church-related projects. When a new Mediterranean policy initiative was launched in 1995 by the EU's Forward Studies Unit, it agreed to proposals by COMECE and CEC to have religion included on the agenda. The resulting Barcelona Declaration acknowledged that 'understanding among major religions' would be a key to closer co-operation in the region. The Unit organised other symposia too, while Church representatives held meetings with each government taking over the EU's rotating half-year presidency. There were no guarantees that church views would acted on. But attitudes appeared to be evolving.

In 1997, the role of churches and faiths was an agenda topic at the EU's Amsterdam summit. After lengthy arguments, a declaration was appended to the Amsterdam Treaty, confirming the EU's acceptance of 'the status under national law of churches and religious associations and communities in member-states'. It was no more than a modest gesture. But it was also a sign that Churches were being listened to.

* * *

That November, a delegation of Polish bishops paid a fact-finding visit to Brussels, and returned home reassured about their country's EU future. Czech and Hungarian Church leaders followed in 1998 and 1999, and came back similarly convinced. Meanwhile, Romania's Orthodox Church came out in support of accession too. What was it that had brought the change of heart?

With conflict still raging in the Balkans and Caucasus, and Russia and its neighbours looking endemically unstable, Western integration looked like the only realistic option. In the early 1990s, there had been talk of a possible East European equivalent to NATO, which might have allowed post-Communist states to approach western integration as a united front. These had come to nothing. Nor had the ideal of a Slavic homeland, with its own distinctive features. The myth of a 'spiritual East' and 'materialistic West' was breaking down. In the East, deeply Catholic Slovaks and Poles lived alongside highly secularised Czechs and eastern Germans. In the West, the irreligious British, French and Swedish coexisted with the devout Austrians, Danes, Greeks, Italians and Portuguese.[10] If religion was in decline, it was not happening in a uniform way. Nor was this an exclusively western phenomenon. In a 1998 survey, eighty-four per cent of Polish priests declared themselves in favour of their country's EU accession. More than a third concurred that the EU should be doing more to support religious life. But two-thirds felt confident that membership would not affect their Church's position. Although integration would lay Poland open to 'materialistic attitudes', more than half were sure the same attitudes would develop even if it remained outside.[11]

There were still conflicts and misunderstandings to sort out among Christians themselves. The Catholic Church had experienced Communist rule differently, depending on its strengths and weaknesses. In Poland, it had been targeted because of its patriotic profile, whereas in the Czech lands and Hungary it had been attacked as reactionary relict of the Habsburgs. In Lithuania, Slovakia and Croatia, it had been identified as a bastion of nationalism. In Ukraine, Romania and Belarus, it had been associated with troublesome minorities. Yet East Europeans complained that western fellow-Christians saw them only as an amorphous bloc. The pre-war Soviet Union had witnessed the mass persecution of Christians. But western Catholics were accused of underestimating communism, and of ignoring the vibrancy of an East European faith which seemed to have exposed their own inadequacies.

Western Catholics, for their part, found it difficult to understand why suffering and persecution were so rooted in the post-war East European identity. They were wary of zealous, missionising priests from Eastern Europe, whose criticisms of 'western materialism' often showed a feeble grasp of the complex spiritual geography of western societies. Some viewed them as a disruptive element, representing an antiquated, authoritarian model of Church-State relations, and a paternalistic approach to faith which jarred with the Church's cautious circumspection in the pluralistic West. Despite much effort, ecumenical relations remained in serious trouble too. In 1991, while the Soviet Union was still intact, the Pope had appointed apostolic administrators (a rank below bishops) for Catholics in European Russia, Siberia and Kazakhstan. The move was intended to give the Church its first proper structure since pre-Soviet times. But it sparked angry Orthodox reactions, which would be repeated when the Pope upgraded the administrations to full dioceses in 2002. Meeting at Santiago in 1991, with the Jesuit Cardinal Carlo Maria Martini of Milan and Anglican Dean John Arnold as co-chairmen, Europe's churches had lamented the 're-establishment of confessional battlelines' and called for an examination of consciences. Religion had not been the cause of war in the Balkans, the assembly insisted. Nor, 'despite appearances', were local churches at war with each other. But the religious disputes of early modern Europe had contributed to unbelief in the nineteenth century. A return to 'rigorous competition' between churches now would merely reinforce it again, in a Europe already 'saturated by consumerist ideology'.

> Not all that long ago, evangelism was regarded as something to do mainly with countries outside Europe. From now on, the missionary vision embraces our own continent too ... The evangelisation of Europeans has a future provided we respect the complex spiritual destiny of this continent. As Christians, we are beginning to rediscover our living roots in the people of Israel. As citizens, we are also the heirs of classical Greece and the Enlightenment. Today, we live side by side with Islam. Our plan envisages no religious monopoly in Europe. It is the proclamation of the grace of God for all men and women.[12]

Tensions between majority and minority faiths had nevertheless flared well beyond Russia. The search for reborn identities was fuelling a debate about the historic rights of dominant churches, especially when two different religious traditions seemed to compete for the title. In most countries, churches had formed national ecumenical councils together in order to speak with a single voice. Although Roman Catholics had generally stayed aloof, they were actively involved in Austria, the Czech Republic and elsewhere. But an effective ecumenical stance was still being impeded by disputes. Most candidate countries for EU accession were predominantly Catholic. There were fears of a new division in Europe between a richer Catholic and Protestant West, and a poorer Orthodox East. If the bloody fate of Yugoslavia taught anything, it was what might happen when that division ran not between countries, but within them.

When the Conference of European Churches had met at Prague in 1992, it had called for a firmer distinction between 'authentic evangelism and destructive proselytism', and a joint inter-faith response to the growing problems of secularisation and atheism. It had urged closer relations with Judaism – something which 'touches the very identity of Christianity' – and a more active dialogue with Islam, which had been present in Europe for more than a thousand years. Above all, it had called for 'philosophers, artists, scientists and theologians' to work together on a common understanding of faith and culture. Christians had been responsible in equal measure for Europe's unity and disunity in history. They could now make sure it was not riven apart again by new ethnic, cultural and religious divisions – and that Europe, the first continent to hear the Gospel, became 'a blessing, and not a curse, to the rest of the world'.[13] Similar anxieties had surfaced when the Catholic CCEE met in Prague a year later to urge a securer balance between 'freedom and solidarity' in facing the challenges of a reunited Europe.

* * *

That quest had also been preoccupying the Pope. Addressing the European Parliament, he had warned against attempts to 'venerate society as a collective supremacy, which swallows up human beings and their irreducible destiny'. States and political powers belonged to the 'shifting and always perfectible framework of the world', the Pope added. They could not last forever. Nor, as the ancient Greeks had discovered, could any democracy which failed to enshrine the rule of law on 'a transcendent standard of what is true and just'. All Europe's schools of thought should reflect on the 'bleak prospects' of excluding God from public life.[14]

In a rare interview with Italy's *La Stampa* daily in 1993, John Paul II hit out at the unacceptable face of contemporary capitalism. Both Karl Marx and Pope Leo XIII, he recalled, had blamed 'unbridled, savage capitalism' for the social ills of the nineteenth century. It had been right to resist the communist system. But it should also be remembered that many workers and intellectuals had initially welcomed it as a gateway to justice and peace. Today, the 'extreme champions of capitalism' dismissed communism's achievement in curbing unemployment and helping the poor. But Leo XIII had been right to recognise that there were 'seeds of truth' in the socialist, or communist, programme. They had helped correct the worst aspects of capitalism; and they should not be 'destroyed or lost', at a time when the transition to a new system in Eastern Europe was exacting a high toll in 'poverty and misery'.

The Church accepted capitalism's basic principles, since they conformed with natural law, John Paul II reaffirmed. But it condemned the 'degenerate aspects of capitalism,' which were the root cause of many social problems troubling the new Europe. After living under atheist rule, Poles and other East Europeans understood what God and religion meant. 'The Eastener has realised this; the prisoner in the Gulag realised it; Solzhenitsyn realised it,' the Pope went on. 'In the West, man does not see this so clearly ... his awareness is largely secularised, and he often sees religion as something alienating.'

> I am not against Poland's membership in Europe, but I am against the attempt to make this membership into a kind of idol, a false idol ... I believe it is a question of vision. The new politicians have lowered theirs rather too much, while the vision of the founding fathers was lofty, comprehensive and total. Yes, confronting the Soviet Union was a strong incentive. They thought not only of economic and political unity, but also of cultural and spiritual unity. Today, I have the impression that everything is reduced to the economic dimension.[15]

Moral attitudes were changing rapidly in Europe, placing the Church's ideals of marriage and family under pressure. Abortion had been legalised in Britain, despite Church protests, in 1967, and in France, West Germany, Italy and Sweden a decade later. The social acceptance of divorce and extra-marital relationships had coincided with a massive increase in single-parent families. Much of this had happened by default, as countries followed each other's legislation, often without exhaustive argumentation. Back in 1979, the Pope had warned against the slavery of a 'materialistic civilisation'.[16] He now took up this theme with a vengeance.

In *Veritatis splendor* (1993), John Paul II warned of an 'alliance between democracy and moral relativism', and an 'overall and systematic calling into question of traditional moral doctrine'. In *Evangelium vitae* (1995), he cautioned against a climate in which personal conscience and responsibility were 'turned over to the civil law', and the state's role was limited to guaranteeing the individual 'complete freedom of choice' on moral issues. Western self-indulgence also threatened European unity. Christianity had helped bring down communism with its religious and moral message, because it had made the protest of workers against injustice – a protest once organised and led by Communists – part of its own teaching. But the roots of totalitarianism, John Paul II added, lay in denying the transcendent dignity of the human person and allowing the 'force of power' to take over.[17] Although communism, the most recent version of totalitarianism, had ended, the danger to fundamental rights was just as great. Some people had convinced themselves that binding moral norms led to authoritarianism and intolerance. They were wrong. Democracy was merely a system, a means to an end. It could not be idolised to the point of becoming 'a substitute or panacea for morality'.

> History has known cases where crimes have been committed in the name of truth. But equally grave crimes and radical denials of freedom have also been committed, and are still being committed, in the name of ethical relativism ... If today we see an almost universal consensus with regard to the value of democracy, this is to be considered a positive 'sign of the times', as the Church's Magisterium has frequently noted. But the value of democracy stands or falls with the values it embodies and promotes.[18]

Visiting Poland in June 1997, the Pope marked the thousandth anniversary of the martyrdom of St Adalbert by meeting the presidents of Poland, Germany, Ukraine, Hungary, Lithuania, Slovakia and the Czech Republic. The concrete and steel of the Berlin Wall had fallen, he told them. But Europe was still divided by an 'invisible wall' – a wall in human hearts 'made out of fear and aggressiveness, lack of understanding for people of different origins, colours and religious convictions, a wall of political and economic sefishness, of weakening sensitivity to the value of human life'. This wall could only be breached, the Pope continued, by a return to Gospel values – by ensuring that 'no nation, not even the least powerful', was excluded from Europe's development, and that an 'elementary solidarity' prevailed over the 'unrestrained desire for profit'. Yet even today the Church was still having to defend itself against charges that it was an enemy of freedom. 'In the name of respect for human rights,' John Paul II went on, 'in the name of liberty, equality and fraternity . . . Do not be afraid! Open the doors to Christ!'[19]

If the Church had harnessed the power of workers, it had now also taken up the slogan of the Revolution. Yet imaginary walls still existed against Christianity too.

In France that August, the Pope beatified Frédéric Ozanam, the nineteenth-century reformer who had urged the Church to embrace social justice and heal its growing alienation from Europe's industrial population. It was an important symbolic statement of the Church's priorities in the new Europe. Two years later, in June 1999, he reminded Poland's parliament, the Sejm, that the collapse of ideological barriers had created a 'historic opportunity' for Europe to regain its unity. But 'if we wish Europe's new unity to last, we must build on the basis of the spiritual values which were once its foundation,' the Pope reiterated, 'keeping in mind the wealth and diversity of the cultures and traditions of individual nations. This must be a great European Community of the Spirit.'[20]

In October, he proclaimed three new patrons for Europe, to add to Saints Benedict, Cyril and Methodius. The honouring of Catherine of Siena (1347–1380), Bridget of Sweden (1303–1373) and the Jewish-born Edith Stein (1891–1942), who died at Auschwitz, could be viewed as a gesture to the equal dignity and authority of women, as well as to Christianity's outreach to all regions and epochs. All three had fought in their time for peace and understanding around Christian values.

* * *

However far Christianity had travelled, the burden of the past would always be with it. At the very beginning of his pontificate, the Pope had looked forward to the year 2000. Many believed it would be an appropriate occasion to atone for past sins and shortcomings. Vatican II's Pastoral Constitution, *Gaudium et spes*, had hinted at this.

> The Church is the faithful spouse of the Lord and will never fail to be a sign of salvation in the world; but it is by no means unaware that down through the centuries there have been among its members, both clerical and lay, some who were disloyal to the Spirit of God. Today as well, the Church is not blind to the discrepancy between the message it proclaims and the human weakness of those to whom the Gospel has been entrusted ... The Church also realises how much it needs the maturing influence of centuries of past experience in order to work out its relationship to the world.[21]

Historic attitudes to the Jews were part of that discrepancy. In 1991, Poland's Bishops Conference had taken up the issue of guilt for the Holocaust, acknowledging Polish indifference to the Jewish fate, while the Pope, visiting Hungary, had branded anti-Semitism and racism 'sins against God and humanity'.[22] In 1997, France's Catholic bishops had gone further, calling on their Church to 'beg forgiveness' for the role of Christian anti-Jewish prejudices in the run-up to the Jewish exterminations. Christianity's Jewish roots, the bishops added, had failed to prevent a 'centuries-long hostility', which had 'stamped its mark in differing ways on Christian doctrine and teaching'. As François Mauriac had written, 'a crime of such proportions falls in no small part on the shoulders of all those witnesses who failed to cry out, and this whatever the reason for their silence'.[23]

'Truth, memory and reconciliation' were the watchwords

proposed by COMECE. As the Millennium approached, other Bishops Conferences issued declarations of regret, while the disputed wartime record of Pope Pius XII was hauled into the open with a 'Reflection on the Shoah' by the Vatican's Papal Commission for Religious Contacts with Judaism. The records of the Inquisition were made available to historians, while Church commissions began examining the work of past reformers. 'The Church should become more conscious of the sinfulness of her childen,' the Pope reaffirmed in an apostolic letter, 'recalling all those times in history when they departed from the spirit of Christ and his Gospel and, instead of offering to the world the witness of a life inspired by values of faith, indulged in ways of thinking and acting which were truly forms of counter-witness and scandal.'[24] The letter, *Tertio millenio adveniente*, listed Church leaders' shared responsibility for 'secularism and relativism', the 'lack of discernment' shown towards human rights violations by totalitarian regimes, and Christian involvement in 'grave forms of injustice and exclusion'.

Repentance became a Millennium theme for other churches too, as a precondition if Christianity was to fulfil its unifying mission in Europe. The Protestant theologian, Wolfhart Pannenberg, called on churches to admit their responsibility for exacerbating national rivalries, as well as for historic events such as the 1054 Great Schism and sixteenth-century Reformation. Protestants should atone, he said, for breaking up the Western Church, and for the 'less helpful aspects of Luther's temper', Catholics for misdeeds against Orthodoxy caused by the 'pride of the Christian West'. The transition to modernity had not been 'a smooth process of unfolding Christian principles'. It would not be easy to persuade modern culture that its problems could be solved by 'rediscovering its Christian origins'.[25]

Not everyone agreed. But most concurred that all churches and denominations would face tough challenges in the Europe of the twenty-first century. By 2000, the Vatican had diplomatic ties with twenty-eight former Warsaw Pact states, including sixteen ex-Soviet republics, and treaties or Concordats regulating the Catholic Church's status with half a dozen. The Pope had visited fourteen, eight times in the case of his homeland. Yet the practical picture was mixed. If Christian life had shown signs of consolidation in Poland, Lithuania, Slovakia, Croatia and the Orthodox countries, it was all but marginalised in traditionally Catholic Hungary, Slovenia and the Czech Republic. Disputes continued over state budget allocations, the status of Church schools and the restitution of Communist-seized properties. Public attitudes to the Church varied widely. So did moral and legal practices. While abortion was effectively banned in Poland, it was widely available in neighbouring countries. Fewer than one in six marriages ended in divorce in Poland, compared to more than half in Lithuania. According to census figures, Catholics dropped from forty per cent to below a quarter of the Czech population in the eight years after 1993, but rose from sixty per cent to sixty-nine per cent over the same period in adjacent Slovakia.[26]

More East European Churches had joined CEC and the Geneva-based World Council of Churches, and Eastern Christianity was better represented at European fora. Yet the differences remained extensive. While priestly vocations were increasing in Poland, they were in crisis in most of Western Europe, dropping by half in Belgium alone in the five years after 1998 and to almost zero in Switzerland. Of Ireland's eight Catholic seminaries, seven were to close by 2003, while almost half of Spain's sixty-eight scored no recruitments at all the same year. In Britain, membership of the Catholic Church fell by a quarter in the fifteen years up to 1990, accompanied by a nineteen per cent drop among Anglicans and a similar decline among Methodists and Baptists. In the Netherlands, Catholic Church attendance plummeted by eighty-one per cent between 1960 and 2001, accompanied by a two-thirds decrease in baptisms, confirmations and church marriages.[27]

Church experts blamed social and cultural change, and sometimes welcomed the shift to a smaller, more committed Church. But internal divisions were multiplying in the Western Church over issues from clerical celibacy and women's ordination, to collegiality and lay participation. Most Protestant Churches had accepted female ministers in the 1970s and 1980s, while the Anglican Church of England voted to follow suit in 1992. The Pope rejected parallel calls in the

Catholic Church, ruling that it had 'no authority whatsoever' to make the change.[28] Even then, the traditionalist Lefebvrist movement went on rejecting the Church's 'liberal direction'. There were, however, signs of dynamism in church life too. Up to one in ten European Catholics belonged to international lay renewal movements with names like Communione e Liberazione, Focolari, Chemin Neuf and Light and Life. Other denominations had movements of their own, like the Orthodox Sindesimos and the Anglican House Church. Retreats and prayer groups were growing in popularity, along with pilgrimages to Europe's great shrines. If secularisation was measured by decreasing day-to-day religious practices, this did not necessarily mean a decline in religious needs.

* * *

There were few differences between the churches when it came to the future of the European Union. In 1993, Europe's Catholic bishops had called on Christians to be 'the thorn in the side of the European conscience'. But the real danger, the bishops warned, came 'not from immorality, but from incapacity'. Since then, co-operation had been improving. A joint committee of COMECE and CEC had criticised the EU's secularism and demanded a more 'structured dialogue' on Christian concerns.[29]

These ranged from unemployment and equal opportunities to life issues and ecology. Immigration and asylum featured prominently too. In the wake of terror attacks on 11 September 2001 against New York and Washington, church organisations warned against allowing 'exaggerated security fears' to unleash a policy of full-scale exclusion. Around 1.4 million immigrants were arriving legally in the EU each year, and there were calls for detention centres and automatic deportations to prevent others from gaining entry. In such a climate, church leaders made clear, the task of Christians was to be the 'voice of the voiceless'. It was also to ensure that the EU, with its growing prosperity, maintained its moral obligations towards the rest of the world, through development aid, fair trade and generous initiatives such as the Millennium goal of halving global poverty by 2015. 'From

184 Rethinking Christendom

now on, the world and its peoples – God's Creation – need and deserve a more coherent approach. In a world where no single power – even the strongest – can or should exert full control worldwide, agreement on a list of basic values and principles is essential,' a COMECE committee reported in 2001. It was headed by Michel Camdessus, former managing director of the World Bank, with input from the World Trade Organisation, International Labour Organisation and Citibank. 'The values and principles which Christians have been given by Christian social teaching – human dignity, responsibility, solidarity, global citizenship, justice, participation, subsidiarity, coherence, transparency and accountability – are shared by many people of good will around the world. They offer the basis for a more humane system of global governance.'[30]

By 2002, the structural funds for social policy and economic development had increased to almost a third of total EU expenditure. Yet there were still glaring disparities. The Church's Caritas charity surveyed forty-three European countries, with populations ranging from the 33,000 of Monaco to 146.2 million in Russia, and gross national incomes varying from Germany's $2103 billion to the $1.5 billion of Moldova. It confirmed that globalisation had raised awareness of the 'inter-relatedness of poverty, population, human rights, health and gender issues'. Yet if East Europeans had experienced poverty with 'much greater difficulty' than their richer western neighbours, in the West too the poor enjoyed the worst education, healthcare and housing, and were often caught in a vicious circle of 'circumscribed options and choices.' Life expectancy across the Continent ranged from seventy-nine years in Sweden to sixty-six in Russia, while infant mortality averaged just half a per cent in the EU compared to three per cent in Albania and four per cent in Turkey. But relative poverty levels in Italy and Britain (13.4 per cent) were higher than in some post-Communist countries, while functional illiteracy in Portugal (forty-eight per cent) was three times the Czech Republic's. The report urged 'multi-sectoral programmes' to recognise 'the central place of the human person'.

The collapse of the Soviet Union has resulted in the emergence of over 150 million 'new poor' and prompted a redrawing of the development map ... Cold, hard facts reveal patterns and trends and highlight disparities both between and within countries. They do not and cannot reveal the depth of human pain and misery experienced by millions of people living on islands of poverty – as pensioners, homeless persons, long-term unemployed, lone parents – amidst a sea of plenty.[31]

Both COMECE and CEC had consistently backed the EU's eastwards expansion, calling for candidate countries to be brought into the consultation process, and making efforts to reassure still-sceptical publics. The projected enlargement, COMECE insisted, would signify the final ending of post-war divisions – the true 'Europeanisation' of the EU. Europe would at last breathe with the 'two lungs' so memorably invoked by the Pope. Having broadly approved, Poland's Catholic Bishops Conference gave official support in March 2002. So did the Ecumenical Council, grouping Poland's seven principal minority denominations. During a ninth pilgrimage that August, the Pope called on his homeland to find its 'proper place' in EU structures, 'not only without losing its identity, but also enriching the continent and world with its traditions'.[32]

There were still misgivings.

In January 2000, six more countries had opened accession negotiations: Bulgaria, Latvia, Lithuania, Romania, Slovakia and Malta. The EU still required reforms to cope with such a big expansion – not least in agriculture, which absorbed forty-four per cent of the Union budget, four times as much as in 1980. A reform programme had been set out in *Agenda 2000*. Yet not even a new Marshall Plan could have come close to closing the East-West gap. After a decade of harsh post-Communist restructuring, Poland's domestic product was still barely a twentieth of neighbouring Germany's. Its annual growth had dropped to two per cent and Poland was saddled with a huge budget deficit, twenty per cent unemployment and worrying social dissatisfaction. Monthly earnings in the candidate countries averaged a fifth of Austria's. Although Slovenia was out in the lead, with twice the salaries of Poland, its citizens earned just forty-one per cent of Austrian wages.[33]

Meanwhile, opinion polls showed fewer than half the EU's citizens favouring enlargement, with similar hesitancy in Eastern Europe. Instead of providing proper information, governments were accused of relying on slogans about 'rejoining the European family'. The case of East Germany had highlighted the hardships likely to follow integration. As awareness grew of what EU accession would mean in hard practical terms, the emotional appeal lessened. Germany and Austria had proposed a seven-year moratorium on East European access to EU labour markets, and there were plans for a ten-year wait until East European farmers gained the same subsidies as their western competitors. In general, the benefits of enlargement seemed weighted in the West's favour.

Under the Treaty of Nice in December 2000, the EU nevertheless agreed to go ahead with enlargement. A new voting system was worked out for the EU's expanded Council of Ministers, and a new allocation of seats for the European Parliament, while the Treaty of Rome was revised to allow changes to other EU institutions. In January 2002, the single currency, or Euro, was adopted in all EU member-states except Britain, Denmark and Sweden. At the Copenhagen summit the following December, formal membership invitations were extended to Lithuania, Latvia, Estonia, Poland, the Czech Republic, Slovakia, Hungary, Slovenia, Cyprus and Malta.

When the historic enlargement took place on 1 May 2004, it gave the European Union twenty-five member-states and a combined population of 455 million. Not everyone was happy. After fifteen years of painful post-Communist adjustment, a new phase of transition now lay ahead. But the move was celebrated all the same. For many, as the Church had foreseen, it symbolised Europe's final reunification.

* * *

While Christian churches were celebrating, they remained determined to ensure the new Europe accorded with Christian values and principles. Meeting in Poland in January 2004, the CCEE and CEC reiterated that expansion had to bring 'justice, solidarity and respect for freedom'. It must mean 'an integrated Europe, not just an enlarged EU', which recognised that the new member-countries were just as 'European' as their richer neighbours.[34] When national referenda had been held in the accession countries in 2003, church leaders had urged citizens to vote. The ballots had been close, even so, with lower turnouts and narrower pro-EU majorities than earlier referenda in Western Europe. Polish citizens cited better employment possibilities as their key motive for supporting accession, followed by 'improved life prospects for future generations', faster economic development and free movement across open borders. As reasons for opposing, they said Poland was unprepared, would be 'bought up by foreign capital' and lose sovereignty in making decisions. Almost half said there had been no 'proper and honest debate'.[35]

In the event, the churches marked the turning point in their own way. In March, 100,000 Christians from Eastern and Central Europe attended a 'Pilgrimage of Peoples' to the Austrian shrine of Mariazell. In April, EU leaders joined Catholic, Protestant and Orthodox delegations from twenty-seven countries on an ecumenical pilgrimage to Santiago. In May, thousands more Christians flocked to Stuttgart for an ecumenical 'Assembly for Europe'.

There were hopes that the accession of East Europeans would strengthen the Christian voice in EU affairs, by bringing well-organised, self-confident churches on to the European stage. All but two of the new members-states – Cyprus and Estonia – were predominantly Catholic by tradition; and several had taken steps to defend themselves against unwelcome western pressures, typefied by a European Parliament vote in July 2002 to demand easy access to abortion throughout the EU. Poland's ex-Communist government had agreed, at Church request, to append a unilateral declaration to its accession treaty, noting that no EU documents would impede the country's sovereign right 'to regulate matters of moral significance or concerning defence of human life'. Similar declarations had been made by Malta and Slovakia. 'As Europe unites, a spiritual struggle is unfolding,' Slovakia's Bishops Conference explained in a pastoral letter. 'Many of those who wield political and cultural influence seek to restrict the Christian faith to the private sphere, to ensure it has no impact at all on the life of society. Yet Holy Scripture tells us a faith without consequences is a dead one.'[36]

Poland's bishops concurred. Having slumped in public esteem in the early 1990s, the Catholic Church had recouped its position here by the Millennium, retreating from political involvements and devising new pastoral strategies. In December 2003, three-quarters of Poles had voiced confidence in the Church, its highest rating since 1989, while almost two-thirds said their country should be governed according to Catholic teaching. Church-State disputes periodically resurfaced. But the confrontations of the past seemed to be over. The bishops were understandably upbeat.

> States which decide to transfer part of their powers to EU institutions receive in return a share in, and a right to co-determine, the fate not just of their own countries, but of other European states too. They gain the right to participate in shaping the spiritual countenance of Europe ... We realize not everyone is guided by Christian motives. But it was the religiously motivated yearning for freedom that materialised in the solidarity impulse in Poland, which contributed to the collapse of the Berlin Wall and later brought about the fall of totalitarian regimes and return of democracy. This experience has made our countries especially sensitive to all forms of injury and injustice. It gives them a special moral right to defend threatened religious and moral values.[37]

Yet this right looked certain to be resisted. Disputes were intensifying in Western Europe over values in public life. Any new-found confidence on the Church's part was bound to provoke reactions.

The May enlargement widened the variety of Church-State models operating in the EU. A third of member-states still recognised Christianity in their constitutions. Germany's, adopted in 1949, opened with the words, 'Aware of its responsibility before God and mankind', and listed religion as a 'fundamental right' in its first article. Italy's stated that Church and State were 'independent and sovereign' in their respective spheres. Greece's, by contrast, enshrined the 'dominance' of Orthodoxy and even required Orthodox consent for Bible translations. In Britain, where the monarch

was head of the established Church of England, Anglican
bishops had a right to sit in parliament.
  In France, by contrast, Church and State had remained
strictly separate since 1905. In 2003, Jean-Pierre Raffarin's
centre-right government had set up a commission to 'reflect on
the application of *Laicité*', after complaints that the Separation
Law was outmoded and discriminatory. But most religious
leaders had advised against changes.
  Religious rights were no longer an East-West issue. Despite
still-unsolved problems, post-Communist countries such as
Hungary and Lithuania scored well in human rights surveys,
whereas Germany, Belgium and other western countries had
come in for criticism over their treatment of new religious
movements. 'Discriminatory legal measures are still being
used in Western Europe, in line with policies which unfairly
equate expressions of religious faith with dangerous cults,' the
US State Department cautioned in its International Religious
Freedom Report. 'Certain countries may serve as a model for
similar acts in other less democratic countries which provide
less security for citizens' rights.'[38]

* * *

In *Tertio millennio adveniente*, the Pope had described the
recovery of Christian unity as a twenty-first century priority.
Progress had remained slow. In one of five meetings with the
Archbishop of Canterbury, Robert Runcie, John Paul II had
agreed that Catholics and Anglicans should resolve their
'doctrinal differences'. Anglicans had been at the forefront of
ecumenism, entering full communion with the Scandinavian
and Baltic Lutheran Churches in the 1990s and taking a
leading role in international initiatives. In practice, however,
relations were hampered by feuds in the Anglican Communion
over women priests and homosexuality. In most areas, theologians tended to run ahead of their churches in efforts at
compromise.
  This was never clearer than in August 2000, when a declaration from the Vatican's Congregation for the Doctrine of
Faith, *Dominus Iesus*, appeared to relegate all non-Catholic
churches to the status of 'ecclesial communities' without the

'fullness of the means of salvation'.[39] The declaration was explained away as an internal church document which had merely recalled the pitfalls of 'religious indifferentism'. But it also highlighted inter-church sensitivities. Many saw it as Catholic intransigence.

In June 1997, 700 church delegations had attended a new European Ecumenical Assembly at Graz, co-organised by the CCEE, CEC and World Council of Churches. Its recommendations covered inter-faith dialogue, social justice, poverty and ecology. But it was criticised for failing to produce firm commitments. The WCC had been plunged into crisis when the Georgian and Bulgarian Orthodox Churches withdrew in protest at the dominance of Protestant concerns, such as women's ordination and 'inclusive language'. Russia's Patriarch Aleksi warned that his own church's continuing participation would depend on the WCC's 'total reconstruction' and an end to Protestant 'mass propaganda'.[40] At its fiftieth anniversary assembly in December 1998, the Council duly agreed to undergo reforms.

Ecumenical progress was not impossible.

In October 1999, Catholics and Lutherans signed a 'Common Declaration on Justification' in Augsburg. In November 2000, the Pope signed a declaration on 'full visible communion' with the Armenian Apostolic Church. Meanwhile, ecumenical accords were not uncommon at national level on long-vexed issues such as baptisms and mixed marriages. Even in the Balkans, inter-faith councils were now at work in Croatia, Bosnia and Kosovo. 'The walls of division don't stretch to heaven,' a Bulgarian metropolitan told the Pope during his visit in 2002. 'People have built them and people must overthrow them.'[41]

In the key area of Catholic-Orthodox relations, however, little had been achieved. In 1997, a new Freedom of Conscience Law in Russia had recognised Christianity, Islam, Buddhism and Judaism as 'traditional faiths'. It had, however, restricted the freedoms of non-Orthodox confessions, Catholics included. During the same year, the Vatican and Moscow Patriarchate set up a working group to tackle religious problems in Ukraine and there was fresh talk of a meeting between the Pope and Patriarch. But top-level tensions continued over claims of proselytism and unfairness. The Russian Orthodox Church's apparent endorsement of President Vladimir Putin's pacification campaign in Chechnya heightened the distrust. In July 2000, when the International Catholic-Orthodox Commission met in Baltimore for the first time since 1993, it broke up over the still 'exceptionally thorny' question of the Greek Catholic Churches.[42]

* * *

Relations with other religions had been a priority too, especially in the case of Muslims, whose rapidly expanding European presence became a focus of attention after the 11 September attacks by Islamic militants in the US. In two decades, Islam had expanded massively, underlining its place as the world's fastest growing religion. France's Muslims made up almost a tenth of the population, while spiralling immigration in Spain had produced large minorities in most cities. Devout Muslims in Britain had come close to equalling the practising membership of the Church of England. The largest of Rome's five mosques had been inaugurated in 1995 in the presence of 650,000 Muslims from Italy, where followers of Islam easily outnumbered all Christian denominations after the Catholic Church. In Belgium, a Brussels-based Islamic Centre was campaigning for the 'Islamicisation of European nations'.

There was potential for disaffection. Germany's two million Muslims ran 2,000 mosques, compared to a mere handful before the Second World War. Unemployment and school drop-out rates, however, were twice the national average, and many had problems finding jobs. Three-quarters were actively religious, and 30,000 belonged to Islamist organisations. Meanwhile, Muslim communities had proliferated in Eastern Europe too. Russia's 20 million Sunnis, mostly concentrated in the Caucasus, operated over 5,000 mosques nationwide, while Ukraine's 240 Muslim associations had 40,000 members in Kiev alone.

Besides becoming the first Pope to visit a Jewish synagogue (Rome, 1986), John Paul II had also been the first to enter a Muslim mosque (Damascus 2001). In a message to world

Muslims in 1991, he had recalled the words of Pope Gregory VII in 1076 to the Muslim ruler of Bijaya, Al-Nasir, about the need for charity and neighbourly love between Christians and Muslims. Both faiths needed a 'sincere, profound and constant dialogue,' the Pope said. Together, they could 'offer mankind a religious alternative to the attractions of power, wealth and material pleasure'.[43]

Although most Christians had little if any knowledge of Islam, many were impressed, even intimidated, by Muslim religiousness. Not everyone, however, was disposed to co-operation. When Turkey had applied for EU membership in 1987, its traditional rival, Greece, had set out to block the move. But other Europeans had opposed it too, citing Turkey's poverty and human rights record, its unequal treatment of women and ethnic minorities, and its unsuitability as a predominantly Muslim country. The eastern Ecumenical Patriarchate had remained in Istanbul (Constantinople) since the Ottoman conquest of 1453, and had survived the creation of a secular Turkish republic in 1923. The acknowledged leader, or *primus inter pares*, of the world's 200 million Orthodox Christians was thus based in a Muslim country. As an outer bastion of European Christianity, the Patriarchate existed on the edge of official tolerance. With Muslim Turkish minorities also living in Western Europe, Turkey's EU bid became something of a test for inter-faith ties.

There was a sharper edge to relations elsewhere. In Cyprus, Christians and Muslims had been divided by a UN-administered 'Green Line' since 1974. In Chechnya, anti-Russian insurgents had reasserted their Muslim identities. The use of religion by politicians to justify ethnic cleansing in Bosnia had brought Christian-Muslim tensions into the heart of Europe. Serb army atrocities against Albanians in Kosovo were cited by some as Christian vengeance for Muslim Ottoman rule. In their reprisals, Albanian guerrillas saw Serbian Orthodox churches and monasteries as symbols of repression.

Amid the Islamophobia which erupted after 11 September, four out of five Germans associated Islam with 'terror, radicalism and fanaticism', while over 41,000 Muslims were reported to have been stop-searched by London police alone in a single year, fuelling bitter complaints of discrimination.[44]

When the EU announced 'anti-terror' measures in December 2001, Europe's Christian churches spoke out against them. The Vatican had set up an international Islamic-Catholic Liaison Committee in 1998, co-chaired by the Nigerian Cardinal Francis Arinze. A separate Islam in Europe Committee, founded by the churches the same year, had called on Christians to abandon 'outdated views' of Islam, which seemed little changed from the time of the Crusades. Islam had posed a particular challenge to Christianity in history, the Committee noted in its reports. Today, however, the time had come to 'encounter each other in truth' and heal 'wounded memories'. The world's two billion Christians and 1.3 billion Muslims jointly made up half its population. They could become 'trail-blazers of peace in the third millennium', against a background of 'secularisation, globalisation and mass migration'.

> The Christian is called by the Gospel to take the first step. If we consider Islam a religious and political system to fight against, we strongly risk placing ourselves in a Church which stands for an aggressive self-sufficiency. We must have courage not to defend the past at all costs, but to see whether we have been as perfect as our history books used to say, and still say ... Our job is not to suppress the differences, but rather to dismantle the psychological barriers between us.[45]

Inter-faith initiatives had increased substantially anyway. In March 2002, a European Council of Religious Leaders, incorporating Christians, Muslims, Jews, Buddhists, Hindus, Sikhs and Zoroastrians, had announced a programme of 'multi-religious action projects'. Similar national bodies had gained a high profile in most European countries. When US-led forces invaded Iraq in Spring 2003, Church leaders rejected claims, provoked by the Christian rhetoric of American politicans, of an anti-Muslim crusade. They also urged the restoration of the United Nations as 'supreme international authority'.[46]

Muslims could be thankful for Christian support. Suicide bomb attacks and beheadings in Iraq further eroded the image of Islam in western societies. It was to be tarnished further by a massacre of schoolchildren by Chechen insurgents at Beslan in September 2004. There had been hopes that a 'European Islam' could find its place in the EU's pluralistic environment by moulding the different traditions brought by three generations of Muslim immigrants into a coherent school. The flow of negative publicity sowed doubts in many minds as to whether Islam would ever be compatible with western democracy. Muslims could fairly complain about the 'cold tolerance' of a western mass culture which appeared more intent on imposing secularist canons than facilitating a pluralism of worldviews. But church leaders complained of a lack of reciprocity. Although Muslims enjoyed civil freedoms in Europe, Islamic countries restricted the rights of Christians. The lack of a central religious authority in Islam made dialogue difficult anyway.

* * *

Relations with Islam had been one of the motors for co-operation between Christian churches. But the real impulse for closer relations was still concern for the future of Europe. In March 2001, a Charta Oecumenica, or ecumenical charter, had been signed by the CCEE and CEC and circulated to local churches. It set out guidelines for an 'ecumenical culture of dialogue' and committed Christians to approach the European Union together. Distrust of religions would deepen among European elites after the attacks of 11 September, while religious and moral convictions would be strained by new legislation on euthanasia, gay unions and therapeutic cloning. Catholic, Orthodox and Anglican leaders put the challenge precisely when they met in Athens in 2003. Defending Christianity would require a united effort.

> At the dawn of a European Union of 25 member-states, 455 million Europeans gaze with hope at a political and human endeavour without precedent ... Assuredly, the Gospel does not pertain exclusively to Europe; yet no one can deny that Europe is thoroughly permeated with it and the experiences it has inspired. Human dignity, freedom, democracy, respect for law and order and for human rights, peace, brotherhood and solidarity are recognised by all as basic values. However, the real and deeper meaning of these values cannot be understood independently of the Gospel of Christ.[47]

In December 2000, a Charter of Fundamental Rights, adopted at the Nice summit, had gone some way to easing Church anxieties. Its articles were organised around six titles: Dignity, Freedoms, Equality, Solidarity, Citizens' Rights and Justice. These reaffirmed the rights to 'freedom of thought, conscience and religion', as well as to marriage and family life, assembly, association and education. They also barred discrimination on grounds of religion or belief, and re-committed the EU to 'respect cultural, religious and linguistic diversity'.

Church leaders were pleased that the Charter recognised the need to 'strengthen the protection of fundamental rights' in the light of social, scientific and technological developments (something the Church had always urged), and to develop 'common values' while respecting diverse cultures and identities. They welcomed its glowing invocation of 'indivisible, universal values' as EU foundation stones, with dignity in first place, and of the individual's place 'at the heart of its activities'. All of these reflected Christian teaching. Yet they were disappointed when a reference to Europe's 'religious heritage' was dropped at the insistence of France's Socialist premier, Lionel Jospin. Jospin insisted it would have infringed his country's secular principles. The EU settled instead for 'spiritual and moral heritage'. It was a foretaste of what was to come.[48]

In the run-up to enlargement, it had been argued that the EU needed a full-scale constitution to draw its laws and treaties together. It was the world's largest trading bloc, and its institutions were evolving amid rival pressures for and against closer unity. The decision to proceed with a Constitutional Treaty was finally taken at the EU's Laeken summit in December 2001. When a European Convention opened in Brussels to draft it that February, a month after the introduction of the Euro, it was clear that Church-related issues would be prominent. The constitution would raise ethical and cultural questions, as well as classifying the EU's relationship with society. For this reason, the churches wanted to see a reference to God, or *invocatio Dei*, in the Constitution's preamble, as well as an acknowledgement of Europe's Christian roots. Most Europeans were still nominally

Christian, they argued; so this would help citizens identify with the EU. But both references were necessary also as a reminder of three essential principles: that public power was not absolute, that human dignity was untouchable, and that fundamental rights were inviolable. These were values for everyone, whether Christians, Muslims, Jews or non-believers.

Among the many depositions sent to the Convention, chaired by France's former president, Valéry Giscard d'Estaing, an explanation of the role of churches and faiths was offered by COMECE:

> Religions provide the foundation and orientation that give meaning to life – they have the potential to inspire innovation in society and governance ... Churches and religious communities are committed to serve society – inter alia, in the fields of education, culture, media and social work – and they play an important role in promoting mutual respect, participation, citizenship, dialogue and reconciliation between the peoples of Europe, East and West. They also emphasise Europe's responsibility not just for its immediate neighbours, but for the whole human family.[49]

Sympathetic members of the European Parliament proposed a formula from Poland's 1997 constitution, drawn from Vatican II's *Gaudium et Spes*. This stated that EU values were shared by 'those who believe in God as the source of truth, justice, goodness and beauty, and those who do not share this faith, but universal values arising from other sources'. The MEPs drummed up hundreds of thousands of signatures for a mass petition, while the churches' demand gained official support from Poland and Italy, as well as Lithuania, Malta, Portugal and Slovakia. Within a year, many church leaders were confident the Convention had come round to the idea. 'The aim is to guarantee freedom, not discriminate over any religion or confession,' explained COMECE's German president, Bishop Josef Homeyer. 'The Church has confirmed its respect for secular states, and the propositions it has tabled before the Convention are a basis for unity, not a source of divisions.'[50]

Yet the demand ran into trouble. There were those, like

Giscard himself, who believed references to God and Christianity would violate 'worldview neutrality'. No one doubted Christianity's importance, Giscard insisted. But references to religion were inappropriate in 'a political system secular to its core'. Christianity could not be singled out without also mentioning Judaism, Islam and 'other religions present on this Continent'. If it was, this would be seen as an act of intolerance towards non-believers and non-Christians.[51]

When a draft preamble was published in May 2003, it made no mention of God or Christianity. Instead, it invoked Europe's 'cultural, religious and humanist inheritance' – 'nourished first by the civilisations of Greece and Rome', and later by 'the philosophical currents of the Enlightenment'. The churches objected, accusing the Convention of doctoring history to suit current ideological preferences. The Pope branded the preamble an 'offence to the fathers of the new Europe', while Russia's Orthodox Moscow Patriarchate deplored its omission of 'the whole period between the fourth and eighteenth centuries when Christianity dominated the Continent'.[52]

References to antiquity and the Enlightenment were left out of a new version, tabled that June. The preamble spoke now of a Europe 'united in diversity', which had 'brought forth civilisation', whose inhabitants, 'arriving in successive waves from earliest times, had 'gradually developed the values underlying humanism: equality of persons, freedom, respect for reason'. The Constitution text was still deeply secular.

Although the text was fine-tuned at a heads of government meeting, disagreements prevented its adoption at the EU's Rome summit in December 2003. Poland and Spain objected to proposed changes to the voting system agreed under the Nice Treaty three years before, which would have given more weight to Britain, France, Germany and Italy at the expense of smaller countries. But the treatment of Christianity contributed to the breakdown. In January 2004, French legislators passed a law banning Muslim veils and 'ostentatious religious symbols' from state schools. It was followed by similar legislative attempts elsewhere, indicating the lines of division over the public presence of religion. When the ban was extended to Baden-Württemberg in Germany, local parliamentarians voted to exempt 'symbols representing Christian and western cultural values'. But this was struck down as discriminatory by Germany's Supreme Court.

When the EU's Constitutional Treaty was approved at Thessaloniki on 18 June 2004, the text and attached protocols and declarations had grown to 784 pages. The revised preamble again made no mention of God or Christianity, opting instead for Europe's 'cultural, religious and humanist inheritance'. Poland's Catholic bishops, still disappointed, lamented what they saw as a 'falsification of historical truth, and a deliberate marginalisation of Christianity'.[53] Yet there was much to be relieved about. The disputed preamble formed only a small symbolic part of the Constitution. Despite repeated disputes over the nature of values, the document had incorporated the Charter of Fundamental Rights, with its listing of the values shared by EU member-states. But the text no longer described them as 'values underlying humanism'. It stated that the Union was open to 'all European states' committed to promoting these values – no country was excluded. Yet merely belonging to Europe was not enough. States could also be suspended from membership for failing to respect these common values.

> Europe, reunited after bitter experiences, intends to continue along the path of civilisation, progress and prosperity, for the good of its inhabitants, including the weakest and most deprived ... While remaining proud of their own national identities and history, the peoples of Europe are determined to transcend their former divisions and, united ever more closely, to forge a common destiny.[54]

Church leaders welcomed Article 1–52, which noted that the EU 'respects and does not prejudice the status of churches in member-states'. Although this repeated the formulation in the 1997 Amsterdam Treaty, it now gave it constitutional status, thus creating a legal basis for Church participation in EU affairs. Meanwhile, the article also committed the EU to maintaining an 'open, transparent and regular dialogue' with churches. It gave equal weight to 'philosophical and non-confessional organisations'. But the pledge was important. For the first time, churches were recognised as full partners in dialogue.

Signed by heads of state and government on 29 October, the Constitution broke new ground in many areas. It introduced 'qualified majority' voting, created the posts of EU president and foreign minister, and again strengthened the European Parliament. In defining the EU's powers, it distinguished fields of 'exclusive competence' (the customs union, competition rules, monetary management in the Euro zone, conservative of marine resources and commercial policy), from areas of 'shared competence' and of 'supporting, co-ordinating and complementary action'.

Yet it was destined to be fought over. Some Europeans saw it as another step towards an EU super-state, which would inexorably usurp the powers of democratically elected parliaments and governments. Others viewed it as a triumph of 'political correctness' and proof that the EU was dominated by a narrow, utilitarian elite.

Christians continued to argue about the Constitution's system of values. Articles 1–2 drew a distinction between values already established (respect for human dignity, freedom, democracy, equality, the rule of law), and values which could only be aspired to (pluralism, non-discrimination, tolerance, justice, solidarity and equality between women and men). But on specific issues, such as bioethics and gay marriages, the Constitution appeared to contain minimal formulations calculated to prove least controversial. Critics said this amounted to a 'sociology of values' only – a list of existing norms, rather than of permanent principles. There was no ontological basis for the Constitution's values – something the *invocatio Dei* would have supplied. Instead, the document codified what was 'common to member-states' thanks to their history, culture, legal codes and citizens' attitudes. If this was a consensus, it seemed to be a consensus of relativism.

Others commended the Constitution as a worthy attempt to find common ground between a myriad of competing viewpoints and convictions. Far from centralising, they argued, it offered a judicious balance between national, regional and continental powers which reflected subsidiarity and proportionality. Even without a metaphysic of values, it echoed the ethical principles embodied in the national constitutions of member-states. If they had not been stated publicly, for fear of discord, they were present all the same, not least in the Charter of Fundamental Rights with its elevation of dignity, freedom, equality and solidarity. Although these were not defined, they were said to be indivisible and universal.

The Commission of EU Catholic Bishops Conference, COMECE, was sure the Constitution reflected the 'Christian view of the human being', and offered 'values and objectives' for the EU. The Conference of European Churches, CEC, concurred that it would be 'an important step towards building a more integrated Europe'.[55]

* * *

The issue of public participation would still pose a crucial test. The Constitution had attempted to counter the EU's 'democratic deficit' by confirming that every citizen had a right to participate in its 'democratic life', and that decisions were to be taken 'as openly and as closely as possible to the citizen'. The EU's institutions would also maintain a dialogue with 'representative associations and civil society'. A new right was established to petition for legislation with a million signatures.[56]

Yet public apathy remained a key problem. June 2004 elections to the newly expanded 732-seat European Parliament saw the lowest ever turnout of just forty-four per cent. Even among the EU's new member-states, fewer than half voted in Lithuania, and barely one in six in Slovakia. Meanwhile, Eurosceptic parties scored well in Britain, France, Belgium and Austria, suggesting widespread disillusionment. Optimists could argue that nine out of ten MEPs were broadly pro-European, with Christian Democrats re-emerging as the principal force in the new Parliament. But the scepticism was growing rather than diminishing, as tabloid newspapers and populist politicians fuelled fears of a steady dilution of national sovereignty and identity.

In January 2005, MEPs voted to approve the new Constitution, with nine EU member-states, including Spain and Germany, following suit by mid-year. Elsewhere in Europe, however, heated arguments raged. When French and

Dutch voters rejected the Constitution in national referenda on 29 May and 1 June, the EU seemed to have been plunged into crisis. In Britain, six out of ten citizens, including young people and professionals, said they favoured renegotiating all EU treaties.[57] As frustration and disillusionment swept the Continent, many argued that the Constitution was dead.

When a new EU Commission president, the Portuguese José Manuel Baroso, had taken office in July 2004, he had pledged to combat 'Euro-apathy' by facing up to the 'challenge of communication'. The preponderance of France and Germany had been further reduced in a new expanded Commission with representatives from the EU's twenty-five member-states. Yet many believed the warning of Europe's churches should have been heeded.

In a sign of the times, Baroso's Italian predecessor, Romano Prodi, had appointed an advisory group in his final months to reflect on Europe's 'spiritual and cultural dimensions'. There was talk of rebuilding a 'Europe of the spirit', as the Pope had urged in the 1990s, and of a moral vision to buttress the authority and popularity of European institutions. Recognition was growing, however belatedly, of the importance of churches, as social forces embracing the Continent which stood as a perpetual reminder of Europe's true origins and aspirations. 'Christianity is indispensable for defining Europe's memory and future hope,' Prodi conceded to a gathering of Christians. 'We need all the values of our tradition, both secular and religious.'[58]

CHAPTER 7

Rediscovering the Soul of a Continent

This celestial city, in its life here on earth, calls to itself citizens of every nation, and forms out of all the peoples one varied society. It is not harassed by differences in customs, laws and institutions, which serve to the attainment or the maintenance of peace on earth. It neither rends not destroys anything but rather guards all and adapts itself to all. However, these things may vary among the nations, they are all directed to the same end of peace on earth as long as they do not hinder the exercise of religion.

St Augustine, *De Civitate Dei,* Book XIX

More visionary politicians might have liked to apply St Augustine's description to the European Union. This was a human institution, not the divine entity of Augustine's fifth century classic. For all the controversies, however, the EU could be proud of its achievements. Its single market programme had been a success. It was a major actor on the world stage. It had helped reintegrate Europe after the Cold War.

Not all barriers had been overcome, not all laws and resolutions observed. Meanwhile, the occupation of Iraq had touched off a damaging row with the United States, pitting France and Germany against Britain, Italy, Spain and the new member-states, and raising awareness of the growing multi-faith sensitivities of Europe's citizens. With millions of words now expended on the Constitution, it was open to debate whether Brussels resembled the City of God or the City of Babel.

In little over half a century, however, the dream of vision-aries from Dante Alighieri to Victor Hugo of a united Europe at peace with itself seemed to have come true. It had been fulfilled, furthermore, by the free will of sovereign nations, without the power and coercion used by imperial rulers from Charlemagne to Stalin and Hitler. Opinions might be divided as to how that will should be expressed in future. But few could reasonably doubt that the EU had been a force for peace and prosperity, and a powerful stimulus for democracy, human rights and the rule of law.

Other countries were queuing for EU membership. Bulgaria and Romania were expected to join in 2007, Croatia in 2009, while Bosnia, Serbia-Montenegro, Ukraine and Georgia also hoped to meet the criteria some day. So did Turkey. It had a long list of conditions, including freedom of speech, equal rights for minorities and recognition of past misdeeds, such as the 1915 genocide of Armenians and 1974 invasion of Cyprus. In December 2004, however, Turkey was invited to begin negotiations. Like other candidate countries, it had something to work for. EU accession was a dynamic process.

Despite this, the EU's premises and purposes were still being assailed. Integration was predominantly a matter of economic and political change. But it had social and cultural aspects too, as the quest for efficiency, openness and tolerance brought changes in how ordinary people lived, worked and interacted. Clearly, room had to be found for a great plural-ity of temperaments, attitudes and outlooks. Yet the debate continued over what kind of Europe was being created – a Europe of purely secular aims, or a Europe with wider spiri-tual aspirations.

This was the area in which the Christian churches had raised their voices. But how strong were these voices? How closely were 'Christian' and 'European' values inter-linked?

As recently as 1900, the critical German Protestant, Adolf von Harnack, had described the Catholic Church as the contin-uation of the Roman Empire – 'the most inclusive and the mightiest structure, the most complicated and yet the most homogeneous, that history as so far known to us has brought forth'. It was a structure, Harnack added, on which 'all the forces of human intellect and soul', all mankind's 'elemental powers', had been expended.[1] The ensuing century had seen much of that structure brought down. The Church no longer had administrators and decrees to enforce its decisions. Science and technology had questioned Christian beliefs; historical research had challenged biblical authority. All that remained to the Church was the power of conviction and testimony.

That power had been resisted too. Christianity had already ceased to be a predominantly European faith by the 1960s, and Europe's dominance in the Church was fast diminishing. In 1978, the year of Pope John Paul II's election, the Continent's 266 million baptised Catholics had comprised a third of the world total; in 2001, its 280 million made up barely a quarter. Traditional rites and practices had been disregarded by a sceptical society.

With over nine-tenths of its thirty-eight million inhabitants declaring themselves Church members, and half attending Mass regularly, Poland shared with Malta the title of Europe's most Catholic society, and offered a striking exception to the Continent's downward affiliations trend. More than one in ten of its 30,000 clergy were working abroad, providing two-thirds of the Catholic priests in Russia and twelve per cent of clergy in Western Europe. In France, by contrast, where baptised Catholics had fallen to around two-thirds of the population of 59 million by the 1990s, fewer than one in ten Catholics ever attended church and forty per cent of inhabitants disclaimed any faith. In Germany, where practising Catholics fell by a third to four million during the same decade, a decline paralleled among Protestants, the Church's Berlin archdiocese had announced plans to pay off a massive debt by closing half its parishes and selling off selected churches.[2]

Yet if traditional religious practices had declined in Europe, this also needed careful explanation. Signs of the Christian faith remained conspicuous in every town and village, while four out of five West Europeans still described themselves as Christians in surveys. In the 1970s and 1980s, Church leaders had called for a 'new evangelisation' to counter secularisation in Europe. Today, many agreed that 're-structuring' was a more accurate term. Although Europe's religious geography was complex and varied, Christianity still provided a common folk identity all around the Continent. Europe's history and culture could not be understood without reference to the Christian faith. Its public discourse would have been incomparably poorer without the presence of Christian voices. Although secular life had long since gained emancipation from religious influences, furthermore, it could be argued that the very idea of secularisation was suspect anyway. Sociologists had identified a process of 're-spiritualisation', beginning in Europe's largest cities, expressed by an increased belief in God and new upturn in religious devotions.[3] It could be seen as a protest against secular life, rather than a return to mainstream churches. But it called in question the assumption that 'modernity' necessarily spelt the rejection of religion. Post-Enlightenment reason and science had clearly failed to eradicate religious and spiritual instincts. Perhaps religiousness was not declining, so much as changing its face.

If true, the re-spiritualisation presented the churches with an opportunity. In France, where nine-tenths of all 230,000 registered historical monuments were Christian in origin, the growing popularity of retreats and pilgrimages suggested a revived interest in Christianity. 'Men cannot do without dogmatical belief,' Alexis de Tocqueville had observed in 1835, when organised religion had survived the onslaught of the Revolution. 'When the religion of a people is destroyed, doubt takes hold of the higher powers of the intellect and half paralyses all the others. Such a condition cannot but enervate the soul, relax the springs of the will and prepare a people for servitude.'[4]

Could the same be said of the present? Could the end of the era of ideologies spell a return to Christianity? Whatever their resilient strengths, Christian churches were no longer setting the moral agenda for European society. In Britain alone, four out of ten children were born out of wedlock in the 1990s and a third of marriages ended in divorce, compared to just a few per cent in 1945. Abortion, though condemned by the Church, was only seriously restricted in Poland and Malta. In 2001, the Netherlands had become the first of several countries to allow euthanasia. By 2004, again following the Dutch lead, half the EU's member-states had tabled legislation to permit same-sex partnerships or gay marriages. These developments had been affected by urbanisation and social mobility, as well as by the changing role of families and social groups and evolving attitudes to authority and tradition.

Yet pressure was also growing for a moral rethink. Under the Lisbon Strategy, adopted in March 2000, heads of state and government had resolved to make the EU 'the most competitive and dynamic knowledge-driven economy' within a decade, by raising employment and productivity, improving education and training, and creating a sustainable 'synergy' of social, economic and environmental aims. By 2005, these targets were in doubt. Among numerous projects, a Mediterranean free trade area, incorporating 700 million people, was to have been completed by 2010. But this seemed likelier to tempt companies to relocate to the cheaper labour markets of North Africa than to generate jobs and opportunities within the EU. There was criticism of the speculative economic planning which threatened, in a French cardinal's words, to 'reduce mankind to a merchandise' and ignore the needs of social cohesion.[5]

There were deeper problems in store too. Falling birthrates, ageing populations and declining health levels threatened to reduce growth to near-stagnant levels and erode Europe's capacity for self-regeneration. By 2050, according to demographic projections, the EU's population would have dropped by more than a quarter. The average age would have risen from thirty-seven to over fifty (compared to thirty-four in the US). Each working citizen would be supporting three at school or in retirement. With a pensions crisis already taking its toll, the result looked certain to be fierce competition for social resources which many viewed as the real motive behind the campaign for euthanasia. Complaints about a 'culture of death', which the Pope had warned against, had been piling up in Europe, uniting members of all faiths and none. It seemed certain to enhance the Church's moral authority, as the last bastion of a countervailing system of values which had not compromised on human dignity and the sanctity of life. In 2004, a third of France's inhabitants thought the Church's influence should be more evident. More than half agreed the Church posed 'important questions', while three-quarters approved of its stance on charity, tolerance, freedom, equality and social justice.[6]

In the complexity of competing social and moral outlooks, the voice of Christianity still had an eager audience. Yet it faced powerful opposition too. The role of Islamic militants in the attacks of 11 September 2001 had deepened distrust for religion among European elites. They appeared the bear out controversial claims by the US analyst, Samuel Huntingdon, that the triumph of western liberal democracy would hasten a 'clash of civilisations'.[7] If that provided a political context for assaulting Christianity, however, there were other reasons for the renewed hostility. Some discerned the advance of new forms of individualism, which sought to bar religion more completely from public life. Others saw a deliberate assault on Christian values by a profit-led consumer establishment, which had seen off other competitors and now viewed churches as a final obstacle. Others complained of a lack of confidence on the part of churches about competing on equal terms with a cynical secular media and indifferent liberal mass culture.

When Rocco Buttiglione, a senior Italian Christian Democrat, was nominated for the Justice and Home Affairs portfolio in José Manuel Baroso's new EU Commission, his Catholic stance on homosexuality and parenthood was used to undermine the appointment in the European Parliament. In Spain, a new anti-clerical Socialist government promised new permissive laws on abortion, divorce and gay issues, and took steps to restrict the Church's presence in education. Programmes like this appeared to strike at the heart of the Christian system of values, and there was little evidence that they enjoyed mass support. Instead, Christians saw the hand of self-appointed, self-serving elites in politics, culture and the media, who were determined to expunge Christian influences in pursuit of their own anti-religious agenda. For all the hopes of religious revival, Europe was still living with its nineteenth-century paradigms, whose modern inheritors persisted in assuming conflict must be inherent between the realms of reason and faith. Like a great actor remembered only for his *Hamlet*, the Church was competing with outdated stereotypes. In some circles, two centuries of change appeared to have passed unnoticed.

The Pope had highlighted the dangers of repudiating Christianity. By 2004, he had devoted all or part of 700 speeches to Europe, compared to 136 delivered by Pius XII, John XXIII and Paul VI together. The Continent's unity and recovery had been central to his pontificate. Yet he had also detected a 'new culture', largely media-influenced, which risked reducing 'the prestigious symbols of the Christian presence' to 'a mere vestige of the past'. The result, John Paul II feared, had been a silent apostasy by people 'who have all they need and live as if God did not exist'. He urged religious Europeans to ignore the pressures and 'wear the signs of faith with pride'.

> There can be no doubt that, in Europe's complex history, Christianity has been a central and defining element, established on the firm foundation of the classical heritage and the multiple contributions of the various ethnic and cultural streams which have succeeded one another down the centuries. The Christian faith has shaped the culture of the Continent and is inextricably bound up with its history, to the extent that Europe's history would be incomprehensible without reference to the events which marked first the great period of evangelisation, and then the long centuries when Christianity, despite the painful division between East and West, came to be the religion of the European peoples. Even in modern and contemporary times, when religious unity progressively disintegrated as a result both of further divisions between Christians and the gradual detachment of cultures from the horizon of faith, the role played by faith has continued to be significant.[8]

There was, on the face of it, little chance that Europe's Christian heritage could be repudiated anyway. Christianity had come slowly to the peoples of Europe, extending and deepening over centuries. But wherever the Christian river had flowed, drawing on its sources in Judaic tradition, Greek philosophy and Roman law, it had also irrigated the European plain, allowing those 'ethnic and cultural streams' both to enrich and be enriched by it. It was Christianity, above all other religions, which had brought down discrimination in the world of antiquity, by rejecting the division between patricians and slaves, civilised and barbarian. All had been equal in the eyes of God, as St Paul told the Ephesians, as 'fellow citizens with the saints and members of the household of God' (Ephesians 2:19–22), with a shared moral status which later became a social status as well.

This was the new Europe which Christianity had created from the ruins of the Roman Empire. But it had not stopped there. Christ had come 'not to abolish the law and the prophets . . . but to fulfil them' (Matthew 5:17). Christianity had imposed standards of justice, virtue and humanity on Europe's rulers. Its saints – Augustine and Benedict, Cyril and Methodius – had drawn on the 'spoil of the pagans', incorporating the best elements of previous traditions, like the bees in St Basil's analogy 'who make honey from the freshest flowers, but fly past others which have less to offer'.[9] In this way, Christianity had transformed the chaos of the barbarian invasions into a *respublica christiana*, based on common culture, a shared rule of law and a unitary European consciousness, which respected the distinctive identities of its many peoples and nations. In 792, when Charlemagne required an oath of allegiance from 'all Christian people', whatever their status, it expressed the principle of equality which Christianity had bequeathed to Europe. At a time when the feudal system had reimposed a hierarchical order, the Christian Church had continued to offer advancement to all, women included. When kings and emperors had overstepped their power, the Church had reminded them there was a sphere of spiritual authority where temporal dictates did not run. It could be viewed as theocracy. But it could also be seen as establishing a vital defence against the whims and phobias of secular rulers in every age.

However it was interpreted, Europe had already had a constitution of sorts a thousand years before the EU's Constitutional Treaty. This was Christianity's creation. What was its legacy for the present?

One was the concept of a natural law, which upheld the inalienable dignity of every individual, irrespective of rank and riches, clan or caste, and predated and superceded all secular laws and statutes.

Another was the notion of a realm of personal conscience, existing independently of the will of the state, which ensured that secular and spiritual power structures were separate and must compete for human loyalties.

Another was the realisation that faith and reason, though autonomous, should be linked in mutual respect.

Knowingly or not, by asserting the moral value of the individual, Christianity had planted the seeds of democracy and human rights. Step by step, it was fated to subvert and undermine every unjust, dictatorial system of rule. Yet this would require long centuries of struggle and conflict. Church leaders would acquiesce in feudalism and absolutism. They would be corrupted by the very same powers and privileges which Christianity had helped undermine. This would be what turned Europe's intellectuals against it, and forced a division between the Church and the new radical democratic forces. Groups like these asserted Christianity's values against the Church itself. In this way, the values became secularised and were turned as a weapon on their own architect. Worship of God was replaced by worship of other idols, dressed up in a variety of ideological colours: state and nation, class and race, science and technology, individualism and free choice.

The lessons of history should have provided the impulse for resolving this great struggle. But it did not end after all. After two centuries of radical secular pressure, the Church could claim to have returned to the 'perpetual centre' commended by Herbert Butterfield, by rediscovering the true democratic, egalitarian spirit of Christian teaching. Having rejected abusive capitalism, it had now also seen off the challenge of totalitarianism, purging itself of its associations with power and privilege and standing alongside common humanity. By them, however, secular forces had moved further along their own separate trajectory, searching without results for a new sense of purpose and meaning.

This was what the Pope had meant when he warned, in *Redemptor hominis*, of a falsely understood freedom – an individualism which made human beings, in Maritain's words, 'appear like so many little gods ... bourgeois ends in themselves with unlimited freedom to own and trade and enjoy'.[10] When Communist rule ended in Europe, it was fashionable to predict the collapse of western relativism and utilitarianism as well. Instead, they appeared to have triumphed. The long-term effect, some argued, would be just as corrosive to democracy and human rights – a confused and misdirected liberalism, which was unable to guide the forces it had unleashed and became poisoned by its own inexorable logic. That was going a bit far. The historian, Christopher Dawson (1889–1970), had warned in the 1950s against allowing profit and consumption to become the new deities of modernity – in a society which viewed religion, with Feuerbach and Marx, as a deception and denial of the truly human, and saw God, with Freud, as an appeaser of guilt and insecurity, the 'universal obsessional neurosis of humanity'.[11] Half a century later, many Europeans seemed to have forgotten their Christian inheritance. Yet even the most anti-Christian remained deeply indebted to it. 'The European, even if he or she is an atheist, remains bound by an ethics and a perception which have deep roots in the Christian tradition', wrote the socio-economic historian, Fernand Braudel. 'He remains of Christian origin, having lost his faith.'[12] If Christianity laboured under the burdens of the past, it also offered creative promises for the future. Its survival was clearest possible proof that contemporary Europe remained truly European, a place of welcome for all faiths and philosophies which shared its essential values.

The new debate on Christianity served a purpose. For one thing, it focused minds on the dangers posed by a new form of secularism, which appeared to be succumbing to the same intolerance and dogmatism which the Church itself had once been accused of. This was not the secularism which Vatican II's Pastoral Constitution, *Gaudium et spes*, had recognised and accepted, when Church and State were separate but nevertheless co-operated for the good of society. It was a secularism which sought only to ridicule and exclude, and which appeared to have turned the one-time persecuted into the new persecutors.

In the wake of the Buttiglione affair, the Vatican's Cardinal Joseph Ratzinger warned against a situation in which Christian values were 'forced underground by secular forces'. Secularism was no longer 'that element of neutrality which opens up space for freedom for all', he added. It was beginning to change into an ideology, 'enforced through politics', which presented itself as 'the only voice of rationality'. Preaching to the cardinals a day before his election as Benedict XVI, Ratzinger talked of the 'small boat' of

Christian thought being tossed by rival winds – 'from Marxism to liberalism, even to libertinism; from collectivism to radical individualism; from atheism to a vague religious mysticism; from agnosticism to syncretism'. 'Today, having a clear faith based on the creed of the Church is often labeled as fundamentalism,' he added. 'We are building a dictatorship of relativism that does not recognize anything as definitive and whose ultimate goal consists solely of one's own ego and desires. We, however, have a different goal: the Son of God, the true man. He is the measure of true humanism.'[13]

There were grounds for optimism. The late Roman Empire had also been a place of luxury, vice, waste and corruption, where Christians had been attacked similarly by elite writers for their irrationality and primitivism. Yet it had been a place of spiritual hunger too, in which Christianity had gained a following through prayerful example, spiritual sharing and works of solidarity. Christianity's end had often been predicted. Yet Christianity was too deeply rooted in the culture and consciousness of Europeans. It had survived the scepticism of the Enlightenment and the positivism and anti-clericalism of the nineteenth century, when Kierkegaard had urged efforts to 'reintroduce Christianity to Christendom'. It had survived fascism and Nazism and Communist rule, when administrative measures had been used against the churches in a climate of hostility and contempt.

In the post-modern era, there were unlikely to be great new political ideas like those of 1789 or 1917, or grand social and moral visions of a new society such as motivated the reformers of the nineteenth century. But the chances were, in the words of one observer, that God was 'much less dead' than was often claimed. 'True religion is slow in growth and, when once planted, is difficult of dislodgement,' the English John Henry Newman had written in the 1850s. 'But its intellectual counterfeit has no root in itself; it springs up suddenly, it suddenly withers.'[14]

* * *

What kind of Christianity would be needed in the Europe of the twenty-first century? Clearly, it had to be a Christianity which placed the human person first and respected the Continent's pluralistic, multi-cultural and multi-faith character. When religion was under attack, it had to be a Christianity which, as Charles Péguy said of the Jewish atheist Bernard-Lazare, possessed 'a heart that bled for the world's ghettos, wheresoever the Jew was persecuted ... for the Orient, for the Occident, for Islam and for Christendom'. When religion was resurgent, it had to be a Christianity which recognised its debt to the streams and currents of history, and rejoiced with the mystic Baron von Hugel: 'What would my religion be without its Jewish figure?... What would my theology be without the Greeks?'[15] Above all, however, it had to be a Christianity which remained true to its humanistic values and impulses, and did not yield to the pressures and strains of a lost and factured society.

Meeting in October 2004 at Whitby, the site of England's famous seventh-century synod, Europe's Catholic bishops again called for ecumenical and inter-faith efforts in evangelising Europe. They were joined by the Anglican Archbishop of Canterbury, Rowan Williams, who urged religious believers to challenge the idea 'that what is neutral and secular is what is natural'. The Christian inspiration was capable, as the Pope had said, 'of transforming political, cultural and economic groupings into a form of coexistence in which all Europeans will feel at home'. It was an 'invitation to everyone, believers and non-believers alike, to blaze new trails to a Europe of the spirit'.[16]

The importance of religion was known instinctively by those at the inter-faith divide, such as the 2,000 Christian, Muslim and Jewish leaders who met with EU officials in the wake of the 2004 Beslan school massacre in Russia, or the six Balkan presidents who, gathering in Albania, highlighted the 'intrinsic value' of inter-religious dialogue for social vibrancy, and urged citizens to 'celebrate, protect and safeguard' their religious heritage. 'Religion is of profound importance to people's identities,' the presidents declared in December 2004. 'There exists an underlying thread of unity connecting the great religious traditions. They each propound basic spiritual truths and standards of behaviour that constitute the very basis of social cohesion and collective purpose.'[17]

Christian leaders spoke out against a resurgence of anti-Semitic attacks in Europe, an alarming trend in a continent where six million Jews had been slaughtered within living memory during the Holocaust. There could, in the words of the German Cardinal Walter Kasper, chairman of the Vatican's Pontifical Council for Promoting Christian Unity, be no such thing as Christian anti-Semitism. 'Anti-Semitism cuts through the roots of Christianity and has no place in the Church,' Kasper told the Organisation on Security and Cooperation in Europe. 'The struggle against it means a struggle for human rights and engagement for peace.'[18]

In May 2004, neo-Nazis attacked Jewish and Roman Catholic cemeteries in Alsace within a day of each other – a sign that all religious groups, Christians too, were potential targets for extremists. When mosques and churches were attacked in the Netherlands the following November, after the murder of a controversial film director by an Islamic militant, the country's Catholic bishops addressed an 'Open Letter to Dutch Society'. It raised questions which would have to be faced throughout the new Europe.

> Far from feeling opposed to Islam, the Catholic Church shares the experience of being religious in a secularising society and the conviction that everything is given us by God. Together, we hold the same belief in the inalienable dignity of every human life, and a striving for justice and peace ... Inculturation and adaptation cannot mean being forced to accept the dictatorship of a politically correct majority view. A society which does not tolerate dissenting religious views gives a token of weakness, not power. Does freedom of speech mean a licence to ridicule the sacred and offend others? The answer to such questions lies not in laws, but in people's consciences.[19]

Jewish leaders would have concurred. In the 1830s, the Jewish poet, Heinrich Heine, had called Christianity 'a blessing for suffering mankind'. It had 'curbed the strong and strengthened the weak', Heine said, 'by linking people through an identity of sentiment and speech'. In 2003, another Jew, Joseph Weiler, who had worked on the EU's Maastricht and Amsterdam treaties, defended the churches for expecting a reference to God and Christianity in the EU Constitution. If they were considered taboo, Europe would be 'in denial', a victim of 'reductionist politics', Weiler insisted. Christians should not make the mistake of 'imposing silence on themselves'. To decline a discussion of Christianity would mean failing to face up to Europe's past. 'Europe' should not become a means of escape – either from the past we are proud and ashamed of, or from the problems of our complicated and contradictory identity ... Christian Europe is not a Europe of exclusion or necessarily a confessional Europe. It is a Europe which in equal measure fully accepts all of her citizens, believers and non-believers, Christians and non-Christians.[20]

European Muslims would have concurred too. When Turkey was invited to negotiate EU accession in December 2004, the Commission of EU Catholic Bishops Conferences (COMECE) called for a 'constructive and amicable develop- ment of relations'. Turkey's predominant Muslim faith posed no obstacle, COMECE insisted. Whether Turkey met the EU's critieria would be 'a political, not a religious question'. There were ironies at work. Under the secular constitution which had been guaranteed by its Army since Turkey's foun- dation as a republic in 1923, religions had been kept on a tight rein. Now, the drive for 'Europeanisation' was being directed by an Islamist government. For religious communities, Europe's Christian legacy seemed to offer greater freedom and security than the whims and prejudices of local politicians and legislators. It was a sign that Christians, Muslims and Jews, people of all faiths and none, could share the same devotion to European values and remind each other, when necessary, of their full meaning and significance.

Those humanistic values – human rights, democracy, pluralism, equality – were the creation of Christianity, and they deserved to be recognised as such. But even if they were not, Christianity would continue to be their protector and guardian, their reference point in the absolute. In a secular age which glorified mankind, there was no point hoping for the rebuilding of Christendom. But it would continue to exist, nevertheless, in hearts and minds, and in the creative rest- lessness which had always been Christianity's genius.

Notes

Introduction

1. Quoted in Denys Hay, *Europe: The Emergence of an Idea*, Edinburgh University Press, 1968, p. 123. Norman Davies, *Europe: A History*, Pimlico, London, 1997, pp. 7–16.
2. Figures from a French government commission; *La Croix*, Paris, 9 August 2002.
3. John Paul II, *Ecclesia in Europa*, no. 19, Catholic Truth Society, London, 2003.
4. *Catechism of the Catholic Church*, nos. 843–8, Geoffrey Chapman, London, 1995.

Chapter 1

1. Quoted in Brian Moynahan, *The Faith: A History of Christianity*, Aurum Press, London, 2002, p. 29.
2. From Justin Martyr's *Apologiae* to the Emperor Marcus Aurelius, 14, 65–66. L. W. Bernard, *Justin Martyr, His Life and Thought*, Cambridge University Press, 1967. Mircea Eliade, *Images and Symbols: Studies in Religious Symbolism*, Princeton University Press, 1991, pp. 160–74.
3. Quoted in Vivian Green, *A New History of Christianity*, Sutton, Stroud, 1996, p. 24.
4. St Augustine, *De Civitate Dei*, Book XIX, 17, Penguin Classics, London, 1984.
5. Text of the Donation in Brian Tierney, *The Crisis of Church and State 1050–1300*, Prentice-Hall, New Jersey, 1964, pp. 21–22. The document was exposed as a forgery in the fifteenth century.
6. Kevin Wilson and Jan van der Dussen (eds), *The History of the Idea of Europe*, Routledge, London, 1995, pp. 26–27.
7. A. S. Atiya, *A History of Eastern Christianity*, Notre Dame University Press, 1968, p. 259. Rollin Armour, *Islam, Christianity and the West: A Troubled History*, Orbis, New York, 2002.
8. Quoted in M. Dobroczyński and J. Stefanowicz, *Tożsamość Europy*, Polski Instytut Wydawniczy, Warsaw, 1979, pp. 20–21. See also

Benjamin Kedar, *Crusade and Mission: European Approaches to the Muslims*, Princeton University Press, 1984, p. 25. J. N. Hillgarth, *Christianity and Paganism 350–750: The Conversion of Western Europe*, Penn Press, Philadelphia, 1985.

9. The instructions of Pope Gregory I, in Bede's *Ecclesiastical History of the English People*, Penguin Classics, Harmondsworth, 2003, Part II, no. 11.
10. From *The Rule of St Benedict*, prologue 45–46, Liturgical Press, Collegeville, 1982.
11. The description is from the historian, Cardinal Cesare Baronius; in Moynahan, op. cit., p. 213.
12. Gregory VII, *Dictatus Papae*, in Sidney Ehler and John Morrall, *Church and State through the Ages: A Collection of Illustrative Documents*, Burns & Oates, London, 1954, pp. 43–44.
13. 'Letter of Henry to the German bishops (1076)', in Tierney, op. cit., pp. 61–2.
14. 'Letter to the prefect Acerbus and the nobles of Tuscany (1198)', in ibid., p. 132.
15. 'Letter to the emperor Leo III (727)', in ibid., p. 20.
16. *Summa Theologica*, II–II, q. 60, in William Baumgarth and Richard Regan, *Saint Thomas Aquinas: On Law, Morality and Politics*, Hacket, Cambridge, 1988, pp. 257–9.
17. *Summa Theologica*, I–II, q. 96 and II–II, q. 10, in ibid., pp. 66–68, 249–55.
18. Josef Pieper, *Guide to Thomas Aquinas*, Pantheon, New York, 1962, p. 132.
19. Boniface VIII, *Unam Sanctam*, in Tierney, op. cit., p. 189.
20. Pius II, *Execrabilis*, in Ehler and Morall, op. cit., p. 133.
21. Erasmus, *Querela Pacis* (1517), in Wilson and van der Dussen, op. cit., p. 37.
22. Hans Küng, *The Catholic Church: A Short History*, Weidenfeld & Nicholson, London, 2001, p. 135.
23. Quoted in Green, op. cit., p. 131.
24. Thomas More, letter to Erasmus, December 1526, in Brian Moynahan, *William Tyndale: If God spare my life*, Abacus, London, 2003, p. 106. More described Tyndale, who was burned as a heretic in Flanders in 1536, as 'a hell-hound in the kennel of the devil ... discharging a filthy foam of blasphemies out of his brutish, beastly mouth'.
25. Quoted in Küng, op. cit., p. 142. Hadrian VI, a Dutchman and the last non-Italian Pope till 1978, lived for barely a year after his election.
26. Eamon Duffy, *Saints and Sinners: A History of the Popes*, Yale University Press, 1997, p. 164.
27. Quoted in Green, op. cit., pp. 182–3. 'The Propaganda' was founded in 1568 as the Congregation for the Conversion of the Infidels.
28. From the Treaty of Osnabrück (24 October 1648), art. V, sec. 1, in Ehler and Morrall, op. cit., pp. 190–1.
29. Innocent X, *Zelo domus Dei*, in ibid., p. 195.
30. 'Revocation of the Edict of Nantes (1685)', in ibid., p. 211.

31. 'Toleration Act of the Emperor Joseph II (1781)', in ibid., p. 227.
32. Pedro Ramet (ed.), *Eastern Christianity and Politics in the Twentieth Century*, Duke University Press, Durham, 1988, p. 52.
33. Quoted in Roy Porter, *Enlightenment: Britain and the Creation of the Modern World*, Penguin, London, 2000, pp. 101–2.
34. Moynahan, op. cit., p. 438.
35. Porter, op. cit., pp. 96–7.
36. Green, op. cit., p. xx. Porter, op. cit., p. 127.
37. Davies, op. cit., p. 7. Hay, op. cit., p. 123.
38. From Voltaire's *Épitres*, in Moynahan, op. cit., p. 595.
39. 'The Civil Constitution of the Clergy (1790)', art. 4, in Ehler and Morall, op. cit., p. 239.
40. Simon Schama, *Citizens: A Chronicle of the French Revolution*, Knopf, New York, 1989, p. 776.
41. Vicomte de Chateaubriand, *Le Génie du Christianisme*, Garnier-Flammarion, Paris, 1996, p. 250.
42. 'Concordat between Pope Pius VII and the First French Republic (1801)', preamble, in Ehler and Morall, op. cit., p. 252.
43. 'Extracts from the Belgian Constitution (1831)', arts. 14–15, in ibid., p. 272.

Chapter 2

1. From *Paroles d'un croyant* (1834), in Thomas Bokenkotter, *Church and Revolution: Catholics in the Struggle for Democracy and Social Justice*, Doubleday, New York, 1998, p. 1.
2. Edmund Burke, *Three letters on the proposals for peace* (1796), in Wilson and van der Dussen, op. cit., p. 67.
3. Friedrich Heer, *Europe, Mother of Revolutions*, Praeger, New York, 1972, p. 5. Antoine de Saint-Just, *Oeuvres complètes*, Folio Histoire, Paris, 2004. Annie Jourdan, *La Révolution: une exception française*, Flammarion, Paris, 2004.
4. From Kingsley's *Letters to the Chartists*, in Moynahan, op. cit., p. 598.
5. Quoted in Frederick B. Artz and William L. Langer (eds), *Reaction and Revolution: The Rise of Modern Europe*, Harper, New York, 1966, p. 195.
6. Pius VI, *Diu satis* (15 May 1800), paras. 14, 16, 25.
7. Alexander Herzen, *From the Other Shore*, Oxford University Press, New York, 1979, p. 149.
8. Green, op. cit., p. 322.
9. Quoted in Denys Hay, op. cit., p. 123. Davies, op. cit., pp. 7–16.
10. Pius VI, *Inscrutabile* (25 December 1775), para. 7.
11. From Massini's *Essays*, in Adam Zamoyski, *Holy Madness: Romantics, Patriots and Revolutionaries, 1776–1871*, Phoenix Press, London, 1999, pp. 289–90, 299.
12. Gregory XVI, *Mirari vos* (15 August 1832), para. 5. Pius VIII, *Traditi humilitati* (24 May 1829), para. 6.
13. Quoted in Heer, op. cit., p. 254.

14. Gregory XVI, *Singulari nos* (25 June 1834), paras. 4,6
15. Heer, op. cit. p. 256.
16. Louis Le Guillou (ed.), *Correspondence Générale*, Librairie Armand Colin, Paris, 1981, pp. 799–800. José Cabanais, *Lacordaire et Quelques Autres: Politique et Religion*, Gallimard, Paris, 1982; p. 102. Montalembert was praised by Guizot for his 'belle docilité Chrétienne'.
17. Pius IX, *Nostis et nobiscum* (8 December 1849), paras. 18, 25.
18. Heer, op. cit., p. 257. Bokenkotter, op. cit., pp. 76, 129.
19. 'For the Polish nation did not die; its body lies in the tomb, while its soul has left the earth . . . And on the third day, the soul will re-enter the body, and the nation will rise from the dead and will liberate all the peoples of Europe from slavery', from Mickiewicz's *Books of the Polish Nation*, in Zamoyski, op. cit., 285–6.
20. Ibid., pp. 408–9. Susan Dunn, *The Deaths of Louis XVI: Regicide and the French Political Imagination*, Princeton University Press, 1994, p. 52.
21. Auguste Comte, *A General View of Positivism*, Robert Speller, New York, 1957, p. 15. Anthony Rhodes, *The Vatican in the Age of the Liberal Democracies, 1870–1922*; Sidgwick and Jackson, London, 1983, p. 12.
22. Heer. op. cit. p. 74. 'To explain history is to depict the passions of mankind, the genius, the active powers, that play their part on the great stage; and the providentially determined process which these exhibit, constitutes what is generally called the "plan" of providence', in Anthony Kenny, *A History of Western Philosophy*, Blackwell, Oxford, 1998, pp. 274–8.
23. From the first paragraph of *The Communist Manifesto*, February 1848, in Jonathan Luxmoore and Jolanta Babiuch, *The Vatican and the Red Flag*, Geoffrey Chapman, London, 1999, p. 2.
24. Karl Marx, *Collected Works*, International Publishers, New York, 1988, p. 354. Paul Misner, *Social Catholicism in Europe: From the Onset of Industrialisation to the First World War*, Darton, Longman and Todd, London, 1991, p 138.
25. Pius IX, *Qui pluribus* (9 November 1846), in Luxmoore and Babiuch, op. cit. p. 2.
26. Pius IX, *Syllabus errorum* (8 December 1864), VI: Nos. 57 and 60, in Ehler and Morrall, op. cit., p. 284.
27. Heer, op. cit., p. 277. Gertrude Himmelfarb, *Lord Acton*, University of Chicago Press, 1960.
28. Pius IX, *Quanta cura* (8 December 1864), para. 4.
29. Ibid., para. 3. In 1846, there had been 8 foreign and 54 Italian cardinals; by 1872, there would be 25 foreign and 39 Italian, along with 200 new bishoprics and 74 new orders for women; Green, op. cit., p. 260.
30. From Gladstone's *The Vatican Decrees and their Bearing on Civil Allegiance*, in Rhodes, op. cit., p. 16.
31. The Italian Law of Guarantees (13 May 1871), Arts. 1, 11–13, in Ehler and Morrall, op. cit., pp. 287–91.
32. Quoted in Green, op. cit., pp. 258–9. Henri Daniel-Rops, *L'Église des*

220 *Rethinking Christendom*

Révolutions: Un combat pour Dieu, Fayard, Paris, 1964, p. 83.
33. Rhodes., op. cit., p. 85.
34. Ibid., p. 92.
35. Leo XIII, *Quod apostolici muneris* (28 December 1878), paras. 4, 6–7, 9–10.
36. Leo XIII, *Immortale Dei* (1 November 1885), paras. 6, 23.
37. Green, op. cit., p. 286.
38. Leo XIII, *Rerum novarum* (15 May 1891), para. 2
39. Ibid., para. 45.
40. Interview with *Le Petit Journal*, Paris (17 February 1892), in Rhodes, op. cit., p. 116.
41. Leo XIII, *Graves de communi* (18 January 1901), para. 8.
42. Friedrich Naumann, *Letters on Religion* (1900), in Heer, op. cit., p. 236. Luxmoore and Babiuch, op. cit., p. 7.
43. Quoted in Adrian Dansette, *Religious History of Modern France*, Nelson, London, 1961, Vol. II, p. 32.
44. Benjamin Martin, *Count Albert de Mun*, University of North Carolina Press, Chapel Hill, 1978, p. 37.
45. Quoted in Bill McSweeney, *Roman Catholicism: The Search for Relevance*, Basil Blackwell, Oxford, 1980, p. 84. Sandor Agocs, *The Troubled Origins of the Catholic Labour Movement, 1878–1914*, Wayne University Press, Detroit, 1988, pp. 126–31.
46. Heer. op. cit., p. 241. Roland N. Stromberg, *Realism, Naturalism and Symbolism*, Macmillan, London, 1968, pp. 25–30, 107–118.
47. Pius X, *Lamentabili sane* (3 July 1907). *Pascendi* (8 September 1907), part III, para. 7.
48. From George Tyrrell, *The Church and the Future*, in Heer, op. cit., p. 296. Alec Vidler, *A Variety of Catholic Modernists*, Cambridge University Press, 1970, p. 119. Lawrence Barmann, *Baron Friedrich von Hugel*, CUP, 1972, p. 219.
49. Quoted in Rhodes, op. cit., p. 202. The Pope's condemnation in *Vehementer nos* (1 February 1906).
50. Tomáš G. Masaryk, *Humanistic Ideals and The New Europe*, in George Kovtun (ed.), *The Spirit of Thomas G. Masaryk*, Macmillan, London, 1990, pp. 154, 216–7.
51. Quoted in Jean Preposiet, *Histoire de l'anarchisme*, Tallandier, Paris, 2002, p. 278.
52. Heer, op. cit., p. 318. Andrzej Walicki, *A History of Russian Thought from the Enlightenment to Marxism*, Clarendon, Oxford, 1988, pp. 268–90.
53. From the preface to *Hellas*, in Zamoyski, op. cit., p. 236.
54. Moynahan, op. cit., p. 665. Robert F. Byrnes, *Pobedonostsev: His Life and Thought*, Indiana University Press, Bloomington, 1969.
55. Green, op. cit., p. 251. A. Boyce Gibson, *The Religion of Dostoevsky*; SCM Press, London, 1973, pp. 52–77.
56. Rhodes, op. cit., pp. 18, 221.

Chapter 3

1 Charles Péguy, *Clio*, from the collection, *Temporal and Eternal*, Harvill Press, London, 1958. For Yeats, see Stromberg, op. cit., p. 242.
2. Green, op. cit., p. 294.
3. Carlo Falconi, *The Popes in the Twentieth Century*, Weidenfeld and Nicholson, London, 1967, p. 118. John Pollard, *The Unknown Pope: Benedict XV and the Pursuit of Peace*, Continuum, London, 1999.
4. Benedict XV, *Dès le Début* (1 August 1917), para. 3.
5. Rhodes, op. cit., pp. 235, 244.
6. Benedict XV, *Pacem Dei Munus Pulcherrimum* (23 May 1920), para 18.
7. Rhodes, op. cit., p. 239. Erzberger was murdered by German nationalists in 1921.
8. Moynahan, op. cit., p. 669.
9. V.I. Lenin, 'The attitude of the Workers Party to religion', in *Collected Works*, Vol. 15, Progress Publishers, Moscow, 1972, pp. 405–10. Arto Luukkanen, *The Party of Unbelief: The Religious Policy of the Bolshevik Party 1917–1929*, Studia Historica, Helsinki, 1994, pp. 193–5. For Solzhenitsyn, see Michael Scammell, *Solzhenitsyn: A Biography*, Paladin, London, 1986, p. 894.
10. Robert Service, *A History of Twentieth-Century Russia*, Penguin, London, 1997, p. 250. Simon Sebag Montefiore, *Stalin: The Court of the Red Tsar*, Weidenfeld and Nicholson, London, 2003.
11. Luxmoore and Babiuch, op. cit., p. 14.
12. Péguy, op. cit.
13. Pius XI, *Ubi Arcano Dei* (23 December 1922), paras. 6, 23.
14. Friedrich Nietzsche, *The Antichrist* (1895), preface, paras. 19, 44. Anthony Kenny, *A Brief History of Western Philosophy*, Blackwell, Oxford, 1998, pp. 292–303.
15. From Hitler's *Mein Kampf*. Joachim Fest, *Hitler: A Biography*, Weidenfeld and Nicholson, London, 1974, p. 211. Alan Bullock, *Hitler and Stalin: Parallel Lives*, HarperCollins, London, 1991, p. 418.
16. Golo Mann, *The History of Germany since 1789*, Pimlico, London, 1996, p. 82.
17. Roberts, op. cit., p. 71.
18. Leslie Murray, 'Modernism and Christian Socialism in the thought of Ottokár Prohászka', *Occasional Papers on Religion in Eastern Europe*, Vol. 12, No. 3, 1992. Luxmoore and Babiuch, op. cit., p. 36.
19. Ibid., p. 32. N. Stone and E. Strouhal (eds), *Czechoslovakia: Crossroads and Crises 1918–88*, Macmillan, London, 1989, pp. 169–82.
20. Pius XI, *Dilectissma Nobis* (3 June 1933), para. 4.
21. Pius XI, *Quadragesimo Anno* (15 May 1931), paras. 113–4, 120.
22. Ibid., paras. 112, 122.
23. Rhodes, op. cit., p. 215.
24. From the Constitution of Eire (29 December 1937), in Ehler and Morrall, op. cit., pp. 595–600.
25. Pius XI, *Divini Redemptoris* (19 March 1937), paras. 6, 26.

26. Green, op. cit., p. 304.
27. Quoted in Guenter Lewy, *The Catholic Church and the Third Reich*, Weidenfeld and Nicholson, London, 1964, pp. 209–10.
28. *Divini Redemptoris*, supra, paras. 2, 82.
29. T.S. Eliot, *Die Einheit der Europäischen Kultur* (1946), in Davies, op. cit., p. 9.
30. Michael Charlton, *The Eagle and the Small Birds: Crisis in the Soviet Empire from Yalta to Solidarity*, BBC Books, London, 1984, p. 13. *Report of the Crimea Conference*, Her Majesty's Stationery Office, London, 1945, pp. 4–5.
31. Moynahan, op. cit., p. 688. Krystyna Kersten, *Jalta w Polskiej Perspektywie*, Aneks, London, 1989. Jan Karski, *Wielkie Mocarstwa wobec Polski 1919–1945*, PiW, Warsaw, 1992.
32. Myron C. Taylor (ed.), *Wartime Correspondence between President Roosevelt and Pope Pius XII*, Macmillan, New York, 1947, pp. 61–2.
33. Rosanna Mulazzi-Giammanco, *The Catholic-Communist Dialogue in Italy*, Praeger, New York, 1989, pp. 55–9. Luxmoore and Babiuch, op. cit., p 100.
34. *Report of the Crimea Conference*, supra, para. 9.
35. Allocution to the Roman Rota (2 October 1945), in Ehler and Worrall, op. cit., p. 604.
36. George Bell, *The Church and Humanity*, Longmans, London, 1946, pp. 177–82. Ronald Jasper, *George Bell: Bishop of Chichester*, Oxford University Press, 1967, pp. 260–6. Davies, op. cit., pp. 922–3.
37. Michael Sturmer, *The German Century*, Orion, London, 1999, p. 221.
38. Cardinal Spellman's reaction to events in 1956, quoted in Robert Gannon, *The Cardinal Spellman Story*, Robert Hale, London, 1963, p. 398.
39. Luxmoore and Babiuch, op. cit. p. 96.
40. Andrea Riccardi, 'The Vatican of Pius XII and the Catholic Party', in *Concilium*, No. 197 (1987), p. 47. Carlo Corradini, *Atteggiamenti del PCI verso la Chiesa Cattolica e la Religione*, Rovigo, Rome, 1978.
41. Corradini, op. cit. William Purdy, *The Church on the Move*, Hollis and Carter, London, 1966, pp. 20–1.
42. Decree of the Sacred Congregation of the Holy Office (1 July 1949), in Ehler and Worrall, op. cit., p. 611.
43. Law on Church Affairs (14 October 1949), ibid., pp. 615–7.
44. *A Freedom Within: The Prison Notes of Stefan Cardinal Wyszyński*, Hodder and Stoughton, London, 1985, pp. 12, 18.
45. Ibid., pp. 13–14. Porozumienie zawarte (14 April 1950), in Peter Raina (ed.), *Kościół w PRL – Dokumenty 1945–1959*, W Drodze, Poznań, 1994, pp. 163–4.
46. Luxmoore and Babiuch, op. cit., p. 105.
47. Quoted in József Közi-Horváth, *Cardinal Mindszenty*, Augustine, Devon, 1979, p. 85. Bohdan Cywiński, *Ogniem Próbowane: I was prześladować będą*, Redakcja Wydawnictw, Lublin, 1990, p. 451.
48. Trevor Beeson, *Discretion and Valour*, Collins, London, 1982, pp. 214–5.

49. Jean Chelini, *L'Église sous Pie XII: l'après-guerre*, Fayard, Paris, 1989, p. 452.
50. Sandro Magister, *La Politica Vaticana e l'Italia 1943–1978*, Editori Riuniti, 1979, pp. 184–5.

Chapter 4

1. Herbert Butterfield, *Christianity and History*, G. Bell, London, 1950, p. 146. Alberto Coll, *The Wisdom of Statecraft: Herbert Butterfield and the Philosophy of International Politics*, Duke University Press, Durham, 1985, pp. 125–38.
2. Treaty establishing a European Coal and Steel Community (18 April 1951), preamble, para. 5. Derek Urwin, *The Community of Europe*, Longman, London, 1995, pp. 44–6. J. Story (ed.), *The New Europe: Politics, Government and Economy since 1945*, Blackwell, Oxford, 1993.
3. Declaration (9 May 1950), paras. 3, 9. John McCormick, *Understanding the European Union*, Palgrave, Basingstoke, 2002, p. 65.
4. Michael Palmer, *European Unity: A Survey of European Organisations*, Allen & Unwin, London, 1968, pp. 110–1. Arnold Zurcher, *The Struggle to Unite Europe 1940–58*, New York University Press, 1958, p. 6.
5. McCormick, op. cit., p. 35. J. Carpentier and F. Lebrun (eds), *Victor Hugo: Histoire de l'Europe*, Gallimard, Paris, 1990, pp. 363–4.
6. Statute of the Council of Europe (5 May 1949), Article 1, para 2.
7. From the Messina Resolution, in David Weigall and Peter Stirk (eds), *The Origins and Development of the European Community*, Pinter, London, 1992, p. 94.
8. Jean Monnet, *Memoirs*, Collins, London, 1978, pp. 287, 310–9. R. Lejeune, *Robert Schuman: Père de l'Europe*, Fayard, Paris, 2000, p. 141.
9. Monnet, op. cit., p. 310.
10. Paul Weymar, *Adenauer*, Dutton and Co., New York, 1957, p. 100.
11. Ibid., pp. 178–9.
12. Luxmoore and Babiuch, op. cit., p. 97. Dermot McKeogh, *Ireland, the Vatican and the Cold War: The Case of Italy 1948*, Woodrow Wilson Center, Washington DC, 1992, p. 35.
13. Katolicka Agencja Informacyjna (KAI), Warsaw, anniversary feature, 17 August 2004.
14. Ibid. Arnold Toybee, *Acquaintances*, Oxford University Press, 1967. E. Tomlin (ed), *Arnold Toynbee: A Selection from his Works*, O.U.P., 1978, pp. 95–101, 280–1.
15. Statute, supra, para. 3.
16. Convention for the Protection of Human Rights and Fundamental Freedoms (4 November 1950), preamble, Article 9.
17. Jacques Maritain, *Freedom in the Modern World*, Charles Scribner's Sons, New York, 1936, pp. 126–7.

224 Rethinking Christendom

18. Jacques Maritain, *True Humanism*, Centenary Press, London, 1939, p. xvi.
19. Bokenkotter, op. cit., pp. 335–401.
20. Ibid., p. 357.
    John Hellman, *Mounier and the New Catholic Left 1930–1950*, University of Toronto Press, 1981, pp. 41–3.
21. Hellman, op. cit., p. 212. Mounier's major works included *Révolution personnaliste et communautaire* (1935) and *Le Personnalisme* (1950).
22. Bokenkotter, op. cit., p. 397.
23. Quoted in Ernest Lefever, *Nairobi to Vancouver: The World Council of Churches and the World*, Ethics and Public Policy Center, Washington DC, 1987, p. xiii. See also John Briggs, M.A. Oduyoye and Georges Tsetsis (eds), *A History of the Ecumenical Movement, 1968–2000*, WCC Publications, Geneva, 2004.
24. Alan Scarfe, 'Patriarch Justinian of Romania: His early social thought', in *Religion in Communist Lands*, Vol. 5, No. 3 (1977), pp. 166–8. Czesław Miłosz, *The Captive Mind*, Penguin, London, 1985, p. 208.
25. The Council's failures have been acknowledged by its former secretary-general, Konrad Raiser. See, for example, 'In dealings with Cold War dissidents, former WCC leader rues failings', Ecumenical News International, Geneva, 22 July 2004.
26. John XXIII, *Ad Petri cathedram* (29 June 1959), paras. 7, 130.
27. *Princeps Pastorum* (28 November 1959), para. 34.
28. *Mater et Magistra* (15 May 1961), paras. 34, 69, 73.
29. Giancarlo Zizola, *The Utopia of Pope John XXIII*, Orbis Books, New York, 1978, pp. 120–1. Peter Hebblethwaite, *John XXIII: The Pope of the Council*, Geoffrey Chapman, London, 1984, pp. 392–4.
30. John XXIII, *Pacem in terris* (11 April 1963), paras. 113–4.
31. Ibid., paras. 43, 159.
32. *Gaudium et Spes* (7 December 1965) paras. 43, 76. See also paras. 9, 26, 41, 73–75.
33. Common Declaration of Pope Paul VI and Patriarch Athenagoras (7 December 1965), para. 4, in Austen Flannery (ed.), *Vatican Council II: The Conciliar and Post-Conciliar Documents*, Costello, New York, 1988, p. 472.
34. *Nostra Aetate* (28 October 1965), paras. 2–4.
35. *Gaudium et Spes*, paras. 19–21.
36. Roger Garaudy, *From Anathema to Dialogue*, Collins, London, 1967, pp. 72–9. Mulazzi-Giammanco, op. cit., p. 62.
37. L.N. Velikovich, in Christopher Read, 'The Soviet Attitude to Christian-Marxist Dialogue', in *Religion in Communist Lands*, Vol. 1, No. 6 (1973), p. 9. Secretariat for Unbelievers, *Humanae personae dignitatem* (28 August 1968), para. II, 2.
38. *New York Times* editorial, 29 March 1967. Paul VI, *Populorum Progressio* (26 March 1967), paras. 1, 21, 23.
39. Orędzie biskupów polskich do ich niemieckich braci w Chrystusowym urzędzie pasterskim (18 November 1965), in Raina, op. cit., p. 362.
40. See Kusý's essay in *A Beseiged Culture: Czechoslovakia Ten Years after Helsinki*, Charta 77 Foundation, Stockholm, 1985, pp. 95–6.

41. Press conference, 5 September 1960, in William Hitchcock, *The Struggle for Europe: A History of the Continent since 1945*, Profile, London, 2004, p. 227.
42. Luxmoore and Babiuch, op. cit., p. 171. See also Agostino Casaroli, *Il Martirio della Pazienza*, Einaudi, Turin, 2000.
43. *L'Osservatore Romano*, 17 October 1975. Dennis Dunn, *Detente in Papal-Communist Relations*, Westview, Boulder, 1979, p. 73.
44. Green, op. cit., p. 357. R. Remond, *Religion and Society in Modern Europe*, Blackwell, Oxford, 1999.
45. Common Declaration by Pope Paul VI and Archbishop Donald Coggan (29 April 1977), para. 9, in Flannery, op. cit., p. 187.

Chapter 5

1. Tadeusz Mazowiecki, *Druga Twarz Europy*, Biblioteka Więzi, Warsaw, 1990, pp. 79, 88-9.
2. Karol Wojtyła, 'Gdzie znajduje się granica Europy?', in *Ethos* (Warsaw), No. 28 (1994), pp. 28-29. Sławomir Sowiński and Radosław Zenderowski (eds), *Europa drogą Kościoła*, Ossolineum, Wrocław, 2003, pp. 15-22. Grzegorz Przebinda, *Większa Europa: Papież wobec Rosji i Ukrainy*, Znak, Kraków, 2001.
3. 'Allocution de Jean-Paul II' (19 December 1978), in Hervé Legrand (ed.), *Les Évêques d'Europe et la Nouvelle Évangelisation*, Cerf, Paris, 1991, pp. 72-4.
4. Tadeusz Mazowiecki, 'Zadania inteligencji katolickiej w Polsce wobec wyboru Jana Pawła II' (1 April 1979), in Zygmunt Hemmerling and Marek Nadolski (eds), *Opozycja demokratyczna w Polsce 1976-1980*, Wydawnictwo Uniwersytetu Warszawskiego, Warsaw, 1994, p. 345. Cardinal Slipyi's declaration, in *Radio Liberty Research Bulletin*, 18 June 1979.
5. John Paul II's statement to Cardinal Wyszyński, in Antoine Wenger, 'La Politique Orientale du Saint-Siège', in Joël-Benoît d'Onorio (ed.), *Le Saint-Siège dans les Relations Internationales*, Cerf, Paris, 1989, p. 183.
6. Karol Wojtyła, 'Teoria-praxis: temat ogólnoludzki i chrześcijański', in *Osoba i czyn*, Polskie Towarzystwo Teologiczne, Kraków, 1969, pp. 465-75.
7. John Paul II, *Redemptor hominis* (4 March 1979), para. 17.
8. Ibid., paras. 17-18.
9. 'Our attitude to the statements of Charter 77' (January 1977), in *Religion in Communist Lands*, Vol. 5, No. 3 (1977), pp. 161-2. Jan Patočka, 'La Charte 77: ce qu'elle est et ce qu'elle n'est pas', in *Cahiers de l'Est* (Paris), Nos. 9-10 (1977), p. 167.
10. *Ausrele*, No. 1 (*samizdat*: 16 February 1978), in Luxmoore and Babiuch, op. cit. p. 185.
11. Pontifical Mass homily, Gniezno (3 June 1979).
12. Address to young people, Gniezno (3 June 1979).

13. 'Oświadczenie KSS KOR w związku z pielgrzymką Jana Pawła II' (1 July 1979), in Hemmerling and Nadolski, op. cit., pp. 592–4.

Andrzej Micewski, *Kościół-Państwo*, Wydawnictwo Szkolne i Pedagogiczne, Warsaw, 1994, p. 65. Communist press reactions in Patrick Michel, *Politics and Religion in Eastern Europe*, Polity Press, Cambridge, 1991, pp. 136–7.

14. Quoted in Scammell, op. cit., pp. 765–7.
15. Lech Wałęsa, *Un chemin d'espoir*, Fayard, Paris, 1987, pp. 274–5.
16. Vatican Radio broadcast (5 December 1980), in Luxmoore and Babiuch, op. cit. p. 229.
17. John Paul II, *Laborem exercens* (14 September 1981), para. 20.
18. Michel, op. cit., p. 3. See also Kołakowski's introduction to *Survey: A Journal of East and West Studies*, London, Vol. 26, No. 3, Part 1 (Summer 1982), pp. 3–5.
19. *Pravda* (Moscow), 19 June 1982. Wojciech Jaruzelski, *Stan Wojenny: Dlaczego*, BGW, Warsaw, 1992, pp. 386–404.
20. 'Opracowanie władz partyjnych' (20 June 1983), in Peter Raina (ed.), *Kościół w PRL: Dokumenty 1975–1989*, W Drodze, Poznań, 1996, pp. 405–7. Mieczysław Rakowski, *Jak to się stało*, BGW, Warsaw, 1991, p. 56.
21. Figures in Luxmoore and Babiuch, op. cit., pp. 255, 262.
22. 'Message des présidents des Conferences Episcopales d'Europe aux fidèles catholiques', Document 32 (8 March 1987); in Legrand, op. cit., pp. 341–2.
23. 'Lettre de Jean-Paul II', Document 31 (2 January 1986), ibid., p. 331.
24. 'Déclaration des évêques d'Europe', Document 11 (28 September 1980), in ibid., pp. 93, 96.
25. 'L'évangelisation de l'Europe, sa nécessité, ses conditions', Document 14 (4 October 1982), in ibid., pp. 118–120.
26. Christine de Montclos-Alix, 'Le Saint-Siège et l'Europe', in D'Onorio, op. cit., pp. 154, 160. Sowiński and Zenderowski, op. cit., pp. 10–15.
27. John Paul II, apostolic letter, *Egregiae Virtutis* (31 December 1980), in Legrand, op. cit., pp. 100–1.
28. For example, *Tribuna* (Prague), 3 January 1985. Luxmoore and Babiuch, op. cit., pp. 258–9.
29. John Paul II, apostolic letter, *Euntes in Mundum* (25 January 1988), Part 5. *Slavorum Apostoli* (2 June 1985), nos. 10–11, 27.
30. Homily at Mass for working people, Zaspa (12 June 1987). Address to representatives of creative milieux, Warsaw (13 June 1987).
31. John Paul II, *Solicitudo rei socialis* (30 December 1987), nos. 22, 41.
32. *Auśra*, No. 28 (*samizdat*, September 1981).
33. I. R. Grigulevich, comments in *Literaturnaya gazeta* (Moscow), 23 December 1981. *Komsomolskaya pravda*, 12 March 1982. See also Moynahan, op. cit., p. 702.
34. Papal address to the Court of Human Rights, Strasbourg (8 October 1988).
35. Mikhail Gorbachev, *Perestroika: New Thinking for Our Country and the World*, Collins, London, 1987, pp. 162–3, 165.

36. Wilson and van der Dussen, op. cit., pp. 90–5, 178. Hans-Magnus Enzensberger, *Ach Europa: Wahrnehmungen aus sieben Ländern*, Suhrkamp, Frankfurt, 1987. Edgar Morin, *Penser l'Europe*, Gallimard, Paris, 1987.
37. Mihály Vajda, 'Ostmitteleuropas Enteuropäisierung', in F. Herterich and C. Semler (eds), *Dazwischen-Ostmitteleuropäische Reflexionen*, Suhrkamp, Frankfurt, 1989, p. 120. Erhard Busek and Emil Brix, *Projekt Mitteleuropa*, Ueberreuter, Vienna, 1986, pp. 118–135.
38. 'Peace with Justice for the whole Creation', final document (2 June 1989), pp. 19–20.
39. Archbishop Ioan Robu of Bucharest, in Jonathan Luxmoore, *After the Fall: Church and State Rebuild 1990–1999*, Catholic International, Baltimore, 2000, pp. 227–8.
40. Catholic News Service interview, 19 March 1997. Gorbachev's column in *La Stampa* (Milan), 3 March 1992.
41. Luxmoore, op. cit., p. 244.
42. Address in St James Cathedral, Compostela (19 August 1989). Speech to Diplomats at the Vatican (13 January 1990).
43. Luxmoore, op. cit., p. 228.
44. Joint declaration, 'Our Unbroken Unity', in ibid., p. 229.
45. Speech to clergy, religious and committed laity, Prague (21 April 1990). *National Catholic Register*, 6 May 1990.
46. *Moscow News* survey, in Luxmoore, op. cit., p. 237.
47. Special Assembly of the Synod of Bishops for Europe (1991), in *Catholic International*, Vol. 3, No. 4, February 1992, pp. 163–4, 178.
48. John Paul II, *Centesimus Annus* (1 May 1991), no. 35.
49. Ibid., Nos. 23, 25.
50. Vadim Zagladin, 'Perestroika: a new way of thinking', in *Catholic International*, Vol. 2, No. 18, October 1991, p. 866.
51. Homily during Mass in Agrykola Park, Warsaw (9 June 1991).
52. Address to the Calvinist Community of Debrecen (18 August 1991).
53. Homily text in Luxmoore, op. cit., pp. 249–50.
54. *Centesimus Annus*, no. 27.
55. Luxmoore, op. cit., p. 55.
56. Cassidy's speech (3 December 1991), in Special Assembly, supra, pp. 156–8.
57. *Izvestia* interview (Moscow), 12 June 1991.
58. Zagladin, 'Perestroika', supra, p. 865.
59. 'Évangeliser l'Europe Sécularisée', Document 27 (7 October 1985), in Legrand, op. cit., pp. 232–4.

Chapter 6

1. Address by Mary Hanafin TD to the COMECE pilgrimage to Santiago, Leon (18 April 2004).
2. *Single European Act*, preamble, paras 3–5, Publications Office, Europa, Brussels, 1987. John Pinder, *The Building of the European Union*,

Oxford University Press, London, 1998, pp. 85-90. Andrew Moravcsik, *The Choice for Europe: Social Purpose and State Power from Messina to Maastricht*, Cornell University Press, Ithaca, 1998, pp. 238-313.

3. *Treaty on European Union*, preamble, Article II-8, Office for Official Publications of the European Communities, Luxembourg, 1992. Andrew Moravcsik, op. cit., pp. 238-313.
4. *Nasz Dziennik* (Warsaw), 21 May 1998.
5. 'The truth will make you free', Pastoral Instruction by the Bishops of Spain, *Catholic International*, Vol. 2, No. 5, March 1991, pp. 225-6.
6. 'Charter of Paris for a New Europe' (21 November 1990), in ibid., pp. 216-223. Kenneth Medhurst, *Faith in Europe*, Churches Together in Britain and Ireland, London, 2004.
7. 'Raffermir l'Espérance et Résister au Mal dans l'Europe d'Aujourd'hui', Document 38 (14 October 1989), in Legrand, op. cit., p. 451.
8. 'Peace with Justice', supra, pp. 19, 26. Noel Treanor, 'The Church and the European Union: COMECE and its Work', speech to an international conference, Warsaw (18 June 1998).
9. 'L'Urgence d'une Évangélisation de l'Europe', Document 39 (12 October 1989), in Legrand, op. cit., p. 459. Aniela Dylus (ed.), *Europa: Droga Integracji*, Fundacja ATK, Warsaw, 1999.
10. Comparative figures in Paul M. Zulehner (ed.), *Kirchen in Übergang in freiheitliche Gesellschaften*, Pastorales Forum, Vienna, 1994. Jonathan Luxmoore and Jolanta Babiuch, 'New Myths for Old', in *Journal of Ecumenical Studies*, Vol. 36, Nos. 1-2, 2000. *Tygodnik Powszechny* (Krakow), 12 February 2003.
11. Centrum Badań Opinii Społecznej (CBOS) survey, in *Rzeczpospolita*, 24 March 1998, and *Polityka*, 28 March 1998. Natalia Jackowska, *Kościół katolicki w Polsce wobec integracji europejskiej*, Gaudentinum, Gniezno, 2003. Jonathan Luxmoore, '*Établir des ponts*', in *Concilium*, No. 286, 2000, pp. 131-40.
12. 'At Thy Word: Mission and Evangelisation in Europe Today', Final Report, *Catholic International*, Vol. 3, No. 2, 1992, pp. 88-93.
13. 'In Christ a New Creation', final message; *Catholic International*, Vol. 3, No. 20, 1992, pp. 968-70. 'Living the Gospel in Freedom and Solidarity', final summary report, CCEE, Prague (12 September 1993).
14. Papal address to the European Parliament, Strasbourg (8 October 1988).
15. *La Stampa*, interview (2 November 1993).
16. *Redemptor hominis*, supra, para. 16.
17. John Paul II, *Veritatis splendor* (6 August 1993), no. 99. *Evangelium vitae* (25 March 1995), no. 69.
18. Ibid., no. 70.
19. Homily in St Adalbert's Square, Message aux présidents, Gniezno (3 June 1977).
20. Luxmoore, *After the Fall*, supra, p. 332.
21. Vatican Council II, *Gaudium et Spes*, supra, para. 55. The Dogmatic Constitution also acknowledged that the Church, 'clasping sinners to her

bosom', was 'at once holy and always in need of purification', *Lumen Gentium*, supra, para. 8.
22. Luxmoore, op. cit., p. 248.
'Shalom: the Saving Presence of God in Human History', Address to the Jewish Community of Hungary, Budapest (18 August 1991).
23. Statement by the French Bishops Conference (30 September 1997), *Catholic International*, Vol. 8, No. 12, 1997, pp. 551–4.
24. Apostolic Letter, *Tertio millennio adveniente* (10 November 1994), Nos. 33–36.
25. Wolfhart Pannenberg, 'The churches and the emergence of European unity', in Grace Davie et al (eds), *Christian Values in Europe*, Westcott House, Cambridge, 1993, pp. 36, 41. P. Pavlovic (ed.), *Churches in the Process of European Integration*, CEC, Geneva, 2001.
26. 'Náboženské vyznanie obyvateľov Slovenska', in *Sme* (Bratislava), 3 November 2001. Jonathan Luxmoore, 'Eastern Europe 1997–2000: A Review of Church Life', in *Religion, State and Society*, Vol. 29, No. 4, 2001.
27. *The Universe* (Manchester), 23 December 2001, Catholic News Service, 19 November 2002 and 12 February 2003. Ecumenical News International, 13 July 2003.
28. Apostolic Letter, *Ordinatio Sacerdotalis* (22 May 1994), no. 4.
29. 'Living the Gospel in Freedom and Solidarity', supra. p. 9.
30. 'Global Governance: our responsibility to make globalisation an opportunity for all', Report of the Bishops of COMECE, Brussels, September 2001.
31. Caritas Europa, 'Report on Poverty in Europe', Brussels, February 2002. 'Poverty has Faces in Europe', Brussels, February 2004.
32. Farewell Speech at Balice Airport, Krakow (19 August 2002), *Gazeta Wyborcza* (Warsaw), 20 August 2002. 'Biskupi polscy wobec integracji europejskiej', Katolicka Agencja Informacyjna report, 21 March 2002.
33. *The Tablet*, 15 December 2000.
34. Ecumenical News International, 4 February 2004.
35. CBOS survey, in *Gazeta Wyborcza*, 9 January 2003, *Rzeczpospolita*, 17 February 2003.
36. 'Pastiersky list biskupov Slovenska na Prvú adventnú nedeľu', 3 November 2003. Catholic News Service, 9 December 2003.
37. 'Słowo biskupów polskich z okazji przyjęcia Polski do Unii Europejskiej', Katolicka Agencja Informacyjna report, 18 March 2004.
38. *Annual Report on International Religious Freedom for 1999*, US Department of State, Washington DC, October 2002. International Helsinki Federation for Human Rights, *Religious Intolerance in Selected OSCE Countries*, Vienna, June 2001, pp. 7–9, 13–15, 16–17.
39. Congregation for the Doctrine of the Faith, *Dominus Iesus* (6 August 2000), no. 22.
40. Luxmoore, *After the Fall*, supra, p. 323.
41. Quoted in Sowiński and Zenderowski, op. cit., p. 22.
42. Joint Communique after the Eighth Plenary Session, Catholic News Service, 27 July 2000. Ecumenical News International, 9 August 2000.

43. Letter to the World's Muslims (3 April 1991), in *The Pope Teaches*, No. 4, 1991, pp. 120–2.
44. *Gazeta Wyborcza* report, 16 November 2004. Ecumenical News International, 7 October 2004.
45. 'Meeting Muslims: Study paper prepared by the Islam in Europe Council of CCEE and CEC', Brussels, April 2003. Catholic News Service, 9 December 2003.
46. Catholic News Service, 20 and 31 March 2003.
47. Ecumenical News International, 12 May 2003. *The Universe*, 18 May 2003.
48. *Le Monde*, 14 October 2000. Katolicka Agencja Informacyjna reports, 12–16 October, 28 November 2000.
49. Catholic News Service, 17 October 2002. 'The Future of Europe: Political Commitment, Values and Religion', COMECE (Brussels), 22 May 2002.
50. *Rzeczpospolita* interview, 24 April 2003.
51. *Gazeta Wyborcza*, 15 February 2003. *Die Zeit* interview (Bonn), 10 March 2003. *Corriere della Sera* (Milan), 30 May 2003.
52. Katolicka Agencja Informacyjna report, 29 November 2003.
53. 'Oświadczenie Prezydium Konferencji Episkopatu Polski', Katolicka Agencja Informacyjna report, 21 June 2004.
54. *Treaty Establishing a Constitution for Europe*, Vol. I, preamble, Council of the European Union, July 2004, p. 11.
55. 'Europe's priority should be its people', COMECE press release (Brussels), 19 November 2004. 'The European Constitution: A major step in the European integration process'; Conference of European Churches press release (Brussels), 19 June 2004.
56. *Treaty Establishing a Constitution*, supra, Articles 1–46, 47.
57. ICM poll for the European Foundation, *The Times* (London), 23 November 2004.
58. 'Letter to the Convention of Christians for Europe' (Barcelona), 6 December 2002. Baroso's speech to the European Parliament; *Le Monde*, 3 August 2004.

Chapter 7

1. From Harnack's *What is Christianity?* (1899–1900), in Heer, op. cit., p. 241.
2. Catholic News Service, 19 November 2002, 12 February, 14–20 November 2003. Ecumenical News International, 13 July 2003.
3. Zulehner, op. cit. *Our Sunday Visitor* (Huntington), 2 December 2001. Catholic cardinals from Europe's capital cities inaugurated an International Congress for the New Evangelisation, *Catholic Herald* (London), 29 October 2004.
4. Alexis de Toqueville, *Democracy in America*, Knopf, New York, 1994. Larry Siedentop, *Democracy in Europe*, Penguin Books, London, 2001, pp. 171–214.

5. Cardinal Bernard Panafieu of Marseille, Catholic News Service, 6 January 2005.
6. *La Vie* survey (Paris), 22 September 2004. *The Economist* survey (London), 22 August 2002. See also demographic data from Eurostat and the UN Commission for Europe.
7. Samuel P. Huntingdon, *The Clash of Civilisations and the Remaking of World Order*, Touchstone Books, London, 1998.
8. John Paul II, Apostolic Exhortation, *Ecclesia in Europa* (28 June 2003), no. 24. *Veritatis Splendor*, supra, no. 106. Apostolic Letter, *Mane Nobiscum Domine* (7 October 2004)
9. Anton Wessels, *Europe: Was it Ever Really Christian?*, SCM Press, London, 1994, p. 23.
10. Jacques Maritain, op. cit., p. 41.
11. Moynahan, op. cit., p. 713. Gerald Russello, *Christianity and European Culture: Selections from the Work of Christopher Dawson*, Catholic University of America Press, Washington DC, 2003.
12. Fernand Braudel, *History of Civilisations*, Penguin, London, 1995, pp. 307–426. *Civilisation and Capitalism*, HarperCollins, London, 1985.
13. Homily at Mass in St Peter's Basilica, 18 April 2005. *La Repubblica* interview (Rome), 19 November 2004. Joseph Ratzinger, *Introduction to Christianity*, Ignatius Press, Fort Collins, 2004. Ratzinger blamed western 'self-hatred' for current hostility to Christianity.
14. From Newman's *Idea of a University* (1853), in Moynahan, op. cit., p. 727. J. Delumeau, *Christianisme: va t-il mourir?* Grasset, Paris, 1977, p. 237.
15. Heer, op. cit., pp. 264, 300.
16. *Ecclesia in Europa*, supra, no. 83, *Catholic Herald*, 8 October 2004.
17. Catholic News Service, 15 December 2004.
18. Statement of Cardinal Walter Kasper, Holy See, OSCE Conference on Anti-Semitism (Berlin), 28 April 2004.
19. 'Open Letter to Dutch Society' (Utrecht), 11 November 2004.
20. J.H.H. Weiler, *Chrześcijańska Europa: Konstytucyjny Imperializm czy Wielokulturowość?* W Drodze, Poznań, 2003, pp. 11, 14.

Index